Creation to Babel

A Commentary for Families

KEN HAM

First printing: October 2021
Third printing: February 2022

ISBN: 978-1-68344-290-5
Digital ISBN: 978-1-61458-789-7
Library of Congress Number: 2021945528

Cover and interior design by Diana Bogardus

Unless otherwise noted, Scripture quotations are from the ESV® Bible (The Holy Bible, English Standard Version®), copyright © 2001 by Crossway, a publishing ministry of Good News Publishers. Used by permission. All rights reserved.

Scripture quotations noted NLT are taken from the Holy Bible, New Living Translation, copyright ©1996, 2004, 2007, 2013, 2015 by Tyndale House Foundation. Used by permission of Tyndale House Publishers, Inc., Carol Stream, Illinois 60188. All rights reserved.

Scripture quotations noted NKJV are taken from the New King James Version, copyright © 1982 by Thomas Nelson, Inc. Used by permission. All rights reserved.

Scripture quotations noted NASB are taken from the New American Standard Bible®, copyright © 1960, 1962, 1963, 1968, 1971, 1972, 1973, 1975, 1977, 1995 by The Lockman Foundation. Used by permission.

Please consider requesting that a copy of this volume be purchased by your local library system.

Printed in the United States of America

Please visit our website for other great titles:
www.masterbooks.com

For information regarding author interviews,
please contact the publicity department at (870) 438-5288.

Illustrations by Bill Looney
except for the following.
Answers in Genesis: pages 40, 64, 72
NLPG staff: pages 8, 85, 162
Getty images: page 77

Dedication

I dedicate this book to all the Christian parents doing their best to raise up godly offspring, and who have that earnest desire to obey God's instruction to enable their children to:

Put on the whole armor of God, that you may be able to stand against the schemes of the devil (Ephesians 6:11).

Thank You

Thank you to AiG writer and speaker Avery Foley for her writing and editorial skills that enhanced this publication.

Table of Contents

Table of Contents

Introduction

This is a unique commentary. We are going to look in detail at the first 11 chapters of Genesis. I will explain what we read in the text, answer many of the most-asked questions people have about these passages, and deal with many of the objections some have. I also want to apply what we learn to our personal lives in the increasingly dark culture we live in.

This commentary will feature apologetics (answers to skeptical questions and objections), how to think foundationally to know what we believe as Christians (doctrine) and why, and how to develop a truly Christian worldview. There is also a devotional aspect throughout as we gain understanding of who God is, what He has done for us, and thus why we should thank and praise Him.

The teaching also will be equipping people to know how to have a correct worldview regarding contemporary issues like gender, gay "marriage," abortion, racism, and others.

As we begin, Genesis chapter one sets the scene for the rest of this book. And there's a recurrent theme throughout the commentary — that of coming to grips with what it means that God is our infinite Creator. So come with me as I "hammer home" the importance of understanding God's infinite greatness compared to our human finite understanding. This is an important key to understanding Genesis 1–11, as it helps us understand that we need to put ourselves under the authority of the text, and not over it!

What an exciting trip through history this will be from creation to Babel!

Chapter 1

Day One

Genesis 1:1-5

In the beginning, God created the heavens and the earth. The earth was without form and void, and darkness was over the face of the deep. And the Spirit of God was hovering over the face of the waters.

And God said, "Let there be light," and there was light. And God saw that the light was good. And God separated the light from the darkness. God called the light Day, and the darkness he called Night. And there was evening and there was morning, the first day.

Genesis 1:1

Let's analyze the first day of creation in detail. It begins with: "In the beginning, God created the heavens and the earth."

This was the first miracle of Jesus recorded in the Bible. In Colossians 1:16 we are told that Jesus (who is God) created all things: *For by him all things were created, in heaven and on earth, visible and invisible, whether thrones or dominions or rulers or authorities — all things were created through him and for him.* The first miracle of Jesus was creation!

"In the beginning God created…" What an exciting statement! If this first verse in God's Word isn't true, then none of the rest of the Bible is true! This is one of the most important sentences in the Bible. If we believe this verse in the Bible, we won't have much trouble believing all the other verses from Genesis (the first book) to Revelation (the last book).

Three Truths from Genesis 1:1

Let me show why this is so by teaching three very important things we can understand from this verse of Scripture.

1. Foundations are important. This word "foundation" essentially means "a base." For instance, consider building a house. Builders construct the foundation, then the floor, and then the walls and roof. But without the foundation, the house would collapse. Or consider four building blocks. If we place one building block on the floor, then this block becomes the **foundation** (or base) for all the blocks that will be placed on top.

If you put a second building block on the first one, then the first block is **foundational** to the second block, and the second block will be **foundational** to all blocks placed on it! Now, if you take a third block and place this on the second block, then the first block is **foundational** to the second and third blocks, and the second block is **foundational** to the third block.

Let's take a fourth block. Once you place the fourth block on top of the third block, you can say that the first block is **foundational** to the second block, and the second block is **foundational** to the third block, and the third block is **foundational** to the fourth block. Okay, now using this block example, let's consider Genesis 1–11 in regard to the topic of foundations.

As we study through the first 11 chapters of Genesis, we learn that the first verse in Genesis is **foundational** to the first chapter, and the first chapter is **foundational** to the first eleven chapters, and the first eleven chapters are **foundational** to the rest of Genesis, and Genesis is **foundational** to the rest of the Bible. Indeed, Genesis 1–11 is **foundational** to all Christian doctrine and to the Christian worldview.

Imagine suddenly pulling the bottom block out from under the other three. The whole structure would collapse. In a similar sort of way, if the **foundational** verse of the Bible is not true, the rest of the Bible would not be true either.

Psalm 11:3 states, *If the **foundations** are destroyed, what can the righteous do?* For instance, if God is not the **foundation** of everything — if there is no God, then trust in Jesus and the Bible would be meaningless. That is why the first verse tells us there is a God — but not just any God, the one true God.

2. The universe had a beginning. This first verse tells us that the universe was brought into existence — it was created by God.

This means that before the universe was made, there was no universe — no earth, no time, and in fact, not even any space! I can't even imagine there being no space. How would we try to describe this? We might say that there was nothing. However, I think most people would still think that nothing would mean an empty black place. But the universe was not even a place before creation — it wasn't black — because it just wasn't!

The only way I have ever been able to describe this, to even try to understand it, is to say there was **not even nothing** (but there was God, and we will learn about this in point number three). We can't even think what **not even nothing** would be like.

Not even nothing! It couldn't be black — because that would be some-thing! This is impossible for us to understand because we are created beings — we were created by God. This means God must be so much more powerful than us, so there are going to be many things we will not understand. This should make us realize more and more how big and powerful God is.

If God made the universe, what did he make it from? The word "cre-ated" used in this first verse really means that God brought into exist-ence materials that had no previous existence to make everything that now exists. God made the universe from materials that He created from "not even nothing."

In the Book of Hebrews in the New Testament we read that, *By faith we understand that the universe [this means everything] was created by the word of God, so that what is seen was not made out of things that are visible*

(Hebrews 11:3). This also teaches us that the things we see now were made from materials that previously did not exist, but God brought them into existence! It helps us to begin to understand how powerful God is.

In Psalm 33:9, we are told about how God does things, *For he spoke, and it came to be; he commanded, and it stood firm.* How does God do things? He just commands it to happen — and it happens. How did He make the universe? He just spoke it into existence! Look at the following verses in Genesis chapter 1:3, 6, 9, 14, 20, 24, and 26. They all start with *And God said* (verse 26 begins with "then God said"). He just spoke, and things happened — things came into existence. He just spoke, and suddenly, from "not even nothing" there was something. Only God could do this.

In Mark 4:39, we are told the account of how Jesus, God's son, was on a boat with the disciples and a great storm arose. He spoke to the wind and sea and they obeyed him! *And he awoke and rebuked the wind and said to the sea, "Peace! Be still!" And the wind ceased, and there was a great calm.*

When the disciples saw this, they said, *"Who then is this, that even the wind and the sea obey him?"* (Mark 4:41). In other words, who is this who can just speak to the wind and sea and they obey Him? Well, the answer is that this is the Creator! This was no ordinary man. Colossians 1:16 tells us that *all things were created through him and for him.* No wonder the sea and the wind obeyed Him — He made them!

If all things were made by Him, it means we were made by Him. Actually, as we will learn further on, God made our first parents and designed them to have children, and their children to have children, and so on. God did not make us directly from dust like He did Adam, but we are all children of Adam. So we can certainly say God made us (Psalm 139:13–14).

Before God spoke the universe into existence, we did not exist, except God knew we would exist. For instance, in Jeremiah 1:5, God said this about Jeremiah, *"Before I formed you in the womb I knew you, and before you were born I consecrated you; I appointed you a prophet to the nations.*" God in eternity knew each one of us just as He knew Jeremiah, before we came into existence. That gives us more of a glimpse of how great God is.

Now we do exist, and we think, and make decisions. And yet our first parents were made from dust that originally did not exist, but which God spoke into existence! Oh, how great God is.

And what did God first create? He created time (*In the beginning*); He created space (*God created the heavens*); He created matter (*and the earth*).

Now the third point I want us to understand from this verse.

3. God had no beginning. The Bible tells us that time, space, and matter (the universe) had a beginning, but that God was just there! How could this be? If God made time, then God had to exist before time. We know that time can be measured. For instance, we measure time with our watches by measuring minutes or hours. Each time we have a birthday, we know that a whole year of time has passed by. As time goes on, we get older — everything that exists gets older. But if God made time and exists outside of time, then He does not age.

Maybe why we find this hard (really impossible) to completely understand is because we were created, just as time was created. The one who created us must understand much more than us. We can't understand everything about God, but God helps us to understand as much as we can.

Look in the Bible at Exodus 3:14. God had spoken to Moses and told him to go to the great Pharaoh of the Egyptians, and tell him to let God's people, the Israelites who were slaves, go free.

Moses wanted to know who he should say sent him to do this. In verse 14 we read, *God said to Moses, "I AM WHO I AM." And he said, "Say this to the people of Israel: 'I AM HAS SENT ME TO YOU.'"*

God said his name was "I AM." Now that might sound like a strange name, but do we know what this means? We were born (had a beginning), which is why we existed in the past and we exist now, and we will continue to exist in our body until we die. Of course, the real us does not cease to exist when we die. If we are a Christian, the Bible teaches us that we will leave our body and go to be with God forever — now that is something to look forward to. We were born, are existing now, and will be existing forever, either with God or sadly, apart from God, if we have not committed our life to Him. We had a beginning.

However, God exists! He did not have a beginning. He is just always there. He doesn't age, because with God there is no time. He made time so He could make us. That is why He says His name is "I AM." Now in Psalm 90:2 we read, *Before the mountains were brought forth, or ever you had formed the earth and the world, from everlasting to everlasting you are God.* God exists in eternity — He didn't have a beginning.

Who Made God?

Some people say, "But surely somehow God had to have a beginning." I've often had children ask me, "Who made God?"

Let's think through this very carefully. Consider a watch. Did someone make the watch? Of course! A watchmaker made the watch. A watch could not come into existence by itself. Now, is the watch more intelligent and greater than the watchmaker? No! The watchmaker is greater than the watch. We know someone had to make the watch — the watchmaker. Yet, the watchmaker is greater than the watch. So who made the watchmaker? Someone greater than the watchmaker. The Bible tells us that this someone is God.

If someone made God, who would that be? A super God. And who made the super God? A super, super God. And who made the super, super God? A super, super, super God! We could keep saying this forever — and we would never get to the end. We would always have to have someone bigger to make someone. This doesn't make sense. It means there must be someone who is the biggest of all. And that's the infinite God!

The Creator God of the Bible exists in eternity, and the Scripture teaches us He is:

Omnipotent (this means He is all-powerful): *For nothing will be impossible with God* (Luke 1:37).

Omniscient (this means He is all-knowing): *in whom [Jesus] are hidden all the treasures of wisdom and knowledge* (Colossians 2:3).

Omnipresent (this means He is everywhere at once): *The eyes of the LORD are in every place, keeping watch on the evil and the good* (Proverbs 15:3).

The word we used to describe God is "infinite." This word means "without end or limit — greater than any amount we could number." If God always exists, and no one made God, then it means His knowledge is infinite. It means His power is infinite. It means His understanding is infinite. It means His wisdom is infinite. It means God had no beginning — He is always there — He is the great I AM. He is the infinite Creator. He knows everything there is to know, and has all power, all wisdom, and all understanding. Everything about God is infinite. His love for us must be infinite. He must be infinitely good. If it was possible, we could say an infinite number of things about God — but then this book would be infinitely long, and no one would be able to finish reading it!

As we read God's Word, remember we are just finite beings. We need to let God, who is infinite, tell us from His Word what He wants us to know. We must do our best to never take our ideas to God's Word and try to make it say what we want it to say.

Another way to understand our finiteness is to think about our education. We have to learn to read and write, and then perhaps go to college, and earn a qualification so we can be a tradesman, scientist, doctor, or teacher, for instance. But God never had to learn anything. He has always known everything. Everything we take a lifetime to learn He knows anyway, and He never has to learn anything more, because there is nothing more for Him to learn. He knows it all.

One But Three

The Hebrew word for God in Genesis 1:1 means God is one but more than one. We learn in the Bible that God is one but three at the same time. Now while there is one being of God, all three members of the Trinity are distinct persons. The three are God the Father, God the Son, and God the Holy Spirit! We use a word to describe the fact that God is one but three — Trinity.

Many times in the Bible we read that God is the Creator, but we also read that Jesus created all things. Colossians 1:16 teaches us that Jesus is the second member of the Trinity and later in the same epistle we read that: *For in him the whole fullness of deity dwells bodily* (Colossians 2:9). In Colossians 2:3, we are told about Jesus that it is He *in whom are hidden all the treasures of wisdom and knowledge*. Jesus, who is God, knows everything. He is infinite. In other words, Jesus is God.

The third member of the trinity is the Holy Spirit: *The grace of the LORD Jesus Christ and the love of God and the fellowship of the Holy Spirit be with you all* (2 Corinthians 13:14).

Can God Really Have No Beginning?

But what about people who say, "It's silly to believe in God, because no one could just have no beginning and always exist." Usually, these people believe that the universe just came into existence by chance — as a result of naturalistic evolutionary processes.

If people don't believe in an infinite God, then we need to ask them where matter came from and where space came from. Many people will say that matter has just always existed. This means they have faith (and it is a faith that lacks credulity) that matter just exists (they believe in eternal matter), whereas we have faith (an objective faith that makes sense of what we observe) that God exists. However, ask them to show you evidence that matter by itself made anything! They can't give any such evidence. It takes intelligence to make things. Man is intelligent — he makes cars, computers, and planes. We need to tell them it is more scientific and logical to believe that an intelligence has always been there rather than their belief that matter always existed.

Some will tell you that matter just appeared out of nowhere. They have faith that matter just came into existence by itself and made everything! No one has observed matter do that! To believe that is to have blind faith. Actually, it's a faith that lacks credulity as it doesn't explain what we observe. It is much more reasonable and scientific to believe an infinite intelligence who has always been there made everything, just as the Bible tells us. Yes, that means we have faith that God who exists in eternity created everything, but it's not blind faith like those who reject God. Our faith makes sense of what we observe, and science confirms it in many ways.

In the New Testament Book of Romans we read: *For his invisible attributes, namely, his eternal power and divine nature, have been clearly perceived, ever since the creation of the world, in the things that have been made. So they are without excuse* (Romans 1:20).

Here we are told that if anyone does not believe in the infinite Creator God, they are without excuse, because God has made it obvious to everyone from just looking around that God the Creator exists. For instance, when we look around at cars, planes, computers, trains, and buildings, we would never think they just arrived here by chance. Matter just did not make these things. Intelligent people made them.

However, trees, flowers, animals, and people are so much more complicated than the things man has made. In fact, a single cell (and we are made of trillions of them) is more complicated than anything man has made. And inside each cell God created a program, similar to a complex computer program, in the DNA molecule to make the cell work and even make copies of itself. If it took intelligence to make simple things like cars, planes, computers, trains, and buildings, what kind of intelligence did it take to make the first trees, flowers, animals, and people and to enable them to make copies of themselves? A much greater intelligence. In fact, an infinite intelligence — the God of the Bible. The God of creation.

God made the first parents, Adam and Eve, and designed them to have children. When we look around the world today and see the trees, flowers, and animals, we need to understand God made the first trees, flowers, and animals, and programmed them to make copies of themselves. So the trees, flowers, and animals today are "copies" (descendants) of the original ones ("kinds," but more on that later) that God made. So, we really can say that God made all the trees, flowers, and animals, as long as we understand that God actually created the original ones and designed them to reproduce (or make copies of) their own kind year after year since the beginning. This is important, because as we come to the event of the Fall (Genesis 3), we must understand the world today has greatly changed from the way it was originally created. Now sin has affected everything, so in the present world, we are not looking at the world God originally made. More on that later.

When you think about it, if we are amazed at the wonderful things man makes, we should be more amazed and give great glory to the One who made man and all things — the God of the Bible. We should kneel down and worship our infinite Creator. And we should recognize that we know almost nothing compared to what God knows. This should put things into perspective as we study God's Word.

Genesis 1:2

The earth was without form and void, and darkness was over the face of the deep. And the Spirit of God was hovering over the face of the waters.

Verse one ends with the phrase "and the earth" and verse two begins with "the earth." One might think this is not a very important phrase, but it really is.

How long ago did God make the heavens and the earth as stated in verse one? Some people think it was billions of years ago. Why? Because many think scientists have proved that the earth is billions of years old.

However, scientists have not proved the earth is billions of years old. There are many scientists who believe the earth is only thousands of years old based on the history recorded for us in the Bible — and nothing in observational science contradicts this. There are lots of dating methods that overwhelmingly confirm the universe is only thousands of years old.

Scientists try to date the earth using complicated methods that have been shown to have enormous problems. For instance, they have used their dating methods on rocks that are known to be only hundreds of years old (or even younger), but their dating method gave a date of millions of years old! This has happened many times and should be a warning to us not to just accept these dates of millions or billions of years.

Really, the only way you would know for sure how old the earth was, is if you knew someone who saw it begin. I know of only one being who saw the earth begin — the God who made it! In the Book of Job, God asked Job a question: *Where were you when I laid the foundation of the earth? Tell me, if you have understanding* (Job 38:4). In other words, God was saying "Were you there, Job? Were you there when I made the earth?" I always tell people that when they hear scientists say the earth is billions of years old, they should politely ask the question, "Were you there?" When they say no, they weren't but tell us neither were we there, then we need to tell them no human was there, but God was, and He has given us in His Word the details about the history of the universe.

The Very Word of God

The Bible claims thousands of times that it is the Word of God (not just the word of men). For instance:

> *And we also thank God constantly for this, that when you received the word of God, which you heard from us, you accepted it not as the word of men but as what it really is, the word of God, which is at work in you believers* (1 Thessalonians 2:13).

All Scripture is breathed out by God and profitable for teaching, for reproof, for correction, and for training in righteousness (2 Timothy 3:16).

Yes, all of what we read in the Bible is God's Word — it's God breathed. The inspired, infallible Word of God.

But Why 6,000 Years?

The Bible records the creation of the world in Genesis, and then gives us all sorts of information that enables us to add up dates to find out when God made the world. For instance, we are told that God made everything in six days. (We will discuss later in detail the fact that these were ordinary days just like we have today). We are then told that the first parents were made on day six, and in passages in the Bible we are told when people were born, and when they died, and so on, just like we read in these verses that are part of the history given in Genesis 5 leading up to a man called Noah:

When Adam had lived 130 years, he fathered a son in his own likeness, after his image, and named him Seth. The days of Adam after he fathered Seth were 800 years; and he had other sons and daughters. Thus all the days that Adam lived were 930 years, and he died.

When Seth had lived 105 years, he fathered Enosh. Seth lived after he fathered Enosh 807 years and had other sons and daughters. Thus all the days of Seth were 912 years, and he died.

When Enosh had lived 90 years, he fathered Kenan. Enosh lived after he fathered Kenan 815 years and had other sons and daughters. Thus all the days of Enosh were 905 years, and he died.

When Kenan had lived 70 years, he fathered Mahalalel. Kenan lived after he fathered Mahalalel 840 years and had other sons and daughters. Thus all the days of Kenan were 910 years, and he died.

When Mahalalel had lived 65 years, he fathered Jared. Mahalalel lived after he fathered Jared 830 years and had other sons and daughters. Thus all the days of Mahalalel were 895 years, and he died.

When Jared had lived 162 years, he fathered Enoch. Jared lived after he fathered Enoch. . . (Genesis 5:3–19).

You can read the entire genealogy from Adam to Noah and his sons in Genesis 5:1–32. You can see that this list tells us when people were born and when they died.

Many great scholars who have spent a lifetime studying the Bible have added up all such dates from these lists and other events and come to the conclusion that God created the world about 4,000 years before Jesus was born as a babe in a manger. I am writing this book in the year 2021 A.D., which means the earth must be about 6,000 years old.

A Gap of Time?

Now what does all this have to do with the word "and" (in verse 1)? Well, as I stated earlier, God knows all things — He has infinite knowledge. Compared to what God knows, even the person who has studied at universities all their life, still knows very little — in fact, hardly anything compared to God.

This means the only way we could ever be sure of being right about how and when this world came into existence was if we had information from someone who had all the answers and has always been there and told us what we need to know. Only God has all the answers and has always been there, and He has told us in His Word (the Bible) what we need to know to have the ability to correctly understand this earth and universe.

Because the Bible is God's Word, it gives information God had written down for us (by inspiring special people over the years) from the One who has all the answers. This mean we should start with God's Word to make sure we will be right in our understanding about the world.

God's Word is the foundation for our worldview. Everyone has a worldview, and it is either founded in God's Word or man's word. Our worldview is like a set of glasses we put on so that we look through those glasses (worldview) to understand the world around us.

Sadly, even many Christians seem to forget that God knows everything. They listen to the fallible scientists who don't know everything, who were not always there, who say the world is billions of years old (based on their beliefs and fallible dating methods that all have problems) and say that Genesis chapter 1 must cover billions of years! Some Christians say that each of the six days of creation must be millions of years long. We will see later on, from the Hebrew language used in the Old Testament, that each of the six days of creation in Genesis chapter 1 can only be an ordinary day as we know it today — approximately 24 hours long. We must let God's Word speak to us, and not us impose our beliefs on God's Word.

Other Christians think that God must have made the heavens and earth that are spoken of in verse 1 billions of years ago and then He made everything else in six days. People who believe this say there is a great gap between Genesis chapter 1 verse 1, and verse 2. But what they are trying to do is to take man's belief about millions of years and add that into the Bible by inventing this gap idea. Such a gap idea compromises God's Word and undermines the authority of the Word of God.

Now, we finally get to the importance of the phrase "and the earth." The Old Testament, which includes Genesis through Malachi, was written in the Hebrew language. People who have studied the Hebrew language for many years tell us that, in the Hebrew, "and the earth" (verse 1) and "the earth" (verse 2) is connected by a particular type of phrase. This means that verse 2 is written as a description of the initial condition of the earth introduced in verse 1. So no one can put billions of years in between these two verses. Actually, the same Hebrew phrase connects verse 1 directly to verse 3. So really, we could read Genesis 1:1–4 this way:

In the beginning, God created the heavens and the earth.

Now the earth God created is described as a watery blob of matter. Everything was dark but the Spirit of God hovered over the waters covering the earth. Then the next thing that happened was this:

> And God said, "Let there be light," and there was light. And God saw that the light was good. And God separated the light from the darkness.

Not only this, but in Exodus 20:11 we read, *For in six days the LORD made the heaven and earth, the sea, and all that in them is, and rested on the seventh day.* This verse tells us that God made the "heaven and the earth," which we read of in verse 1, and then everything else listed in all of chapter 1, all in six days. So you can see that you certainly cannot put billions of years between the creation of the heaven and earth and everything else. This also means Genesis 1:1 is not a summary verse — it's part of the first day of creation.

Where Does a Week Come From?

Verse 11 of Exodus 20 (quoted above) is part of the fourth commandment which tells us that because God worked for six days in creating the world and rested for one day, so we should copy this pattern and work for six days and rest for one.

We all use a seven-day week! And Christians set one of these seven days aside as a special rest day to think about God. We go to church and worship our Creator. It is a special day set aside for Him. It's also interesting to note that the only place the seven-day week comes from is the Bible! It's not based on any astronomical observations, but based on the fact that God created everything in six days and rested for one. Consider:

Where does our day of approximately 24 hours come from? This is the time it takes the earth to rotate on its axis.

Where does a year come from? This is the time it takes for the earth to go around the sun.

Where does a month come from? This has to do with the relationship between the earth and the moon.

Where does a seven-day week come from? Nowhere — except the Bible! The fact that we use a seven-day week is actually confirming the truth of the Bible.

Now if God made everything in six million years and rested for one million years, we would have a very long week and that wouldn't make sense. It only makes sense if God really did make the universe in six ordinary days and rested for one ordinary day.

Earth Was Without Form and Void

Now look back at verse 2. *The earth was without form and void.* This means that at this stage, there was no life (it was "void") and the earth had not been given its final shape and features. It would have been like a watery blob.

In the last part of the verse, we are told *And the Spirit of God was hovering over the face of the waters.* This tells us the earth began covered with water, which means it could not have been very hot (as the evolutionary model predicts). If it was hot, the water would turn into steam.

When I went to school, my teachers, who believed in evolution, taught me that the earth supposedly began as a hot, molten blob without any water. In other words, all the material that makes up the rocks and soil we have today would have been liquid, just like when you see hot lava flowing out of a volcano. If the whole earth was originally like this, there would not have been any liquid water.

My teachers also told me that the earth was formed from all sorts of material swirling in space. They taught that billions of stars were formed millions of years before the earth. Yet Genesis tells us the earth was created on day one, and the sun, moon, and stars weren't created until day four (Genesis 1:16).

They taught me that all of this first began with a big bang. However, they never did tell me what caused this supposed big bang. And they also never told me where the material came from so the big bang could happen. And they never told me how from a big bang you could get such a beautiful universe with so much order and complexity with programmed information and codes for life. How could such design and complexity form as a result of supposed natural processes causing a supposed big bang?

Imagine putting sticks of dynamite into a big pile of bricks and then setting off an explosion. Do we think the bricks would all arrange themselves into a wonderful order and build a fence or a building? We know that would be ridiculous. And yet, many scientists think that is basically how the universe formed (which is much more complicated than a fence or building!).

By the way, the question we could ask a person who insists that the big bang brought the universe into existence is the same question I mentioned earlier, "Were you there?" And our point is God has always been there and has told us in His Word how the universe came into being.

God Didn't Use the Big Bang

When Christians claim God could have used the big bang to create the universe, we know that can't be so as that idea contradicts God's Word. The supposed order of events in the big bang model clearly contradict what God's Word tells us about the formation of the universe, the earth, and then all the other heavenly bodies. It also contradicts what God's Word tells us about the initial conditions of the earth.

Even God's Word in the New Testament confirms the earth was originally covered in water. In 2 Peter 3:3–10, Peter tells us that there will be a time when many people will make fun of those of us who believe that Jesus Christ, the One who created the world and came and died on a Cross, will be coming back one day to judge the world.

Peter informs us that these people that scoff will not believe that God made the earth and that *the earth was formed out of water and through water.* This seems to say that the original substance from which God made the bodies in the universe was water. And it's very obvious from this passage that the earth was not a hot molten blob to start with, as those who believe in the big bang claim.

Now look at 2 Peter 3:10. Here Peter states that these same people who scoff at us will not believe that this earth is going to be judged in the future by fire. Consider Peter's description, that *then the heavens will pass away with a roar, and the heavenly bodies will be burned up and dissolved, and the earth and the works that are done on it will be exposed.*

Actually, we could say that a big bang did not make the universe, but a very different sort of big bang is going to end it when God judges this earth by fire, and then makes a new heaven and earth. For those of us who are Christians, that is something we look forward to.

Let me ask a question here. Has God judged the earth at any time in the past? He certainly did, but not by fire; it was with water at the time of Noah. We will study about this later on, when we get to the event of the worldwide flood of Noah's day in Genesis 6–9. But think about this: the water God made when He created the earth, was the same water that He used later to judge the earth. And this is the same water we swim in down at the beach! Think about that the next time you take a swim.

Darkness Was Over the Deep

Now look back at Genesis 1:2 again: *...and darkness was over the face of the deep.* When God first created the earth, there was no light — it was dark. Remember, there was no sun or moon. There were no stars. There was just space, and the earth which was like a watery blob. And it was dark. We can't even imagine how dark it was. Let's go on to verse 3.

Genesis 1:3

And God said, "Let there be light," and there was light.

God spoke light into existence. Remember, God is infinite. He just has to speak, and it happens. (*For he spoke, and it came to be; he commanded, and it stood firm.* Psalm 33:9). So suddenly light flooded the earth. But if there was no sun yet, where did the light come from?

The Bible does not tell us where the light came from. It certainly could not have been from the sun, because the sun was not created until three days later. The light did not come from any of the stars we see in space, because they were made on the same day as the sun (the fourth day of creation). But we do know this — because there was an "evening and the morning" as described in verse 5, the light could only shine on the earth from one direction, and the earth must have been spinning around so there could be day and night. You don't need the sun and moon for day and night. You need light and darkness which is what existed on day 1.

So What Was the Light?

Some people have suggested that the light may have come from God Himself. For instance, in Revelation 22:5, we read about the new heavens and earth: *And night will be no more. They will need no light of lamp or sun, for the LORD God will be their light, and they will reign forever and ever.* There are many passages in the Bible that tell us that God is light, and in him is no darkness at all (1 John 1:5).

However, because God was there before He said, "let there be light," I think this light must have been a specially created light made just for the earth. God doesn't tell us where the light came from. We don't know what source it had. But that shouldn't worry us, because if God told us everything, we would have an infinite amount of information. And because we are created beings, we could never learn an infinite amount of information. But God has given us all the information we need to have. There are times when we have to admit we don't have all the answers, but we have God's Word, and we need to believe what He tells us. There will always be a faith aspect to everything we believe, as only God knows everything.

So be ready for the fact there will always be questions we cannot answer. The exciting thing though is that God has given us the answers we need. He has given us all the information that is important for us. And it is just the right amount of information for us to understand the truth about the world and what it is all about.

By the way, if you are familiar with the account in Exodus of how God led His people out of Egypt, you would know that the LORD provided a special light He made for His people. *And the LORD went before them by day in a pillar of cloud to lead them along the way, and by night in a pillar of fire to give them light, that they might travel by day and by night* (Exodus 13:21).

Why would God create a source of light for the earth before He created the sun, moon, and stars on day four? I often think about the fact that, through the ages, cultures have tended to worship the sun. So I often wonder if God was reminding us to worship the God who made everything, and not to worship the sun and the moon which He created as His tools to rule the day and night (which already existed on day one) from day four of creation onward. *And God made the two great lights — the greater light to rule the day and the lesser light to rule the night — and the stars* (Genesis 1:16).

Genesis 1:4-5

And God saw that the light was good. And God separated the light from the darkness. God called the light Day, and the darkness he called Night. And there was evening and there was morning, the first day.

God described the light as "good." He tells us a number of times that what He made was "good." Look at verses 10, 12, 17, 21, 25, and 31. What does God mean by "good"?

In Psalm 25:8, we read *Good and upright is the LORD*. In Psalm 34:8, we also read *Oh, taste and see that the LORD is good*.

God describes Himself as "good." Therefore, if we want to understand what God means by "good," we need to understand what God is like. In Luke we read how Jesus answered when a ruler asked Him, "*Good Teacher, what must I do to inherit eternal life?" And Jesus said to him, "Why do you call me good? No one is good except God alone*" (Luke 18:18–19).

Jesus was telling the man asking the question that He (Jesus) is God, as only God is good. God is infinitely good, and the source of all goodness. There are numerous passages that teach us about the goodness of God.

> *The Lord passed before him and proclaimed, "The Lord, the Lord, a God merciful and gracious, slow to anger, and abounding in steadfast love and faithfulness* (Exodus 34:6).

Look again at what Jesus said: *No one is good except God alone.* Only God is good.

What Does "Good" Mean?

There are many passages in the Bible that help us understand what God is like, and thus what "good" means.

In Matthew 6:28–31 we read: *And why are you anxious about clothing? Consider the lilies of the field, how they grow: they neither toil nor spin, yet I tell you, even Solomon in all his glory was not arrayed like one of these. But if God so clothes the grass of the field, which today is alive and tomorrow is thrown into the oven, will he not much more clothe you, O you of little faith? Therefore do not be anxious, saying, "What shall we eat?" or "What shall we drink?" or "What shall we wear?"* God cares about even the little things. He took the trouble to make the lilies beautiful, and if we love Him, He promises to care for and look after us.

The Bible says we are made in God's image (Genesis 1:27). If God looks after the lilies, how much more will He care for us who are made in His image. I suggest reading Psalm 139. After reading these passages, we understand that God's thoughts about us each day are more than we could number: *O Lord, you have searched me and known me! You know when I sit down and when I rise up; you discern my thoughts from afar. You search out my path and my lying down and are acquainted with all my ways. Even before a word is on my tongue, behold, O Lord, you know it altogether* (Psalm 139:1–4). Even though there are billions of people in the world, His thoughts each day about each one of us are infinite in number. That's difficult for us to comprehend but it means God is watching us and listening to us all the time. What a comfort to know He cares for us so much.

No wonder David says, *How precious to me are your thoughts, O God! How vast is the sum of them! If I would count them, they are more than the sand. I awake, and I am still with you* (Psalm 139:17–18). God knows everything about us. He even knows what we are going to say before we say it. He knew us even before we were born, even before we developed in our mother's womb.

Further on, in the Book of Matthew, we read, *Are not two sparrows sold for a penny? And not one of them will fall to the ground apart from your Father. But even the hairs of your head are all numbered* (Matthew 10:29–30). God sees every sparrow that falls to the ground. He knows the number of all the hairs on our head (Luke 12:7). He really does care for us.

There is another passage in the Bible that tells us how great God's thoughts are, and it reminds us that God knows so much more than we'll ever know. *For my thoughts are not your thoughts, neither are your ways my ways, declares the Lord. For as the heavens are higher than the earth, so are my ways higher than your ways and my thoughts than your thoughts* (Isaiah 55:8–9).

Let's look at some other passages in the Bible that tell us how the Creator, Jesus Christ, acted toward people.

> *And a leper came to him, imploring him, and kneeling said to him, "If you will, you can make me clean." Moved with pity, he stretched out his hand and touched him and said to him, "I will; be clean." And immediately the leprosy left him, and he was made clean* (Mark 1:40–42).

We read in the New Testament where Jesus healed the blind, the lame, the sick, the deaf, and raised the dead. In John 11:35, the shortest verse in the Bible, we read that "Jesus wept" when He looked on the grave of Lazarus. Then He raised him from the dead. Jesus wept because of death. He had compassion on people because they were sick, and He healed them. *When he went ashore he saw a great crowd, and he had compassion on them and healed their sick* (Matthew 14:14).

God makes it clear in His Word that the reason for sickness, pain, and suffering is because we live in a groaning world as a result of our sin: *For we know that the whole creation has been groaning together in the pains of childbirth until now* (Romans 8:22).

We are also told that one day there will be a restoration of all things (Acts 3:21). We read of this restoration: *He will wipe away every tear from their eyes, and death shall be no more, neither shall there be mourning, nor crying, nor pain anymore, for the former things have passed away* (Revelation 21:4).

We also read in the Old Testament in Leviticus and Deuteronomy that the animals that were to be sacrificed to God because of sin could not have any defects because God was holy and perfect, and needed a perfect sacrifice.

Obviously, when God describes something as "good," it must be beautiful, perfect, without any defects, and certainly death, disease, bloodshed, and suffering would not fit the description of good.

After he finished creating everything, God declared all He made as "very good." There was no death, suffering, or disease. Now this fact is one that those who believe the fossil record was laid down over millions of years before man need to consider carefully. The fossil record is a record of death, with evidence of animals eating each other and evidence of diseases like cancer in the bones of creatures. If a Christian believes the fossil record is millions of years old, then they are in essence stating that God calls death and disease "very good." Such compromise with millions of years is a direct attack on the character of God and undermines the gospel message because death is a result of sin, not a result of millions of years of evolutionary processes.

Many Christians think that God could have used evolution to create everything including all life. However, the idea of evolution requires death and struggle over millions of years leading up to man. And most of the fossil record is the supposed evidence of these millions of years. But we will learn that most of the fossil record is actually the graveyard of the judgment of the Flood of Noah's day. The imagined evolutionary process was one of suffering, disease, animals fighting each other — a violent and terrible world over millions of years. This does not fit with a creation described by God as "good." There is no way the idea of evolution/millions of years fits with God's character.

Look back at verse 4. God describes the light as good. It must have been perfect and beautiful. Each time God describes something as good it must fit with how perfect God is.

What Is a Day?

Verse 4 also tells us that God separated the light from the darkness. This was so that there would be night and day on the earth. It seems that the earth then must have been spinning around, with light shining on the earth, so that as it spun, there would be night and day, just like we have today. Remember, we aren't told where the light came from, but it wasn't the sun at this stage. Presumably God made a special source for light until the fourth day. The sun was created and made to shine light on the earth from day four onward. Note what God's Word states: *And God set them in the expanse of the heavens to give light on the earth, **to rule over the day and over the night*** (Genesis 1:17–18, emphasis added). God made sun and moon to rule the day and night that already existed.

When God first made the earth (remember it was a watery blob at this stage), everything was dark. This means the first day started with darkness. The Bible states at the end of Genesis 1:5, *And there was evening and there was morning, the first day.* Many scholars state that the Hebrew word used for "first" day, really means "one" day. In other words, this was the first of the six days of creation, but it was also defining what one day in this series of six is — a literal approximately 24-hour day.

So, a day is described as having darkness first, then light. You will be interested to know that the Israelites measured their day starting from sunset (the start of darkness) and ending at the beginning of the next sunset. Thus "evening" (the start of the period of darkness) and "morning" (the start of the light period) describe an ordinary day.

Many other cultures measured their day this way. However, most nations of the world today measure a day from midnight through to the next midnight. Nonetheless, the day is always approximately 24 hours in length — the time it takes for the earth to rotate once on its axis.

I have an exercise for the family. Obtain a globe and a flashlight, hold the flashlight out from the globe so it can act as the source of light from the earth. Now place a piece of paper on the globe to represent your starting point.

Keep the flashlight switched off at this stage and turn the globe half-way around from your starting point. This would represent half of the first day of creation. Now turn on your flashlight. This represents God saying, "Let there be light." Now turn the globe around the rest of the way back to your starting point. This represents the next half of the first day.

You have just demonstrated a dark period followed by a light period. The first day of creation.

But When Is a Day a Day?

As we look at each of the six days of creation, I am going to give you some important information so you can know that these days were ordinary days of approximately 24 hours, just as we have today. This is important, because some Christians think these six days of creation in Genesis could be millions of years long and were not ordinary days at all. Usually people who say this do so because they think scientists have proved the earth to be billions of years old. As I said earlier, scientists have not proved this at all.

There are many scientists who have investigated evidence that confirms the earth being only thousands of years old. You can find information on this by going to the AnswersinGenesis.org website. However, the ultimate "evidence" is the Bible itself, as it is God's record of history for us.

Because God is perfect, and He does not tell a lie, and He is the only one who knows everything, it is important that we accept His Word as truth. If you take God at His word, it is obvious that each of the days of creation are ordinary days. God communicates through language. When He made the first man, Adam, He had already "programmed" Adam with a language, so there could be communication. Human language consists of words used in a specific context that relates to the entire reality around us. Thus, God can reveal things to man, and man can communicate with God, because words have meaning and convey an understandable message. If this were not so, how could any of us communicate with each other or with God?

The Old Testament was originally written in the Hebrew language. The Hebrew word for "day" in Genesis chapter one is *yom*.

What does the Bible tell us about the meaning of "day" in Genesis 1? A word can have more than one meaning, depending on the context. The reason it is necessary to understand this is because words do have different meanings, and it is how they are used that determines which meaning is the correct one. Because I am an Australian, let me give you an Australian example to explain this.

In the state of Queensland in Australia, people use the word "port" to mean a suitcase, or a place where ships come in, or a type of wine, or the left side of a ship. Now if you said, "I am taking my port to the aeroplane" (the Australian word for airplane), by "port" you would obviously mean your suitcase. However, if you said, "I'm going down to the port to meet a friend," it's obvious you would be going down to where the ships come in, and not to visit your suitcase!

In the same sort of way, the manner in which words are used in the Bible determine exactly what they mean, because many words can have more than one meaning. Even the word day (*yom*) can have a number of different meanings, but as we will see, the way it is used in Genesis chapter 1 tells us that it means an ordinary day.

Now the English word "day" can have perhaps 14 different meanings. For example, consider the following sentence: "Back in my grandfather's day, it took 12 days to drive across the country during the day."

Here the first use of "day" means "time" in a general sense. The second "day," where a number is used, refers to an ordinary day of 24 hours, and the third refers to the daylight portion of the 24-hour period. The point is that words can have more than one meaning, depending on the context.

To understand the meaning of "day" in Genesis 1, we need to determine how the Hebrew word for "day," *yom*, is used in the context of Scripture. Consider the following:

> A typical Hebrew dictionary will illustrate that *yom* can have a range of meanings: a period of light as contrasted to night, a 24-hour period, time, a specific point of time, or a year.

> A classic, well-respected Hebrew-English dictionary (Brown, Driver, Briggs) has seven headings and many subheadings for the meaning of *yom* — but it defines the creation days of Genesis 1 as ordinary days under the heading "day as defined by evening and morning."

> A number and the phrase "evening and morning" are used with each of the six days of creation (Genesis 1:5, 8, 13, 19, 23, 31).

> Outside of Genesis 1, *yom* is used with a number 410 times,

and each time it means an ordinary day. Why would Genesis 1 be the exception?

Outside of Genesis 1, *yom* is used with the word "evening" or "morning" 23 times. "Evening" and "morning" appear in association, but without *yom*, 38 times. All 61 times the text refers to an ordinary day. Why would Genesis 1 be the exception?

In Genesis 1:5, *yom* occurs in context with the word "night." Outside of Genesis 1, "night" is used with *yom* 53 times, and each time it means an ordinary day. Why would Genesis 1 be the exception? Even the use of the word "light" with *yom* in this passage determines the meaning as an ordinary day.

The plural of *yom*, which does not appear in Genesis 1, can be used to communicate a longer time period, such as "in those days." Adding a number here wouldn't make sense. But, in Exodus 20:11, where a number is used with "days," it is referring to the six earth-rotation days of the creation week.

There are words in biblical Hebrew (such as *olam* or *qedem*) that are very suitable for communicating long periods of time, or indefinite time, but *none* of these words are used in Genesis 1.

From the meaning of the word for *day* in Hebrew and how it's used in Genesis 1 for each of the six days of creation, it is very clear they are six ordinary days of approximately 24 hours each.

Is A Day Like 1,000 Years?

In 2 Peter 3:8 we read, *But do not overlook this one fact, beloved, that with the LORD one day is as a thousand years, and a thousand years as one day.*

Some people point to this verse to try to say that the word "day" used in Genesis chapter 1 can't mean an ordinary day. But look carefully at the verse. It does not say a day is a thousand years, it says that **with the LORD one day is as a thousand years**. This actually means that to God, one day is like a thousand years (and a thousand years is like a day) because God is outside of time and God created time, so He does not age. There is no time as far as God is concerned.

The context of this passage is the Second Coming of Jesus Christ. Peter is saying that in the last days (and ever since Jesus stepped into history to be Jesus Christ the Godman we've been in the last days) scoffers will say Jesus is not coming back. They will claim things just go on and on. But God through Peter is saying that what we may think is a long time is not to God, as He is outside of time. And the reason He hasn't come back yet is because, He is *patient toward you, not wishing that any should perish, but that all should reach repentance* (2 Peter 3:9).

By the way, if you say that one day is a thousand years because of what Peter said, then he also says that a thousand years are as one day. This would mean that if every time you read the word day it meant a thousand years, then every time you read a thousand years it would mean a day! This would not make sense at all. And saying that a day is a thousand years doesn't help those who claim the days of creation are millions of years long anyway! Also, it's interesting when people use that "day as a thousand years" argument to try to justify rejecting literal days of creation, they only apply this argument to Genesis 1. To be consistent they should then apply their argument to all the uses of "day" in the Old Testament. So then Jonah was in the great fish 3,000 years? People often just don't logically think through positions they hold to!

Imagine reading Genesis 5:5 where it says that Adam died when he was 930 years old. If each day in Genesis was a thousand years (a day is like a thousand years), then Adam was created on day six, lived through day seven and died when he was 930 years old. Obviously, this does not make sense.

And you can't use a phrase from the New Testament, taken out of context, to determine the meaning of a Hebrew word (*yom*) in Genesis! The meaning of a Hebrew word depends on the rules of the Hebrew language. And as we know, the Hebrew word for day, *yom*, means an ordinary day in Genesis chapter 1 for each of the six days, because it is used each time with a number and the phrase "evening and morning." The days referred to in Genesis chapter 1 are definitely ordinary days of approximately 24 hours each.

A Symbolic Day?

Some people have claimed the word "day" in Genesis 1 is used symbolically. But a word can't be a symbol until it first has a literal meaning. When Jesus said *I am the door*, we know what that means because the word "door" has a literal meaning and, in this context, it is being used symbolically. The first time the word "day" is used is Genesis 1:5, it is given a literal meaning. It can't be a symbol the first time it's used.

Was Earth "Not Good" Because It Was a Blob?

Before we finish with day one, there is one more thing I want to explain. Some people think that because the earth was shapeless (a watery blob) when God first made it, that it was NOT perfect. But God said it was "good."

What we need to understand, is that even though earth was a watery blob (remember the phrase "without form and void" in Genesis 1:2), it doesn't mean there was something wrong with it — it just means it was not finished.

Consider a builder building a house. First, he obtains all of the materials. Then he builds the foundation for the house to sit on. Then he proceeds to build the walls, and then the roof, and then he finishes the inside of the house. Just because the house is unfinished while he is building it does not mean there is something wrong with it. At first, with all the materials dumped on the land, and the foundation in the ground, we could even say it was rather shapeless.

In a similar sort of way, we need to realize that God deliberately took six days to make the universe and the world with all its living creatures. For each of the first five days of creation, it was not finished — everything He did was perfect — He just had not completed it all until the end of the sixth day. Then He said it was "very good" (Genesis 1:31). We then read in Genesis 2:2 that on the seventh day of creation God had "finished" His work of creation.

Day Two

Chapter 2

Genesis 1:6-8

And God said, "Let there be an expanse in the midst of the waters, and let it separate the waters from the waters." And God made the expanse and separated the waters that were under the expanse from the waters that were above the expanse. And it was so. And God called the expanse Heaven. And there was evening and there was morning, the second day.

What Was "the Expanse"?

To understand this passage, we also need to read the following verses:

And God said, "Let the waters swarm with swarms of living creatures, and let birds fly above the earth across the expanse of the heavens (Genesis 1:20).

Note that the birds fly "across" the expanse, or as the NKJV more literally says, "across the face of the expanse."

*…and let them [stars] be lights **in the expanse** of the heavens to give light upon the earth." And it was so. And God made the two great lights — the greater light to rule the day and the lesser light to rule the night — and the stars. And God **set them in the expanse of the heavens** to give light on the earth (Genesis 1:15–17, emphasis added).*

So the flying creatures were to fly across the expanse, and the sun, moon, and stars were in the expanse.

So what does all this mean? Let me summarize and then I'll explain:

1. The "expanse" is outer space, where the sun, moon, and stars are.
2. The "waters above the expanse" are at the outer boundary of the universe.
3. The phrase "across the face of expanse of the heavens" means in the atmosphere where birds fly.
4. The waters "under the expanse" are the waters covering the surface of the earth.

So, on day two of creation week God made the expanse (or some translations say "firmament") which is really outer space. Then God separated the water that covered the earth to make two areas of water, with space between the waters above and the waters below. He called the expanse "heaven." All this is difficult to explain briefly because we need to look carefully at the Hebrew words used here and elsewhere in the Bible. For instance, the Hebrew word for heaven, like our English word for heaven, has different meanings depending on how it is used in a sentence. Despite the difficulty for me in explaining it succinctly, the Bible is clear on these points. God says that on day two He separated the water that, on day one, covered the earth to be two areas of water, by putting a space between the waters. So, there was water below this "firmament" or "expanse," covering the earth (which on day three became the seas separated from the dry land), and there was water above the firmament.

Now, on day four God says three times (in vv. 14, 15, and 17) that He put the sun, moon, and stars *in* the firmament that He made on day two. Then the Bible tells us that on day five God created the birds to fly *across the face* of the expanse (firmament). So after much more study of other verses that talk about this expanse/firmament, we can say that the expanse/firmament is the sky, which includes both the blue sky we see the birds flying in and the clouds floating in (what we call the atmosphere of the earth), and the night sky where the sun, moon, and stars are (what we call outer space).

And as difficult as it is for our finite minds to grasp, it seems that the waters above the firmament are at the outer edge of outer space. In fact, Psalm 148:3–4 says that water is still above the heavens where the sun, moon and stars are. It's also interesting to note that in 2 Peter 3:5 we read that "the heavens existed long ago, and the earth was formed out of water and through water by the word of God." Many biblical scholars believe this is teaching that water was the main element for the creation.

For those who are wondering about the water vapor canopy model that was popularized by many of the older generation biblical creationists, I have reproduced an article entitled "What Is the State of the Water Vapor Canopy Model?" in Appendix 4.

Getting Earth Ready for Life

So as part of what happened on day two, God was obviously preparing the atmosphere for living things. On days three, five, and six of creation week, we will find that God made all sorts of living things — plants, flying creatures, sea creatures, and land animals. We know that all living creatures need air so they can live. Most living things need oxygen. Every time you breathe in, your body takes the gas oxygen out of the air so your body can function.

We obtain our food from animals (in a post-Fall world) and/or plants. Even the animals we eat get their food from plants, or they eat animals that in turn eat plants. So, really, our food ultimately comes from plants. Plants use the gas oxygen, but they also use another gas called carbon dioxide. Both of these are part of the air we breathe. Plants also use water. They use a combination of carbon dioxide, water, and sunlight to make food so animals and people can eat them to get their food.

On day three of creation, God made all the plants. So when He was preparing this atmosphere on day two, He must have put oxygen and carbon dioxide around the earth so the plants and later the animals would be able to live.

We know oxygen had to be in the air when the earth was just over one day old. This means there was oxygen around the earth from almost the beginning.

Creation vs. Evolution –
The Order of Events Doesn't Agree

People who believe in evolution do not believe the air around the earth had oxygen in it when the earth first existed. They believe that the air was very poisonous, made up of gases like methane and ammonia, for example. If the air today was full of these gases, there would be no life on this planet.

Now why do evolutionists believe the first atmosphere had these poisonous gases? Well, because the substances (chemicals) that make up living things could not evolve if there was oxygen in the air. They would, in a sense, just "burn up" and life from non-life would be impossible. You see, evolutionists believe that chemicals just came together by chance to make all the very complex substances (including DNA, which is really an information system and language system) that are a part of living systems. But they also know that this could not happen if there was oxygen. And yet, for most living things, they need oxygen to live!

Now scientists have discovered oxygen in rocks they believe were supposedly part of the earth when the earth first existed. So, from their own evolutionary story, evolutionists have to accept that there must have been oxygen in the air from the beginning of the world — which is contradictory to their evolutionary worldview.

Heavier Than Air

Have you ever thought about why the air stays around the earth? Why doesn't the air just escape into space? If it did this, then we would have no air to breathe, and everything living would die.

The air is kept around the earth by an invisible force called gravity.

The remarkable thing is that scientists know gravity exists. They see it work — for example, if you throw something into the air, it will fall back to earth because the force of gravity brings it back to earth — but they don't really know why it works. They don't understand it.

When you hop on a scale to weigh yourself, the force of gravity pulls you down on the scale, and that is what gives you weight. When the astronauts went to the moon, they did not have much weight there because the force of gravity is much less on the moon. That is one reason why there is no air on the moon — there is not enough gravity for the air to stay there.

Air consists of particles called molecules that make up a number of different gases. If these particles are pulled down by this invisible force, then they must have weight. Scientists know that air has weight. But did you know the Bible had this information in it before scientists discovered it? Job 28:25 states, *To make the weight for the winds* (KJV). God told Job (who likely lived around the time of Abraham) the air had weight!

Our Goldilocks Atmosphere

Other planets in our solar system, like Venus and Jupiter, have an atmosphere — but their atmospheres are full of poisonous gases. Only the earth has exactly the right atmosphere for life. In fact, it looks like it was designed just right! That is what we would expect if God made the world. Actually, there is a word that describes the fact that the earth is just right in so many ways — just the right distance from the sun, just the right atmosphere, just the right substances like liquid water, and so on, that our planet has just the right conditions for life. This is called the "anthropic principle."

Scientists who are evolutionists believe that if life evolved on earth, it must have evolved on other planets. The more they are able to send spacecraft to Venus, Mars, and some of the other planets in our solar system, the more they find that it is only on earth that everything is just right for life. These other planets all have poisonous gases, or they are too hot or too cold for life. God did not make life on other planets — only on the earth. We will discuss this in more detail when we look at day four. However, evolutionists continue looking for life in outer space as they believe life had to evolve elsewhere in the universe. They can't believe life is special to earth because they reject that God is the Creator as the Bible tells us. These evolutionists believe that matter (of course, they don't ultimately explain where matter came from) somehow has this ability to form life if the right conditions exist. But matter can never, and has never been observed to, form life by itself. Such a belief is called "naturalism," which is, in reality, the religion of atheism. But life had to arise from an intelligent Creator; it can't come about by natural processes.

Just Pure Air

Now air is important for many things. Birds would not be able to fly if there was no air, as it is the air that rushes over their wings as they flap them that makes them fly. We would not be able to have airplanes if there was no air. There would be no wind to keep us cool and bring rain if there was no air. When God first made this air, it must have been perfect. The cleanest that air could ever be. Sadly, today, a lot of the air in the world is polluted from cars, factories, and other activities of man that put poisonous gases and other substances into the air. Because of the way we live, we can't help polluting the air, but we should try to keep it as clean as possible. After all, it is God's world, and as we will learn, God told man to look after it for Him. Now that doesn't mean we shouldn't have cars and factories, but we should do our best to keep the air pure. But actually, God set up the earth with the land, rain, air, and oceans to be a very complex system to keep conditions right for life to exist here. That's why it's so reassuring that God told Noah after the flood that, *While the earth remains, seedtime and harvest, cold and heat, summer and winter, day and night, shall not cease* (Genesis 8:22).

He's Coming in the Air

One day something very important is going to happen in the air around the earth. Jesus Christ, the Creator of this air, is one day coming back to take those who love and serve Him to heaven to live with Him forever. We read about this in the book of 1 Thessalonians 4:16–17, *For the Lord himself shall descend from heaven with a shout, with the voice of the archangel, and with the trump of God: and the dead in Christ shall rise first: Then we which are alive and remain shall be caught up together with them in the clouds, to meet the Lord in the air: and so shall we ever be with the Lord* (KJV).

When God was preparing the atmosphere for life, He knew that man would sin, and one day Jesus would ascend to heaven by going up into the atmosphere, and that He would return one day when He comes back for His bride (the church).

> *And when he had said these things, as they were looking on, he was lifted up, and a cloud took him out of their sight. And while they were gazing into heaven as he went, behold, two men stood by them in white robes, and said, "Men of Galilee, why do you stand looking into heaven? This Jesus, who was taken up from you into heaven, will come in the same way as you saw him go into heaven"* (Acts 1:9–11).

Was Day Two Not "Good"?

So on day two, we now have an earth that is still a watery blob, but there is an atmosphere around the earth, but no living things yet, and outer space, but with no other planets, moons, stars, or other heavenly bodies.

God has completed another part of the earth as He continues getting this earth ready for plants and animals, and ultimately humans, to live on it.

Genesis 1:8 ends with *And there was evening and there was morning, the second day.*

Now notice that at the end of the second day, God doesn't say that it was "good," as He does for the other five creation days. I believe this could be because He didn't create anything totally new on day two. He just separated what was already created, as explained earlier, and He was preparing for all that would happen on the next four days of creation. But regardless, while day two was not specifically called "good," we know the day, and what God did on that day, was good because Genesis 1:31 tells us that everything God made at the end of the creative process was "very good." This, of course, would include day two and everything God did on that day.

When Were Angels Created?

I think it would be interesting at this stage to mention angels. Many Christians who have studied the Bible for a long time think that the angels, who are created beings, were made sometime early in the creation week, perhaps on the first or second day. For instance, in Exodus 20:11, we read that God made everything in six days. Presumably this included the angels, as we read in Colossians 1:16 that *For by him all things were created, in heaven and on earth, visible and invisible, whether thrones or dominions or rulers or authorities — all things were created through him and for him.*

The Bible doesn't tell us much about angels as it is primarily a book about God and His relationship with man. But we do know from passages such as Hebrews 1:14, that they were made for a purpose associated with this earth and the people that live here: *Are they [angels] not all ministering spirits sent out to serve for the sake of those who are to inherit salvation?*

Many biblical scholars believe Job 38:7 is referring to all the angels who rejoiced when the foundations of the earth were laid, *when the morning stars sang together and all the sons of God shouted for joy.* If so, this passage could be telling us that the angels saw God making the earth. This would also mean that Satan, who is a created angel, was one of those that sang for joy. If so, this would mean Satan's rebellion had to be after this time — in fact, after everything God had created was called "very good." So when was Satan's rebellion? I think it's possible it could have been at the time he tempted Eve. Others think it would have had to happen before he tempted Eve and this act was what came from the rebellion. We don't know for sure, but it's interesting to think about this.

God had now finished the second day of creation — so let's move on to day three.

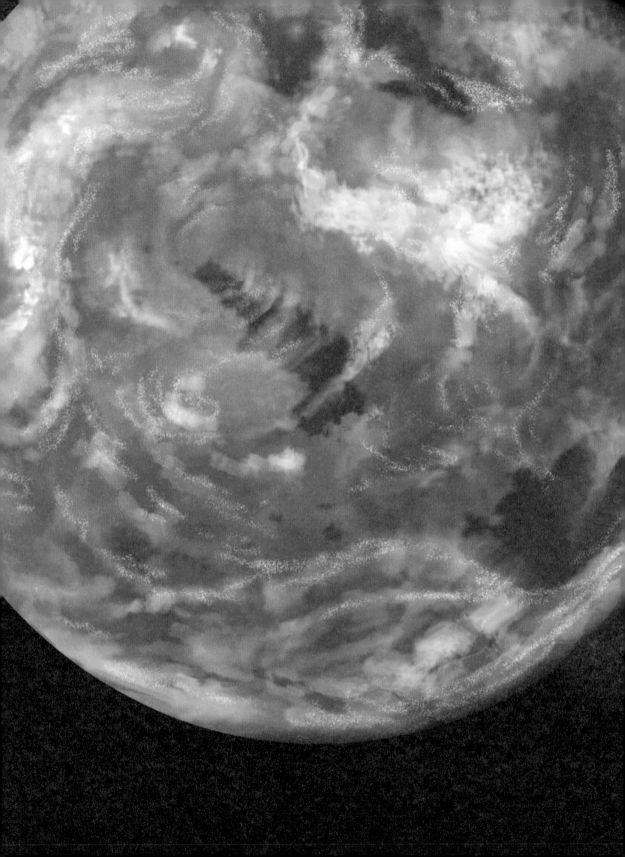

Chapter 3

Day Three

Genesis 1:9-13

And God said, "Let the waters under the heavens be gathered together into one place, and let the dry land appear." And it was so. God called the dry land Earth, and the waters that were gathered together he called Seas. And God saw that it was good.

And God said, "Let the earth sprout vegetation, plants yielding seed, and fruit trees bearing fruit in which is their seed, each according to its kind, on the earth." And it was so. The earth brought forth vegetation, plants yielding seed according to their own kinds, and trees bearing fruit in which is their seed, each according to its kind. And God saw that it was good. And there was evening and there was morning, the third day.

On day three, God was making the earth take on definite shape as He commanded the land to rise up out of the water. Later, on this same day, He commanded the plants to be brought forth. As these plants would be growing on this land surface, God must have made this dry land with beautiful, nutritious soil to provide what the plants needed.

One Continent?

Because God said that he gathered the waters "together unto one place," creation scientists believe that the land would also have been in one place. What I mean by this is the possibility that there was actually only one continent originally — one major land mass on the earth when it was first made. This continent may have had a variety of shapes around its coast, with long narrow areas jutting out, and so on.

The shape of the land may have divided up the water around the globe so that the areas of water could be called "seas" — which means there was more than one sea. Think about the continent of Australia today. On the east side we have what is called the "Pacific Ocean," on the west side the "Indian Ocean," and in the south the "Great Southern Ocean." So, we have a number of different oceans, but it is one body of water. Thus, even if the original earth only had one continent, there could still be a number of "seas."

If there was only one continent originally, then something has obviously happened to break up this one land mass to form all of the various continents that exist today. This likely happened during the catastrophic event of Noah's Flood (this will be discussed when we get to chapters 6 through 9).

High Mountains?

What was the land surface like when it was first made? For instance, would there have been high mountains like we have today? I doubt there were really high mountains, because we are told later on that the waters from the great flood covered "all the high hills under the whole heaven" (Gen 7:19, NKJV). Now there's not enough water in the oceans to cover all the mountains that exist today. But scientists have calculated that if all of the land surface and the ocean basins that exist today were leveled out so that there were no hills, valleys, deep ocean trenches, etc., the water in the oceans would cover the entire earth to a depth of almost two miles. So, if the oceans were not as deep as they are now, and the mountains not as high, there would have been enough water to cover the entire earth just as it says in Genesis chapter 7. This would mean the high mountains and the deep oceans were formed toward the end of the Flood and even after the Flood.

Now Psalm 104 is a psalm that David wrote that tells us a lot about creation. In fact, David puts a lot of the information about creation in this psalm in the same order as the days of creation in Genesis chapter 1. He also adds in lots of other information for us as well. For instance, in verses 6–9, some scholars believe David might be referring to what happened at the end of Noah's Flood.

> *He set the earth on its foundations, so that it should never be moved. You covered it with the deep as with a garment; the waters stood above the mountains. At your rebuke they fled; at the sound of your thunder they took to flight. The mountains rose, the valleys sank down to the place that you appointed for them. You set a boundary that they may not pass, so that they might not again cover the earth* (Psalm 104:5–9).

In these verses, David seems to be saying that after the water covered the entire earth, God raised up the mountains and then sunk the ocean floor so that the water could run off the earth. This would also explain why there are marine fossils on the tops of mountains like the Himalayas. The creatures were buried during the Flood and then the sediments were raised up as mountains formed at the end of the Flood. He then tells us that God set a boundary so the water would never again cover the earth. This fits with the end of the Flood as described in Genesis 9:11: *I establish my covenant with you, that never again shall all flesh be cut off by the waters of the flood, and never again shall there be a flood to destroy the earth.*

God promises He will never again judge the earth with such a global flood. Now we have seen many local floods since this time, so this verse is obviously referring to God never judging again with a global flood. We know though that the earth is going to be judged again, but with fire next time (2 Peter 3:10).

So it seems that at the end of Noah's Flood, God raised up the mountains and made the deep oceans. This means the water from Noah's Flood is in today's oceans. Remember that the next time you are looking at the ocean! You are looking at the water that once destroyed the entire earth — the water that God used to judge this earth because of wickedness. We could even use the ocean as a topic to witness to people, sharing how God judges wickedness as a righteous judge, but provides a way of salvation for those who obey His Word.

What did this original land surface look like then? Well, we know there were hills, because Genesis 7:19 says that the "high mountains" were covered with water during the Flood. The mountains though (some translations say "hills," which is a better word) were nowhere near as high as the mountains we have today, as I have explained. So there were probably hills, valleys, flat areas, lakes, and rivers. In Genesis 2:10 we are told about a river in the Garden of Eden. There must have been plenty of places like rivers and lakes with lots of fresh, clean water, because God made many kinds of land animals to live on the earth on day six.

Salty Seas?

I've also often wondered what the seas were like. Was the water as salty as it is today? Well, scientists can measure how much salt drains into today's oceans from the land (due to erosion by rivers, rain, etc.) and they can measure how much salt leaves the oceans. If all the water in all the oceans was fresh water, with no salt, when the oceans were first formed, then evolutionists have another big problem. They say the oceans are hundreds of millions of years old. But even if there was no salt at all in the oceans to start with, the amount of salt in them today would not take anywhere near hundreds of millions of years to accumulate. In other words, the oceans would be so salty by now that life would be impossible! This means the oceans can't be millions of years old. Another big problem for evolution.

I believe there would have been some salt in the oceans to start with, as God made the oceans ready for all the sea animals that He created on day five. However, it may have been that it wasn't as salty when it was first made as it is now. It is possible that during the great Flood, a lot of salt from the earth was added into the oceans.

Our Great God

Now this verse reminds us of how great (infinite) our creator God is:

> *Who has measured the waters in the hollow of his hand and marked off the heavens with a span, enclosed the dust of the earth in a measure and weighed the mountains in scales and the hills in a balance?* (Isaiah 40:12).

God knows how much water is in the oceans, how big the universe is, and how much material makes up the mountains and hills! This is beyond our understanding — but it helps us to understand how great God is as we discussed in regard to the first verse of Genesis 1.

How did God make the seas? Look at Genesis 1:9 again. *And God said...* He spoke, and it happened. This helps us understand what happened in Mark 4:39–41, where a storm was battering the boat with the disciples and Jesus on board. Jesus stood up and said, *Peace! Be still!* The wind and the sea immediately became calm. The disciples said, *Who then is this, that even the wind and the sea obey him?* (Mark 4:41). Who is this? Jesus the Creator. What did the Creator do when He looked at the storm? He spoke. What did the sea do? The sea obeyed the voice of the Creator — it had to, because He made it.

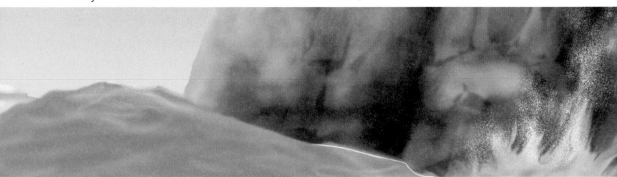

This should make us think about ourselves. We should obey the words of the Creator because He made us also.

Think of another time when the land obeyed God because He wanted it to do something for Him. In Numbers 16 we read about a man called Korah who rebelled against Moses. We are told that because of his rebellion *the ground under them split apart. And the earth opened its mouth and swallowed them up, with their households and all the people who belonged to Korah and all their goods* (Numbers 16:31–32). God made the land open up and swallow all those that followed Korah in that rebellion. God told the land what to do, and it obeyed, because God was its Creator.

This should make us all realize how much we should obey our Creator.

What Shape Is Earth?

Now when God raised up the land surface and made the seas on day three, the earth was now taking on a definite shape. It was no longer a watery blob. It was no longer "without form and void" as we read in verse 2. What shape did God make the earth?

Because scientists have traveled all over the earth, and have seen the earth from outer space, we know the earth is a sphere. We also know it hangs in space. The pictures of the earth taken by the astronauts who landed on the moon show the earth as a beautiful, colorful sphere hanging in space. Before scientists had done a lot of study on the earth or had been able to see the earth from outer space, some people actually believed the earth was flat or that it sat on pillars!

We laugh at this now because we know that it is not true. But did you know we could have learned that the earth was a sphere hanging in space by reading the Bible? God had people write this information in the Bible before modern scientists understood it, long before man invented airplanes, satellites, and other spacecraft. Remember, God has always been there, He knows everything, and He doesn't tell a lie.

Many scientists who had read and believed God's Word became famous because of the exciting discoveries they made. I'll discuss one of these scientists after we look at the Bible verses that teach us that the earth is a sphere hanging in space.

> *When he established the heavens, I was there; when he drew a circle* [set a compass] *on the face of the deep. . .* (Proverbs 8:27).

> *It is he who sits above the circle of the earth, and its inhabitants are like grasshoppers. . .* (Isaiah 40:22).

The words **compass** and **circle** in the above verses can mean circle or sphere. God is telling us that the earth is round/spherical — it is not flat. In the Book of Job 26:7 we read, *He stretches out the north over the void and hangs the earth on nothing.* The Bible tells us what scientists now know to be true — the earth does not rest on anything; it hangs on nothing. It hangs in space. If only people had read and believed the Bible, they would not have believed such ridiculous ideas as the earth being flat or sitting on pillars. I have a Christian friend who is a space shuttle commander and has been on the International Space Station orbiting the earth — he's even done space walks. He has sent me videos of the earth taken from space, and you see the spherical earth spinning. So amazing!

A Flat Earth?

Maybe some of you are thinking, "Well why does the Bible say in 1 Samuel 2:8, *For the pillars of the earth are the LORD's, and he hath set the world upon them*" (KJV)? Does this contradict the other passage of the Bible that teaches us the earth hangs on nothing? No, it certainly does not. This quote is from a prayer of Hannah, Samuel's mother. Hannah is using the term "pillars of the earth" in a spiritual sense. Remember, words can have different meanings depending on context. This section in Samuel is not an account of history concerning cosmology. It's a prayer.

The phrase "pillars of the earth" used in this prayer actually refers to the strength of God Himself as He holds everything together. The only reason that we and everything else exists, is because God's power holds everything together. The Bible teaches this to us in Hebrews 1:3 where we are told that God is *upholding all things by the word of his power* (KJV). In Colossians 1:17 we read, *And he is before all things, and by him all things consist* (KJV). This means God holds everything together. Hannah is recognizing God's great power in her prayer.

Some of you may have read another interesting verse in the Bible that seems to contradict the idea that the earth is a sphere. In Isaiah 11:12 and Revelation 7:1, we read about "the four corners of the earth." Some think this means the Bible says the earth is flat. This is not true at all. Let me explain what the phrase "four corners of the earth" means here in these passages.

If you take an apple and cut it across one way and then the other, you will end up with four even pieces. You have cut the apple into quarters. The earth, being a sphere, could also be divided up into four quarters. This is what the phrase "four corners of the earth" means.

Because our English Bibles have been translated from the original language, and because English words change their meanings over a period of time, we could believe wrong things if we did not study the Bible properly and carefully look at the Hebrew and Greek words and how they're used in context.

No wonder God tells us to *Do your best to present yourself to God as one approved, a worker who has no need to be ashamed, rightly handling the word of truth* (2 Timothy 2:15).

The Paths of the Seas

To finish up discussing the seas God made on day three, here is an interesting fact of history.

Matthew Maury lived during the 19th century. He read in the Bible in Psalm 8 verse 8, *whatever passes along the paths of the seas*. He loved the sea, and this verse was very special to him. If God said there were paths in the sea, he believed there must be paths, as God knows everything. So he set out to find them. Maury charted the winds and currents of the Atlantic Ocean, mapping out what he believed these "paths" in the sea were. He was known as "the Pathfinder of the Seas." Because of his work, the modern sciences of hydrography and oceanography began. Psalm 8, and other Bible verses, are referenced on his tombstone!

The First Life

On the third day of creation, God also made the first living things — plant life. The text tells us God made three basic types of plants — grasses, shrubs (herbs), and trees. God did not make seeds and plant them so they would grow into plants. He made the plants fully formed. For instance, the fruit trees already had fruit on them with seeds in them. The plants were mature.

In Genesis 1:29–30 we're told that Adam and Eve were to eat fruit (plants) and that the animals were also plant eaters. Obviously, God made plants ready for humans and the animals He would create just a few days later to eat. Imagine if God had only made seeds and planted them in the ground, and then three days later the land animals and the first two people needed food to eat! Adam and Eve couldn't wait for years while the fruit trees grew to bear fruit so they could have their first meal!

We don't know how many plants God made, but I presume He must have made enough trees, shrubs, and grasses to cover the entire land surface.

When I am in my native country of Australia, I like to visit the Australian tropical rainforest. In the rainforest there are lots of trees, vines, shrubs, and grasses. Everything is so green, lush, and moist. There are often streams of clear, cool water running through the rainforest, with lots of beautiful ferns growing on the bank and orchids with colorful flowers in the trees. It is so peaceful. I like to sit in the rainforest and just think about God. As I look around, I like to think about what the world was like when God first made it. Maybe some of the land surface would have been something like this rainforest. I think there would also have been lots of areas that just had green grass for grazing animals. Everything must have been so beautiful.

Carrying Out God's Instructions

Notice that God created the plants so they would reproduce (or make copies of) themselves. God said the plants He made had seeds. Imagine planting a small seed that you can hardly see into the ground, and then watching the plant grow from that seed into an enormous tree. Every time I see that happen, I am so amazed that all the information about the tree is in that tiny seed. When God created the various plant kinds, He created all the information in the DNA molecules for each of those different kinds. That's just beyond my understanding.

When builders design a building, all their plans and instructions for just one large building might take up hundreds of pages of diagrams and written information. Do you realize that if you could write out all the information in one seed that grows into a tree, it would probably take hundreds or thousands of books, each with hundreds of pages? God put all the instructions on how the tree is built and how it is to grow in the seed — and then, the remarkable thing is the seed then carries out the instructions. It does it all by itself!

We've never seen a building just build itself from the plans. It doesn't happen. But a plant can do it. Not only that, but a plant grows and then makes more seeds so it can make copies of itself. We've never seen a building after it was built, make its own plans so it can copy itself to make more buildings. The more I think about just a tiny seed, the more I just want to praise the God of creation who created all this.

Now the plants we have today were not made directly by God. God made the first plants directly, but He made them to make copies of themselves. Because plants only live for a certain number of years, the plants have had to make copies over and over and over again for thousands of years since they were made. So the plants we see today are copies (with variation due to created diversity in each plant kind's

DNA) of the original plants. But we can still say that God made all the plants, because all the information that builds a plant was made by God in the first place.

From Day Three to Golgotha

Now here is something to ponder. One of the kinds of trees God created made copies of itself many times over, so there were trees of the same kind when Jesus came to earth as the Godman. One of these trees that was a descendant of the original kind God made was used by Roman soldiers to make into a cross. Jesus Christ, the Creator, was nailed on the Cross to die for our sins.

So when God made the trees, He knew one of those trees was the ancestor of the tree that many thousands of years later would be used to make His Cross. God knows everything, so He must have known this. The Bible even tells us that God did know this. In Revelation 13:8, we read about Jesus who is said to be the "Lamb of God" and *everyone whose name has not been written before the foundation of the world in the book of life of the Lamb who was slain.*

God knew that He would send His Son, the LORD Jesus Christ, to die on a Cross for our sin of rebelling against God. He knew this before He made the world. Even knowing this, He still made the world.

According to Its Kind

In Genesis 1, we read the phrase "according to its kind" or "according to their (own) kinds" a total of ten times.

So God made plants (and later animals) after their kind, which implies they would reproduce after their own kind. We will discuss the word "kind" in much more detail when we deal with the creation of animals. But our research shows there can be great variation within a kind, but one kind can never change into a totally different kind. Now, with animals, we know cats only reproduce cats and horses only reproduce horses. There can be many different types (varieties) of horses (i.e., zebras, donkeys, miniature ponies, etc.), but they remain horses. God also made plants in kinds, with each kind being able to reproduce its own kind. God made different kinds of fruit trees with each kind being able to produce variation in fruit, but only within its own kind. Obviously, coconut trees could never produce oranges — they belong to different kinds.

Now people who believe in evolution think that one kind of animal changed into a totally different kind of animal over millions of years. For instance, they believe that animals like dinosaurs changed into birds, and ape-like creatures evolved into people.

The fact that God uses the phrases "after its kind," or "after their (own) kind," ten times in Genesis 1, shows He is emphasizing to us that all the plants and animals He made were all made as separate kinds. None of them evolved from a different kind. He created living things so there would be variation within any kind, but they would always stay within their own kind.

So we could say this: God made the original kinds of animals and plants as separate kinds to reproduce after their own kind, so one kind would not change into another kind but there would be variation within a kind — which is why we see all the kinds of organisms (and great variety within each kind) we have today.

Organizing Life

This reminds me of a famous scientist I learned about when I went to school. Carolus Linnaeus in the 18th century believed the Bible when it said that God made the animals and plants in kinds (or groups). He invented a system to name animals and plants in groups because of this (this is called taxonomy). When you study science, you always learn about Carolus Linnaeus because he invented this idea of naming living things in groups. We still, by and large, follow his taxonomy today, classifying living things by kingdom, phylum, class, order, family, genus, and species. He became a very famous scientist because he started with the Bible, believing God's Word. Now, initially, he thought "species" corresponded to kind, but later realized this was not so in most instances. We now realize the "family" level of classification usually corresponds to what is called a kind. Sometimes it is at the "order" level, but mainly it is at the "family" level of classification.

Which Came First?

Sadly, some Christians think that God used evolution to make life! Here is a big problem for people who try to accept this idea.

The evolutionary story states that life first evolved in the sea. Evolutionists say that chemicals in the ocean somehow came together by natural processes to make the first life. Notice that on day three of creation week, the first living things God made were land plants. The evolutionary story and what God states in the Bible are totally different.

Have you ever heard of the yucca plant? These tough plants grow very well in Mexico. Now, for the yucca plant to produce seeds so it can make copies of itself, pollen (that orange sticky stuff you see on flowers) from one plant must get to another yucca plant — otherwise yucca plants would all die out.

Now plants are often pollinated by insects, but most insects can't pollinate yuccas. However, there is a special moth called the yucca moth. It is only the yucca moth that can pollinate a yucca plant. Remember, the plant can't do it by itself. And, by the way, the yucca moth needs the yucca plant so it can live and reproduce. The yucca plant can't live without the yucca moth, and the yucca moth can't live without the yucca plant. So how could evolution explain this?

Here's the problem for those who try and add millions of years into the Bible. If the moth was not created at the same time as the yucca plant (it was likely created day five or six), and if each day of creation was thousands or millions of years long as some Christians believe, then how could the yucca plant survive if God made it on day three, but the yucca moth was not made until day five or six, thousands or millions of years later? This would not work at all. Instead of adding man's ideas into God's Word, let's start with God's Word.

Day Four

Chapter 4

Genesis 1:14-19

And God said, "Let there be lights in the expanse of the heavens to separate the day from the night. And let them be for signs and for seasons, and for days and years, and let them be lights in the expanse of the heavens to give light upon the earth." And it was so. And God made the two great lights — the greater light to rule the day and the lesser light to rule the night — and the stars. And God set them in the expanse of the heavens to give light on the earth, to rule over the day and over the night, and to separate the light from the darkness. And God saw that it was good. And there was evening and there was morning, the fourth day.

Now on the first day of creation God said *let there be light*. In other words, he made the entity of light. Presumably this would include the entire electromagnetic spectrum, including infrared, X-rays, visible light, and ultraviolet light.

Now on day four of creation week, God made "lights." The Hebrew word for "lights" means "light givers." He made sources for the light that He had already created. Now the main purpose for light was given on day one — to divide the day and the night. And light has many other functions including providing heat and enabling plants to produce chemical energy through photosynthesis.

The lights that have the most significance are called the greater light (the sun) to rule the day, and the lesser light (the moon) to rule the night. The sun is a gigantic body that produces its own light. The moon reflects the light of the sun, so although it doesn't produce its own light, it still is a source of light reflecting light from the sun.

Let It Shine

The Bible tells us *God is light, and in him is no darkness at all* (1 John 1:5).

Jesus tells us, that *You are the light of the world. A city set on a hill cannot be hidden. Nor do people light a lamp and put it under a basket, but on a stand, and it gives light to all in the house. In the same way, let your light shine before others, so that they may see your good works and give glory to your Father who is in heaven* (Matthew 5:14–16).

I remember my mother teaching me that, in a way, the sun is like Jesus. Jesus as God is the source of "light" (holiness, righteousness, goodness, and all truth). Now this is the opposite of darkness, meaning the darkness of sin and evil, and thus He is the opposite of the evil one (the devil) who is the "father of lies" (John 8:44). The sun is its own source of light, whereas the moon reflects the sun's light. So for us, as humans, to be the "light of the world," we need to be like the moon — reflecting the light of the Lord Jesus in everything we do.

My mum and dad taught us a popular chorus based on Mathew 5:15, *Nor do people light a lamp and put it under a basket [bushel], but on a stand, and it gives light to all in the house.* I still remember the words to this day. I know there are different versions of the lyrics, but this is what my parents taught me and my siblings, along with numerous kids in Sunday school, along with actions — and I like this version the best, of course. We can sing it as kids or adults!

> See this little light of mine,
>
> I'm going to let it shine.
>
> See this little light of mine,
>
> I'm going to let it shine, let it shine, let it shine, let it shine.

Hide it under a bushel, NO.

I'm going to let it shine.

Hide it under a bushel, NO.

I'm going to let it shine, let it shine, let it shine, let it shine.

Don't let Satan blow it out,

I'm going to let it shine.

Don't let Satan blow it out,

I'm going to let it shine, let it shine, let it shine, let it shine.

Let it shine till Jesus comes,

I'm going to let it shine.

Let it shine till Jesus comes,

I'm going to let it shine, let it shine, let it shine, let it shine.

A Big Bang Origin?

Now, remember, those who believe in the big bang idea for the origin of the universe believe the sun came before the earth. But as I stated earlier, God's Word makes it clear the sun was created after the earth, so we know the big bang idea is wrong.

He Made the Stars Also

Along with the sun and the moon, we are told God made the stars on day four. I love how the King James Bible translation states it in Genesis 1:16:

He made the stars also.

How many stars are in the universe? No one knows, but some scientists estimate there are 100 billion stars in the Milky Way galaxy alone and then 1,000,000,000,000,000,000,000,000 in the universe. To try to count them would be like trying to count the grains of sand on all the beaches in the world. The point is, the number of stars is so great we can't even comprehend it.

But think about this. *He determines the number of the stars; he gives to all of them their names* (Psalm 147:4). So God knows the number of stars and has a name for each one. Once again, we get a little inkling of what it means that God is the infinite Creator.

God even tells us we can't count the number of stars or the number of grains of sand. This reminds us of how finite we are compared to God:

> *As the host of heaven cannot be numbered and the sands of the sea cannot be measured, so I will multiply the offspring of David my servant, and the Levitical priests who minister to me* (Jeremiah 33:22).

And when I think about the fact that all we're told is "he made the stars also," I think it's almost as if God is saying, "Oh, by the way, you see all those stars you can't count? I made them too." And when you think about how powerful just our one star (the sun) in our solar system is, I can't even imagine the power it took to create all these stars, and many of them so much bigger than our sun! So why did God create so many stars?

Well, the Bible tells us why God made the stars:

> *The heavens declare the glory of God, and the sky above proclaims his handiwork. Day to day pours out speech, and night to night reveals knowledge. There is no speech, nor are there words, whose voice is not heard. Their voice goes out through all the earth, and their words to the end of the world* (Psalm 19:1–4).

God made the stars to declare His glory! And as we consider the number of stars and the energy they produce and the vastness of space, we start to again get a tiny understanding of what it means that God is infinite in power.

Is Anyone Out There?

Another point to ponder is that the earth was made first. The earth was specially created, is unique, and is the focus of God's attention:

> *Thus says the LORD: "Heaven is my throne, and the earth is my footstool"* (Isaiah 66:1).

> *The heavens are the LORD's heavens, but the earth he has given to the children of man* (Psalm 115:16).

Why is this important? Well, we know life did not evolve but was specially created by God on this earth, as we've seen on day three and will find out more about on days five and six. And the sun and moon were created for signs and our seasons in relation to the earth — and to declare the glory of God. Earth was specifically formed for life, particularly human life. Because of all this, Christians certainly shouldn't expect alien life to be cropping up across the universe as evolutionists claim we should find. Now it's true the Bible doesn't say whether or not there is animal or plant life in outer space. I certainly suspect not. I'll discuss more about the topic of whether there could be aliens in the universe when we learn about the gospel message in Genesis chapter 3.

Really Old Light?

Some Christians believe that because the universe is so big and has so many stars, the universe must be billions of years old. They claim it would take light billions of years to reach Earth from the farthest star. But we really don't understand light or deep space — there's so much we don't know. Not only that, but the processes God used to create were finished at the end of the sixth day of creation. So there's an enormous amount (actually an infinite amount) we don't understand. What we do know is God created the stars so they would be seen on earth from day four onward. With God nothing is impossible. *For nothing will be impossible with God* (Luke 1:37).

Astronomical Signs

The sun, moon, and stars were *created for signs and for seasons, and for days and years.*

We know that the sun gives light on the earth, and the rotating earth results in a light period and a dark period. One rotation is a 24-hour day. The moon was made to rule the night — we don't really see the moon (unless under special circumstances) during the daylight portion of a day. We also know the time it takes for the earth to go around the sun is one year (roughly 365 days). During this time the amount of sunlight on the earth changes, resulting in seasons. The seasons we have today are probably more extreme than they were originally because the Flood of Noah's day caused catastrophic changes. The relationship of the moon to the earth enables us to calculate months. The moon also has an important function in producing tides so the ocean waters can cleanse themselves and provide the right conditions for all sorts of fascinating animals and plants.

God also tells us that seasons and days and nights will never cease until the Lord Jesus returns. So even though we need to look after the earth, no matter what happens there will always be seasons and always be day and night:

> *While the earth remains, seedtime and harvest, cold and heat, summer and winter, day and night, shall not cease* (Genesis 8:22).

> *Thus says the LORD: If you can break my covenant with the day and my covenant with the night, so that day and night will not come at their appointed time, then also my covenant with David my servant may be broken, so that he shall not have a son to reign on his throne, and my covenant with the Levitical priests my ministers* (Jeremiah 33:20–21).

Down through the ages, people have used the stars to navigate, using them as signs. God referred to certain star clusters (constellations) to remind Job of how great God is as He does things we human beings can't explain:

> *Can you bind the chains of the Pleiades or loose the cords of Orion? Can you lead forth the Mazzaroth in their season, or can you guide the Bear with its children? Do you know the ordinances of the heavens? Can you establish their rule on the earth?* (Job 38:31–33).

And God used a special event in the heavens as one of the greatest signs ever:

> *Now after Jesus was born in Bethlehem of Judea in the days of Herod the king, behold, wise men from the east came to Jerusalem, saying, "Where is he who has been born king of the Jews? For we saw his star when it rose and have come to worship him"* (Matthew 2:1–2).

> *After listening to the king, they went on their way. And behold, the star that they had seen when it rose went before them until it came to rest over the place where the child was* (Matthew 2:9).

Yes, the heavens declare the glory of God.

Day Five

Chapter 5

Genesis 1:20-23

And God said, "Let the waters swarm with swarms of living creatures, and let birds [flying creatures] fly above the earth across the expanse of the heavens." So God created the great sea creatures and every living creature that moves, with which the waters swarm, according to their kinds, and every winged bird according to its kind. And God saw that it was good. And God blessed them, saying, "Be fruitful and multiply and fill the waters in the seas, and let birds multiply on the earth." And there was evening and there was morning, the fifth day.

On the fifth day of creation God made the flying creatures and the sea creatures. Some translations use "birds" in Genesis 1:20, but the better translation is "flying creatures." This would include birds, flying mammals such as bats, and flying reptiles like the pterodactyls and rhamphorhynchoids. Today these are considered by secular scientists to be "prehistoric creatures." But from a biblical worldview there's really no such thing as prehistoric, as history began from when it was recorded in Genesis 1:1. These creatures are also not flying dinosaurs as some people think. The word "dinosaur" wasn't invented until 1841, and it was a name chosen for particular groups of animals that walk on the land. We'll deal with that topic later.

Now there are some creatures that do glide through the air, such as flying squirrels, sugar gliders, and gliding lizards. But they are not free-flying creatures, so they would likely have been created on day six.

Insects on Day Five?

The Bible doesn't specifically tell us on which day God created insects (or spiders, bacteria, viruses, etc.). Many insects have important functions associated with plants. Many insects fly. Perhaps God created some on day five (when creatures that fly were created) and others on day six. It's possible that insects and spiders were included under the term "creeping things" on day six. We are just not told. God's classification system is very different from ours and God doesn't tell us all the specifics, but gives us the big picture. We do know God created all living things originally.

Which Came First?

In Genesis 1:21 we read that God created the sea creatures and flying creatures according to their respective kinds. So God created specific kinds of sea creatures and flying creatures to produce their own kinds. However, God put a lot of information in the DNA of each kind so there would be great variability. For instance, we know that the domesticated fowl, turkeys, and pheasants belong to the landfowl kind (order Galliformes). We know that because scientists can document how they are all interrelated. This brings me to a well-known question I'm sure we've all heard, "Which came first—the chicken or the egg?"

Well, a chicken today is a descendant of the original animals God made for the landfowl kind. Now after God made the flying creatures, He told them to "multiply on the earth." They would have laid eggs so the next generation of landfowls would be produced. So, we can say the chicken (meaning the bird) came before the egg.

Birds Obey the Creator

There's another lesson to learn about birds. Because God created the birds, He owns them, and He can tell them what to do. In 1 Kings 17:6 we read how

74

God sent birds to feed Elijah: *And the ravens brought him bread and meat in the morning, and bread and meat in the evening, and he drank from the brook.* When God created the dove kind (order Columbiformes) from which doves descended, God knew that one day Noah would send a dove out toward the end of the Flood and it would come back with an olive branch in its beak. Just a reminder that God knows everything and knew before He created the world everything that would happen in this universe.

Are Birds Dinosaurs?

Another important topic to discuss in relation to birds concerns the land animals we refer to as dinosaurs. Evolutionists believe dinosaurs evolved into birds. Many evolutionists claim when you see birds in your backyard, you are actually looking at dinosaurs. This is ridiculous.

First of all, the Bible makes it clear birds were created on day five, before the land animals (which would include the animal kinds we today call dinosaurs) that were created on day six. So God is making it clear to us the evolutionists are wrong.

Secondly, think of what would have to happen for a dinosaur to evolve into a bird. Scales (folds in the skin) would need to evolve into feathers (complex structures that grow from a follicle), and a reptile lung would have to evolve into a totally different lung like birds have. These vast changes would be impossible (there is no known mechanism that can add the brand-new genetic information required into the genome). Besides, although some evolutionists claim they have supposedly found dinosaur fossils with feathers, other scientists vehemently disagree with these "feathered dinosaur" claims, pointing out some of these "feathered dinosaurs" are really just birds that evolutionists are claiming are dinosaurs. Evolutionists make all sorts of outrageous claims because they just don't want to believe God created them and thus owns them and has a right to tell them what they should do.

Genesis is clear that God didn't make birds from pre-existing dinosaurs. In fact, dinosaurs (certain land animal kinds made on day six) came *after* winged creatures made on day five, according to the Bible. Both biblically and scientifically, chicken eaters around the world can rest easy — they aren't eating mutant dinosaurs.

Oceans Teeming with Life

God also created all life to live in the seas. Remember that evolutionists believe the first living things supposedly evolved in the primeval oceans before plants. But God's Word tell us plants were created before anything lived in the seas! Once again, the evolutionary story is wrong!

This sea life God created would include all the vast array of aquatic creatures including fish, sea mammals like whales and dolphins/porpoises, sea reptiles like turtles, plesiosaurs, ichthyosaurs, crocodiles, and so many more.

Many marine reptiles are now extinct. Again, creatures like plesiosaurs are not called dinosaurs, as they lived in water. And they are not prehistoric creatures, as there's really no such thing as prehistory as we've already discussed.

Another problem for evolutionists is that they believe after land animals evolved from a fish ancestor, something like a dog went back to the ocean, evolving into an aquatic mammal (like a whale). This is how they explain the origin of marine mammals. But the Bible makes it clear that marine mammals were created on day five before land animals that were created on day six. One certainly cannot try to add the evolutionary story to the Bible as some Christians sadly try to do — it just doesn't fit!

An Aquatic Sign Pointing to Christ

We don't know which particular kind of sea creature it was, but God knew that one day he would prepare one to swallow a man called Jonah: *And the LORD appointed a great fish to swallow up Jonah. And Jonah was in the belly of the fish three days and three nights* (Jonah 1:17). And God knew that what happened to Jonah would be used by the Lord Jesus Christ, our Creator, as a teaching point for the rebellious people who did not believe He was the Son of God when He was on earth. Jesus used Jonah to tell them about a sign that He really was the Messiah, the Son of God. That sign would be His Resurrection on the third day after being crucified.

> *An evil and adulterous generation seeks for a sign, but no sign will be given to it except the sign of the prophet Jonah. For just as Jonah was three days and three nights in the belly of the great fish, so will the Son of Man be three days and three nights in the heart of the earth* (Matthew 12:39–40).

First *Nephesh* Life

Now there is one last, very important subject to cover before we move on to day six. In Genesis 1:20 we read the term "living creatures." The word "living" is translated from the Hebrew word "*nephesh*." This term means "life" and is used for the first time in this verse. It is the word used for the soul of man and the life of animals. Plants do not have *nephesh,* which means in the biblical sense, plants are not considered alive or having real life. We will find out later on that plants were given to man and the animals for food. Man and the animals were vegetarian originally. There was no *nephesh* death before sin. God didn't tell man to eat animals until after the Flood (Genesis 9:3).

God Cares for His Creation

Note that God gave a special blessing to the all the sea creatures and land creatures: *And God blessed them.* Even in the fallen world we see God's care and concern for animals: *Are not two sparrows sold for a penny? And not one of them will fall to the ground apart from your Father* (Matthew 10:29); *Look at the birds of the air: they neither sow nor reap nor gather into barns, and yet your heavenly Father feeds them* (Matthew 6:26).

God also told these creatures to *"Be fruitful and multiply and fill the waters in the seas and let birds [flying creatures] multiply on the earth"* (Genesis 1:22).

Chapter 6

Day Six

Genesis 1:24-25

And God said, "Let the earth bring forth living creatures according to their kinds — livestock and creeping things and beasts of the earth according to their kinds." And it was so. And God made the beasts of the earth according to their kinds and the livestock according to their kinds, and everything that creeps on the ground according to its kind. And God saw that it was good.

On day six, God made the land animals and two humans. He made the land animals first and once again we read the phrase "according to their kinds." The implication is that each kind was created to reproduce its own kind. And that's what we observe today. Dogs only produce dogs, cats only produce cats, elephants only produce elephants, and so on. One kind did not, and cannot, evolve into a totally different kind. Now, there can be great variation within a kind because of all the information God placed in the DNA of the original animals of each kind God created.

How Many Kinds?

We've already discussed the word "kind" as it is an important concept to understand. Evolutionists mock creationists who say Noah took representatives of each kind of land-dwelling, air-breathing animal on the Ark. They claim there would be too many to fit. But we will find in Genesis 6 that two of each kind and seven pairs of some went onboard

the Ark. Now creation scientists have determined that, in most instances, the word "kind" is referring to the "family" level of classification. So only two of the dog family, and two of the cat family, etc., were on the Ark. When we work out how many kinds were actually needed, we find, at the most, only around 1,400 kinds were needed. For various reasons, many creation scientists believe there may actually be only 1,000, or even less, land-dwelling, air-breathing kinds. So there would have been plenty of room on the Ark.

Now God's classification system is different from ours. So when we read that God created the livestock, the creeping things, and the beasts of the earth, this would have included all the land-dwelling, air-breathing animals.

Nephesh Chayyah

Once again the Hebrew word *nephesh* (soul) is used for these living creatures. Humans and animals are described in Genesis as having, or being, *nephesh* in Genesis 1:20–21, 24, where the Hebrew words *nephesh chayyah* are translated "living creatures." In Genesis 2:7, the same Hebrew words are used to describe that Adam became a "living soul."

The word *nephesh* has the basic idea of a "breathing creature." It is never used of non-breathing animals like insects and is sometimes combined with another Hebrew word *ruach* which means "breath" or "spirit." Most of the time when the word "soul" appears in the Old Testament, the word is also *nephesh*. Therefore, the Bible actually does teach that animals have souls. However, animal souls are not the same as human souls. For animals, the soul is only the animating force, and there is no indication in the Bible that it is an eternal soul. For mankind, the soul is the animating factor, plus the seat of logic and reason, emotion and conscience, and all the rest of what makes up a person. And the human soul is eternal, but an animal's soul is not.

God explains this in Ecclesiastes 3:21: *Who knows whether the spirit of man goes upward and the spirit of the beast goes down into the earth?*

Though animals have *nephesh*, they were not created in the image of God (as we will see in Genesis 1:27), which means they do not have an eternal soul, as humans do. Because of Adam's disobedience and the subsequent entrance of sin and death into the world (Romans 5:12), the entire creation was corrupted (Romans 8:22) and animals die for various reasons. Jesus died and rose again to remove the penalty of sin for humans — not animals. God's Son became the God-man, not a God-animal. This also reminds us that man is not just an animal — humans didn't evolve from animals. We will see in the next chapter that humans are totally separate from the animals.

So God had created all things, but He left the pinnacle of His creation to be last — the creation of human beings. This must mean God has a unique place and role for humans in the creation.

We All Like Sheep

When God created the animal kinds, he knew that he would refer to the *tsoan* kind (which includes sheep) to describe humans:

> *All we like sheep have gone astray; we have turned — every one — to his own way; and the L*ORD *has laid on him the iniquity of us all* (Isaiah 53:6).

This verse not only describes us and our sin problem, but is a prophecy concerning the Lord Jesus Christ who would pay the penalty for our sin. Jesus, as the Godman, said:

> *Truly, truly, I say to you, I am the door of the sheep. All who came before me are thieves and robbers, but the sheep did not listen to them. I am the door. If anyone enters by me, he will be saved and will go in and out and find pasture* (John 10:7–9).

When God gave coats and skins to Adam and Eve (as we will see in Genesis 3), and thus carried out the first blood sacrifice which was a picture of what was to come in Jesus, *the Lamb of God, who takes away the sin of the world* (John 1:29), I wonder whether the animals God used for this were of the *tsoan* kind (which includes sheep).

As God made those animal kinds,
He knew all of this would happen
in history.

Chapter 7

Day Six

Genesis 1:26-27

Then God said, "Let us make man in our image, after our likeness. And let them have dominion over the fish of the sea and over the birds of the heavens and over the livestock and over all the earth and over every creeping thing that creeps on the earth." So God created man in his own image, in the image of God he created him; male and female he created them (Genesis 1:26–27).

Something special occurred when God created man. Something very different from how the animals were created. When God created the animals, He gave a command, *Let the earth bring forth.* But when God created man he said, *Let us make man.* Remember, the word for "God" means He is one but more than one. So this verse tells us that in eternity, God the Father, God the Son and God the Holy Spirit counseled together to create man. This must mean that humans are very special.

Made in the Image of God

Then we read three times (so this must also be something unique and special) that God made man in His image. The animals weren't made in God's image, only humans were. So what does this mean? An atheist once asked me on a radio program, "So what do you mean when you say God created humans in His image?" For a quick answer I said, "Well visit the local zoo and have a conversation with the apes and you will quickly learn what it means that the humans — and not animals — are made in God's image."

The image of God is not simply the human body. The body is frail, and does share some similarities with animals and other forms of life. But only humans can use their minds to use logic and reason. Only humans can use language, both to communicate needs and abstract (difficult concepts) ideas. Animals can use objects as tools, but humans create tools and use tools to make tools. Humans can design and build numerous types of structures, invent machines, write music and play musical instruments, and do beautiful paintings. Humans have a conscience, knowing right and wrong, and God tells us this in Romans 2:15, *The work of the law is written on their hearts, while their conscience also bears witness.*

Humans can also express love. But because we now live in a world affected by sin, we also see humans who hate and do terrible things.

God Is Spirit

Now God is spirit as we read in His Word: *God is spirit, and those who worship him must worship in spirit and truth* (John 4:24). God is not limited to a physical body like us. That's why He can be everywhere at once (omnipresent). And even though God does not have a body like us, we know that:

God laughs: *He who sits in the heavens laughs* (Psalm 2:4).

God sees: *The eyes of the LORD are in every place, keeping watch on the evil and the good* (Proverbs 15:3).

God smells: *And when the LORD smelled the pleasing aroma…* (Genesis 8:21).

God hears: *And this is the confidence that we have toward him, that if we ask anything according to his will he hears us* (1 John 5:14).

God speaks: *…we ourselves heard this very voice borne from heaven* (2 Peter 1:18).

God touches: *Therefore to this day the people of Israel do not eat the sinew of the thigh that is on the hip socket, because he touched the socket of Jacob's hip on the sinew of the thigh* (Genesis 32:32).

But we also know that when God appeared in physical form to men, He did so in the form of a human body. This is also true of the angels. So the human body must have been designed by God with this in mind.

And the Lord appeared to him by the oaks of Mamre, as he sat at the door of his tent in the heat of the day. He lifted up his eyes and looked, and behold, three men were standing in front of him (Genesis 18:1–2).

And while they were gazing into heaven as he went, behold, two men stood by them in white robes (Acts 1:10).

And think about this. When God designed the human body, He knew (as this was planned before the universe was created) that about 4,000 years later, the Son of God would take on human flesh.

Consequently, when Christ came into the world, he said, "Sacrifices and offerings you have not desired, but a body have you prepared for me" (Hebrews 10:5).

This all helps us understand these verses of Scripture even more because Jesus was made in likeness of men just as man had been made in the likeness of God!

… but emptied himself, by taking the form of a servant, being born in the likeness of men (Philippians 2:7).

So Jesus was himself the image of God: *He is the image of the invisible God, the firstborn of all creation* (Colossians 1:15).

The word translated "man" is the Hebrew word *adam*. This word is related to the Hebrew word for earth (*adamah*). Man was made from the earth, which is why his name in Genesis is Adam.

God Made Two Types of Humans

One final point before we move to the rest of day six, and this is a very important topic. God uses the word "man" (*adam*) to include both male and female. We read that *male and female he created them* (Genesis 1:27). God only made two genders. A human being is either male or female. A female can't change into a male and a male can't change into a female. God put the information into the DNA of the first two people so that one was male and the other female. In our cells we have chromosomes that contain DNA which contains all the information to build a human. In males, two of the 46 chromosomes (the 23rd pair) are labeled XY. In the females, the 23rd pair are labeled XX. So males have an XY and females have an XX. Now in today's world, because of sin, a very small number of people can have problems with these chromosomes. But that doesn't change the fact there are only two genders that God made for humans.

Now let's look at the rest of day six.

> *And God blessed them. And God said to them, "Be fruitful and multiply and fill the earth and subdue it, and have dominion over the fish of the sea and over the birds of the heavens and over every living thing that moves on the earth"* (Genesis 1:28).

The Dominion Mandate

Subdue it and have dominion. We call this the "dominion mandate." The term "dominion" is given to the role of man as a caretaker in the pre-Fall world. Man was to take care of the animals, and was to dress and keep the garden God had placed him in. So man was instructed to work. This means that in the perfect world before sin, God mandated the doctrine of work. Now we will read later that, after sin, work became very hard. So work, looking after the garden God made, would have been very different than the work in today's world.

As part of the dominion mandate, man was placed in charge of the environment in a stewardship role. This means we can and should use the resources God has placed in His creation, but we should not abuse it. Good stewardship means conserving the resources we have, using them thriftily, to best honor the Creator. We are to use the resources for man's good and God's glory. The principle of stewardship is found throughout Scripture because, as Psalm 24:1, says, *The earth is the* LORD's *and the fulness thereof, the world and those who dwell therein.* We are on God's earth, and God instructed us to be caretakers. If we are to be honoring to God, we should take good care of what is His.

This impacts our understanding of environmentalism as well. Humans are not a plague on the earth as some of the modern environmentalists claim. The earth and all that is in it was created for man to use. This also means nature has value. We've already discussed that God knows every sparrow that falls. But humans have far more value in God's eyes than those sparrows: *Fear not; you are of more value than many sparrows* (Luke 12:7).

As stewards of God's creation, we absolutely should be taking care of the earth. However, we should not panic over doomsday claims. The LORD has told us how the world will end, and it will not be due to overpopulation, or an abundance of greenhouse gases, or supposed man-made climate change. God will end it with a judgment by fire. And remember, in Genesis 8:22 after the Flood, God said, *While the earth remains, seedtime and harvest, cold and heat, summer and winter, day and night, shall not cease.* We can be 100 percent confident in God's promise. Man can never and will never destroy the earth.

But, at the same time, it is important to balance the needs of mankind with the stewardship of God's creation. We should use as we have need, but not waste what we have been given. In a practical sense, this can mean something as simple as picking up your trash and placing it in the trash can or picking up litter from the roadside. In a larger sense, this means cleaning up oil spills and other forms of pollution. We should not be destructive just because we can. We should only impact the environment when necessary to benefit humanity. And note that God gave man dominion over the animals and the environment. Much of the modern evolutionary environmental movement places animals and the environment over man!

There's another aspect of environmentalism that applies today because we live in a world where the ground has been cursed, and weeds and thorns grow. This means sin has adversely affected the environment. Much of the modern evolutionary environmental movement looks on the environment as good. Now it was all "very good" before sin. But now it's not good! And this means man can do things to improve the environment and help overcome some of the effects of sin and curse. For instance, periodically burning underbrush can protect forests. Harvesting trees for man's good but having planted forests to replace the trees harvested is good stewardship.

Be Fruitful and Overpopulate?

Some people claim that because God told man and the animals to *be fruitful and fill the earth,* that this would lead to overpopulation for animals and humans. But consider:

1. God can do anything. Nothing is impossible for God. If sin and death had not entered the creation, man and animals would have filled the earth, not overfilled it. As the infinite Creator, He would have had a perfect solution if the earth was filled. But God also knew man would sin, so He designed life to cope in a fallen world. We tend to analyze things from a perspective of finite human limitations instead of from the perspective of who God is.

2. God knew that man would sin, and that death would enter the world. He obviously designed into the creation what was needed for animals and man to live in a fallen world. And regardless of what we're told, the earth is nowhere close to being overpopulated. With proper management and care there could easily be enough food produced to feed all the people and many more on earth. The problem is that man is a sinner, so man's own selfish ambitions get in the way and so we see many people starving and impoverished. The real answer to this is the saving gospel. When leaders of nations and people trust Christ for salvation and build their worldview on God's Word this will dramatically change things for good.

No Filet Mignon in the Garden

And God said, "Behold, I have given you every plant yielding seed that is on the face of all the earth, and every tree with seed in its fruit. You shall have them for food. And to every beast of the earth and to every bird of the heavens and to everything that creeps on the earth, everything that has the breath of life, I have given every green plant for food." And it was so. And God saw everything that he had made, and behold, it was very good. And there was evening and there was morning, the sixth day (Genesis 1:29–31).

God's Word clearly tells us in Genesis 1:29–30 that originally man and animals were vegetarian. There was no death, violence, or bloodshed before sin. Some people claim these verses don't say man and animals were not to eat meat. But that doesn't fit with Genesis 9:3 where, after the Flood, God said:

Every moving thing that lives shall be food for you. And as I gave you the green plants, I give you everything.

This verse clearly teaches that for man, God gave plants to eat originally (Genesis 1:29), but now God is changing man's diet to be able to eat animals (in fact, anything). Genesis 1:30 is written in a similar way to Genesis 1:29, but is in regard to the animals eating plants. So it makes sense that originally man and animals were all vegetarian.

Millions of Years of Bloodshed?

Think about it! Hebrews 9:22 states, *Without the shedding of blood there is no forgiveness of sins.* For those Christians who believe in millions of years, they believe animals were killing and dying for millions of years before man. So that would mean blood was shed for millions of years before man sinned. But the first blood was shed when God set up the sacrificial system in Genesis 3:21 when He gave coats of skins to Adam and Eve. And if there was bloodshed for millions of years before sin then that makes the shedding of blood meaningless in regard to sin. This undermines the gospel message.

Also, for those Christians who believe in millions of years, they believe the fossil record was laid down millions of years before man. But in the fossil record there's lots of evidence of animals eating each other (e.g., teeth marks on bones, bones in stomachs, etc.) and, in this view, that would mean animal carnivory came before man and before sin. But after God made the animals and man, He told us their diet was plants — vegetarian.

Now some people object and say that many animals have sharp teeth, so they're obviously meat eaters. But just because an animal has sharp teeth, does not mean it's a meat eater, or has always been a meat eater, it just means it has sharp teeth! There are many animals today with sharp teeth that eat only or mainly plants. For instance, the fruit bat in Australia has sharp, savage-looking teeth but it only eats fruit. The giant panda has big, sharp-looking teeth, but mainly eats bamboo. Bears have sharp teeth, somewhat like a lion's teeth, but most bears are primarily vegetarian. Even alligators and crocodiles will eat fruit, and great white sharks are known to eat kelp (a plant that grows in the ocean). Originally, all animals ate only plants. This fits with the fact that at the end of the sixth day God describes everything He made as "very good." There was no sin or death in the world. There was no violence. There was no bloodshed. There was no fossil record with bones showing evidence of disease or violence and bloodshed.

A "Very Good" Creation

When we go to the last book of the Bible (Revelation) we read what the new heavens and earth will be like when God restores them from the effects of sin, death, and the curse:

> He will wipe away every tear from their eyes, and death shall be no more, neither shall there be mourning, nor crying, nor pain anymore, for the former things have passed away (Revelation 21:4).

If God used millions of years of death, disease, suffering, and bloodshed as part of His process of creating all life, then what we see around us today with all the death, disease, suffering, and bloodshed should be called "very good." And if God is going to restore this present earth to what it was supposedly like, originally filled with death, then the new heavens and earth would be full of death, disease, suffering, and bloodshed. This makes no sense and does not fit with what God's Word clearly teaches.

No! At the end of the creation week everything was "very good." It was perfect! So different from today's world. Also, God had reached the pinnacle of creation, His purpose for creating the universe with the earth and life — to create man in His image. As Psalm 115:16 states: *The heavens are the LORD's heavens, but the earth he has given to the children of man.* Yes, the earth was designed for Adam and his descendants, to live in it, to till it, and enjoy the fruits of it.

Genesis 1 and 2 – A Contradiction?

Before we move to chapter two, we need to deal with two particular objections some people make about taking Genesis as literal history.

1. The claim is sometimes made that Genesis chapters 1 and 2 are two different accounts of creation and contradict each other.

But take a step back and look at it this way. Genesis chapter 1 is actually an overview of the creation of life and the universe in chronological order. We are told what happened on each day — 1st day followed by 2nd day, through day six. Genesis chapter 2 is focused on the sixth day of creation, specifically the creation of man and woman and what God instructed Adam to do, setting the scene for Genesis chapter 3 where we learn about the entrance of sin and death because of Adam's rebellion. In Genesis 1:27 we are told that God made man, and He made a male and female. We are not given much detail. Now in Genesis chapter 2 we are given the details on how God made Adam, how He showed Adam he was different from the animals, and then how God made Eve. We then learn God made the first marriage, Adam and Eve — a male and female. Consider this: in Matthew 19:4–5, when Jesus was asked about marriage, He said in verse 4:

Have you not read that he who created them from the beginning made them male and female?

That's a quote from Genesis 1:27 concerning the fact God made man and made a male and a female.

Then in verse 5 Jesus said:

Therefore a man shall leave his father and his mother and hold fast to his wife, and the two shall become one flesh.

Now that's a quote from Genesis 2:24. So Jesus, who is the truth and the Word, quotes from Genesis 1 and Genesis chapter 2 in discussing marriage about one man and one woman. Jesus is connecting Genesis 1:27 to Genesis 2:24, thus talking about the same one man and woman. This is illustrating that Genesis chapters 1 and 2 are not contradictory accounts of creation, but complementary accounts. Genesis chapter 2 is primarily a detailed account of the creation of man and woman.

A Cosmic Poem?

2. The claim is sometimes made that Genesis is poetry and not meant to be taken as literal history. But Genesis is written as typical historical narrative. Even if it was poetry (which it is not), that doesn't mean it's not true. Poetic language is used in the Bible in the Psalms. Certainly, poetry includes symbolism (and it's obvious when that is so and obvious what it means), but consider just this one verse from the Psalms:

…but overthrew Pharaoh and his host in the Red Sea, for his steadfast love endures forever (Psalm 136:15).

Yes, it's poetry but teaching about a real event that happened.

However, Genesis is not written like the Psalms.

Genesis chapters 1–11 are historical narrative for a number of reasons. Both Jesus Christ and the apostles treated the first 11 chapters of Genesis as literal history. They quoted from this section as real history. The vast majority of the early church leaders and teachers accepted Genesis as real history. Genesis contains only a small amount of figurative or symbolic language, and the Hebrew verb forms used are consistent with a narrative, not a poetic, approach. Now there is some figurative language, certainly, but just because figurative language exists does not mean that the entire narrative is figurative. For example, Adam's statement about Eve being "bone of my bones and flesh of my flesh" (Genesis 2:23) is figurative. But this does not mean the entire narrative is figurative. And what Adam said was true, as Eve was made from Adam. In fact, these are the first recorded words of the first man as he describes the first woman.

Further, typical Hebrew poetry has parallelism, which is almost completely absent from the text in Genesis 1–11, despite some scholars' attempts to force it into the text. Genesis 1–11 is written in the same manner as the rest of the historical narratives in the Bible, such as 1 and 2 Chronicles, 1 and 2 Kings, and so on. It makes much more sense to accept Genesis 1–11 as historical narrative.

As we come to the end of Genesis 1, I would like us just to pause and remember our recurring theme throughout this chapter — God is infinite. Contemplate these verses of Scripture:

> *For my thoughts are not your thoughts, neither are your ways my ways, declares the LORD. For as the heavens are higher than the earth, so are my ways higher than your ways and my thoughts than your thoughts* (Isaiah 55:8–9).

> *Great is our LORD, and abundant in power; his understanding is beyond measure* (Psalm 147:5).

> *When I look at your heavens, the work of your fingers, the moon and the stars, which you have set in place, what is man that you are mindful of him, and the son of man that you care for him?* (Psalm 8:3–4).

Now on to chapter two.

Chapter 8

Genesis 2

Genesis 2:1-3

Thus the heavens and the earth were finished, and all the host of them. And on the seventh day God finished his work that he had done, and he rested on the seventh day from all his work that he had done. So God blessed the seventh day and made it holy, because on it God rested from all his work that he had done in creation (Genesis 2:1–3).

Now God stopped His work of creation, and "rested." Note that it doesn't say "resting." This doesn't mean God was tired. It's just that His work of creation was finished! Now we are up to the seventh day — a special day of rest. There was no need to add "evening and morning" for the seventh day, as each day continues on from this seventh day with no more work of creation. This seventh day had special significance for the Israelites as God told them:

You shall remember that you were a slave in the land of Egypt, and the LORD your God brought you out from there with a mighty hand and an outstretched arm. Therefore the LORD your God commanded you to keep the Sabbath day (Deuteronomy 5:15).

The fourth commandment found in Exodus 20:11 refers to the six days of creation and one day of rest.

Even though God's work of creation was finished, God works today in the fallen world, but it's a totally different type of work. His work now is one of reconciliation and redemption because we sinned in Adam. There is another time in Scripture when we read that God's work was "finished." On the Cross, Jesus said, *"It is finished," and he bowed his head and gave up his spirit* (John 19:30). That's when He finished paying the penalty for our sin. Then He rose from the dead so we may receive the free gift of salvation.

The Generations Of

These are the generations of the heavens and the earth when they were created, in the day that the LORD God made the earth and the heavens (Genesis 2:4).

The word "generations" (or it can also be translated "account") comes from the Hebrew word *toledoth*. This *toledoth* phrase (the generations of, or the account of) appears 11 times in the Book of Genesis, and nearly all Bible scholars agree that these phrases tie the whole book together as a unity. Some scholars believe they are a reference to who wrote the previous section. If so, for Genesis 2:4, this would be referring to the section before that God presumably revealed to Adam. In Genesis 5:1, this would refer to the previous section perhaps recorded by Adam. But regardless, we know that this is the Word of God and thus is an infallible account of the history of the universe.

The word "day" here is not qualified with "evening" or "morning" or a number or "night." In context here the word *day* basically means time. In other words, in the time God created everything — meaning in the time of six days just given.

Earth Before Man

When no bush of the field was yet in the land and no small plant of the field had yet sprung up — for the LORD God had not caused it to rain on the land, and there was no man to work the ground, and a mist was going up from the land and was watering the whole face of the ground (Genesis 2:5–6).

At first, this section can seem confusing to many. What does it mean? Well, we need to understand it in the whole context of this second chapter. After this section, we read details about the creation of the first man, Adam, the planting of a garden and Adam's role to look after it, the command and warning given to Adam, the naming of the animals, the creation of the first woman, and thus the first marriage. This means the first section of the chapter must be focused on finishing the previous section and then leading us up to the details of the creation of man and the roles and instructions God gave him.

God had created the plants on day three. Now God didn't just plant seeds so the plants could grow. The plants were obviously mature and fruit trees had fruit on them, as God had told man to eat fruit on the sixth day. But until man was created, no human tilled the ground to grow plants for food, and God had a different watering system in place until the hydrological cycle we see today was fully functioning.

Man of the Dust

…then the LORD God formed the man of dust from the ground and breathed into his nostrils the breath of life, and the man became a living creature (Genesis 2:7).

We are now given more detail in regard to how God created the first man. He created him from the "dust of the ground." Remember, Adam comes from the word meaning "earth." God "breathed into his nostrils the breath of life." God didn't do this for the animals, so obviously man was different from the animals. Also notice, the man did not become a "living creature" (the Hebrew word discussed earlier is used here: *nephesh*) until after God breathed into him. The animals were created before man and were created as living creatures. So God certainly did not take an animal and make it into a human, or take an animal and evolve it into a human.

In the New Testament, what we read in 1 Corinthians 15:47 confirms the history in Genesis that Adam was the first man and was made from the earth — from dust:

The first man was from the earth, a man of dust; the second man is from heaven (1 Corinthians 15:47).

Some people try to claim that the "dust" in Genesis 2:7 represents the so-called "ape-man" that God used to make Adam. But in Genesis 3:19 we read about the judgment of death God placed on the human race: *for you are dust, and to dust you shall return.* We don't return to an ape-man when we die, we return to dust! We also read this in Job 10:9: *Remember that you have made me like clay; and will you return me to the dust?*

A Special Garden

And the LORD God planted a garden in Eden, in the east, and there he put the man whom he had formed. And out of the ground the LORD God made to spring up every tree that is pleasant to the sight and good for food. The tree of life was in the midst of the garden, and the tree of the knowledge of good and evil. A river flowed out of Eden to water the garden, and there it divided and became four rivers. The name of the first is the Pishon. It is the one that flowed around the whole land of Havilah, where there is gold. And the gold of that land is good; bdellium and onyx stone are there. The name of the second

river is the Gihon. It is the one that flowed around the whole land of Cush. And the name of the third river is the Tigris, which flows east of Assyria. And the fourth river is the Euphrates (Genesis 2:8–14).

God planted a special garden with mature plants and trees. We will see that God gave Adam a special role in the garden to look after it. Also, in this garden, God put two trees leading up to the test of obedience God would give to Adam.

Where in the World Was Eden?

Now where was this garden?

Most Bible commentaries state that the site of the Garden of Eden was in the Middle East, situated somewhere near where the Tigris and Euphrates Rivers are today. This is based on the description given in Genesis 2:8–14 (above).

Even the great theologian John Calvin struggled over the exact location of the Garden of Eden. In his commentary on Genesis he states:

Moses says that one river flowed to water the garden, which

afterwards would divide itself into four heads. It is sufficiently agreed among all, that two of these heads are the Euphrates and the Tigris; for no one disputes that... (Hiddekel) is the Tigris. But there is a great controversy respecting the other two. Many think that Pison and Gihon are the Ganges and the Nile; the error, however, of these men is abundantly refuted by the distance of the positions of these rivers. Persons are not wanting who fly across even to the Danube; as if indeed the habitation of one man stretched itself from the most remote part of Asia to the extremity of Europe. But since many other celebrated rivers flow by the region of which we are speaking, there is greater probability in the opinion of those who believe that two of these rivers are pointed out, although their names are now obsolete. Be this as it may, the difficulty is not yet solved. For Moses divides the one river which flowed by the garden into four heads. Yet it appears, that the fountains of the Euphrates and the Tigris were far distant from each other.[1]

Calvin recognized that the description given in Genesis 2 concerning the location of the Garden of Eden does not fit with what is observed regarding the present Tigris and Euphrates Rivers. God's Word makes it clear that the Garden of Eden was located where there were four rivers coming from one head. No matter how one tries to fit this location in the Middle East today, it just can't be done.

Interestingly, Calvin goes on to say: "From this difficulty, some would free themselves by saying that the surface of the globe may have been changed by the deluge.[2]"

This is a major consideration that needs to be taken into account. The worldwide, catastrophic Flood of Noah's day would have destroyed the surface of the earth. If most of the sedimentary strata over the earth's surface (many thousands of feet thick in places) is the result of this global catastrophe, as creationists believe, then we would have no

---

1. John Calvin, *Commentary on Genesis*, Volume 1, online at: www.ccel.org/ccel/calvin/calcom01.viii.i.html.
2. Ibid.

idea where the Garden of Eden was originally located — the earth's surface totally changed as a result of the Flood.

Not only this, but underneath the region where the present Tigris and Euphrates Rivers are located there exists hundreds of feet of sedimentary strata — a significant amount of which is fossiliferous. Such fossil-bearing strata had to be laid down at the time of the Flood.

Therefore, no one can logically suggest that the area where the Tigris and Euphrates Rivers are today is the location of the Garden of Eden, for this area is sitting on Flood strata containing billions of dead things (fossils). The perfect Garden of Eden couldn't have been sitting on billions of dead things (fossils) before sin entered the world! This being the case, the question then is why are there rivers named Tigris and Euphrates in the Middle East today?

In my native country of Australia, one will recognize many names that are also used in England (e.g., Newcastle, Perth). The reason is that when the settlers came out from England to Australia, they used names they were familiar with in England to name new places/towns in Australia.

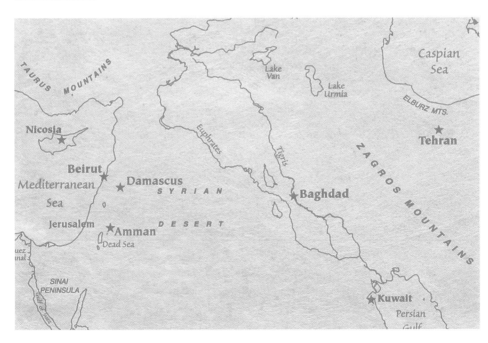

Another example is the names given to many rivers in the United States. There is the Thames River in Connecticut, the Severn River in Maryland, and the Trent River in North Carolina — all named for prominent rivers in the UK.

In a similar way, when Noah and his family came out of the Ark after it landed in the area we today call the Middle East (the region of the Mountains of Ararat), it would not have been surprising for them to use names they were familiar with from the pre-Flood world (e.g., Tigris and Euphrates), to name places and rivers, etc., in the world after the Flood.

Ultimately, we don't know where the Garden of Eden was located. To insist that the garden was located in the area around the present Tigris and Euphrates Rivers is to deny the catastrophic effects of the global Flood of Noah's day, and to allow for death before sin.

The Doctrine of Work

The LORD God took the man and put him in the garden of Eden to work it and keep it. And the LORD God commanded the man, saying, "You may surely eat of every tree of the garden, but of the tree of the knowledge of good and evil you shall not eat, for in the day that you eat of it you shall surely die" (Genesis 2:15–17).

Here we have the foundation of the doctrine of work. Man was to work even before sin. But the work would not have been stressful work. Adam was to look after the garden. He wouldn't have had to deal with weeds or thorns, as they didn't exist until after sin and the curse. The ground wasn't cursed at this stage, so plants would grow in perfect conditions. We will find that because of sin, work changed to being laborious — hard. After sin, man would have to deal with weeds, thorns, and a cursed ground. Man has always been required to do work. And in the New Testament in a fallen world, we are told, *For even when we were with you, we would give you this command: If anyone is not willing to work, let him not eat* (2 Thessalonians 3:10).

Don't Eat from One Tree

Genesis 2:9 states that *the tree of life was in the midst of the garden, and the tree of the knowledge of good and evil.* Now these were real trees that each had real fruit. God gave Adam permission to eat from every tree, which would have included the tree of life, but Adam was instructed not to eat the fruit from one tree — the tree of the knowledge of good and evil. Adam was given a warning that if he ate from that tree, he would die.

Even though the tree of life was a real tree, it also had a symbolic purpose in that while man had access to the tree, then he would have eternal life and blessing given by God. This tree was in the center of the garden and was to teach Adam and Eve that they were to have their lives centered on God. We also find references to the tree of life in Ezekiel 47:12 and Revelation 22:2. It's also fascinating that in Proverbs we find wisdom (Proverbs 3:18), the "fruit of righteousness" (Proverbs 11:30), and a "gentle tongue" compared to a tree of life. This helps us understand that the tree of life was a real tree, but it symbolized God's blessings of eternal life, joy, wisdom, and so on. And if Adam and Eve obeyed God's test of obedience, such blessings would be for generation after generation. In other words, if Adam passed the test God gave to him, then he and all his descendants would have eternal life in his present state. If he didn't pass the test he would die.

It wasn't something in the fruit of the tree of life that would give Adam eternal life. The fruit was real but had a symbolic purpose. There wasn't anything in the actual fruit of the tree of knowledge of good and evil that would cause Adam to die. The fruit was real but had a symbolic purpose.

God gave Adam a test. He was not to eat from the tree of knowledge of good and evil. God didn't make Adam like a puppet to force him to love and obey his Creator. God gave Adam the free will to make that choice. God did this even knowing Adam would disobey.

The Lord Had Formed?

Then the LORD *God said, "It is not good that the man should be alone; I will make him a helper fit for him." Now out of the ground the* LORD *God had formed every beast of the field and every bird of the heavens and brought them to the man to see what he would call them. And whatever the man called every living creature, that was its name. The man gave names to all livestock and to the birds of the heavens and to every beast of the field. But for Adam there was not found a helper fit for him (Genesis 2:18–20).*

At this stage of the sixth day, God had created the land animals and one human being — Adam. God said Adam was alone. He wasn't lonely as if Adam was sad. He lived in a perfect world that God described as "good." However, Adam didn't have a mate. To teach Adam he was alone, God brought certain animal kinds to Adam to name.

Now some translations of Genesis 2:19 state *"the* LORD *God formed every beast."* As this appears in Genesis 2, after the account of the creation of Adam, some people think this contradicts the order given in Genesis 1 where we read God made the land animals before Adam.

However, in the ESV translation used above we read *"the* LORD *God **had** formed every beast"* (emphasis added). Reading it this way makes it clear that God had already formed the animals — past tense. Because the Bible is God's Word there will not be a contradiction, as it's infallible. So why do some translations put "had formed" and others just "formed"?

Well, in biblical Hebrew (modern Hebrew is different), there were only two tenses — one meaning a completed action and one meaning an action that was not completed. Now context determines which tense is being used. In this instance, Genesis 1 gives a chronological summary of creation (first day, second day, etc.), Genesis 2 is not a detailed chronological account, but an account of the details of the creation of the first man and woman. So, using and understanding the context of Genesis 1, it's easy to understand that when God said in Genesis 2 that He "formed" the land animals, this means a completed action. In other words, He "had formed" the animals before He created Adam.

Adam Names the Animals

God brought animals to Adam for him to name. One of the purposes of this was so Adam could see he was alone. Now, God didn't bring all the land animals to be named. In Genesis 1, we are told that on day five God created flying creatures and sea creatures, and on day six He created cattle (livestock), the beasts of the earth, and the creeping things.

When God brought animals to Adam to name, He brought flying creatures and livestock (cattle) and beasts of the field — not beasts of the earth. He didn't bring the creeping things or the sea creatures. So God obviously limited the kinds He brought to be named (in other words, Adam didn't have to name every single animal kind God had created, only the specific groups of kinds God brought to him). Also, we are not told how many animals of these groups God brought to Adam. He brought enough for Adam to name and to understand he was alone as there was no mate for him to be found. Being the first man, and with a perfect brain, I'm sure Adam could have named animals very quickly and remembered those names.

Woman Came from Man

So the LORD God caused a deep sleep to fall upon the man, and while he slept took one of his ribs and closed up its place with flesh. And the rib that the LORD God had taken from the man he made into a woman and brought her to the man. Then the man said, "This at last is bone of my bones and flesh of my flesh; she shall be called Woman, because she was taken out of Man" (Genesis 2:21–23).

God put Adam to sleep to conduct an operation, using part of Adam's rib to make the first woman. Some people state that this can't be true as it would mean men would have one less rib than women and they don't. I had someone ask me once at a church why men don't have one less rib than women. I replied, "If a man had an accident and lost his leg, and sometime later got married and had kids, would his kids have one less leg?" Of course not; such things are genetically determined. Adam's descendants would not have one less rib, and Adam didn't have to have one less rib. If a rib is removed, but the tissue around the bone (called periosteum) is left, then the rib can grow again.

Adam was made from dust and the woman was made from Adam. This makes it clear that one cannot add man's evolutionary idea that man and woman supposedly evolved from some ape-like creature to the Bible. Also, in the New Testament, Paul clearly states in 1 Corinthians 11:9 and 12 that woman came from man. This attests to the fact that Paul accepted Genesis as literal history.

The Origin of Marriage

Therefore a man shall leave his father and his mother and hold fast to his wife, and they shall become one flesh (Genesis 2:24).

This verse was quoted by Jesus as recorded in Matthew 19:5 and Mark 10:7–8 in regard to the meaning of marriage. This passage of Genesis, is the origin of marriage. Marriage is a God-ordained institution and began when God made the first man from dust and the first woman from his side. In other words, the only true marriage is one man and one woman.

In this era, our Western world has seen nations legalize what they call gay "marriage." However, there's really no such thing as gay "marriage," as marriage is an institution God created and ordained, and this happened in Genesis 2:24. For so-called gay "marriage," we find people having two men or two women in a relationship. But why do they even have two? Why not three, or four, or whatever combination? Why not one man with many "wives" or one woman with many "husbands"? The stipulation of two in marriage comes from the Bible! Satan will do all he can to pervert what God has done. The more people abandon God's Word for their worldview, the more we will see them abandon marriage. Now we are observing increasing polyamorous relationships — any combination of male and female as people themselves decide. Now that the door has been opened to reinterpret marriage from being one man and one woman, we see people pushing to legalize polygamy.

Some people claim that as long as people love each other, it doesn't matter whether it's two men or two women. However, it's not love that determines how to define marriage, it's God who defines marriage, and He defines it very clearly as between one man and one woman. God's Word — not feelings or ever-changing cultural standards — defines truth.

Naked and Not Ashamed

And the man and his wife were both naked and were not ashamed (Genesis 2:25).

When God created Adam and Eve, they didn't wear clothes. We have to understand things were very different in a perfect world. Adam and Eve weren't affected by sin, so they wouldn't have had any moral guilt. They would not have experienced the sin of lust, for instance. Some people have claimed Adam and Eve must have been covered in light so they wouldn't see each other's bodies. But the Bible states they were "naked." And we must remember, we live in a world affected by sin; we just cannot understand what it was like before sin in a perfect situation. So, by wanting to cover them in light really is just because, we as sinful people, recognize their nakedness would be a problem for us. It was a very different world in many ways, but all that is about to change with the events of Genesis 3.

Chapter 9

Genesis 3

Genesis 3:1

Now the serpent was more crafty than any other beast of the field that the LORD God had made. He said to the woman, "Did God actually say, 'You shall not eat of any tree in the garden'?"

We don't know exactly what the animal looked like that the devil used to tempt Eve. Most people think it was a snake, often arguing that snakes don't have legs and therefore they think the serpent the devil used did. But nowhere does the biblical text say the serpent had legs. Whatever animal it was, it was certainly beautiful. Being an animal that was a "beast of the field," means it was from the group of animals that Adam named. It would seem Adam would have been familiar with this creature.

Often, people say that they can't believe the serpent in Genesis 3 spoke because they claim animals don't speak! Now, many types of parrots talk by mimicking, so it would be illogical to think that God didn't give this mimicking ability to other animals — especially in a perfect world. However, speaking intelligently with human-sounding words is not the same. But there is one other example of an animal speaking in Scripture — Balaam's donkey was specially enabled by the power of *God* to speak intelligently to Balaam.

Because there is no other place in Scripture that reveals Satan or demons can cause animals to speak, it's certainly possible that the serpent could make the sounds capable of speech, and the devil used this to his advantage. If so, the devil likely used this feature that the original serpent had and caused it to say what he wanted.

Now the serpent was "crafty" (clever) when it spoke. It made *sense* to the woman. Since the devil was the one who influenced the serpent (Revelation 12:9, 20:2), then it makes sense why the serpent could deliver a message capable of deceiving her. The serpent apparently cooperated and was an instrument in the deception and so deserved a punishment, which God justly gave.

But why wasn't Eve shocked when she heard this serpent speak? Well, everything in the Garden of Eden was new to the first couple — they'd only been alive for a short time. Even a bug, cat, or what we today call dinosaurs would all be new, so perhaps they wouldn't have been shocked at a talking serpent. Regardless, the devil used the serpent and spoke to Eve.

Did God Actually Say?

The devil's first words were a question, *"Did God actually say?"* Note that the first thing the devil did was to question God's Word in an attempt to create doubt and undermine God's Word. This was a direct attack on the authority of the Word of God. Doubt leads to unbelief. The devil wanted to get Eve to doubt God's Word and be led to not believe God's Word.

Here is a warning for all of us. In 2 Corinthians 11:3, God warns us:

> *But I am afraid that as the serpent deceived Eve by his cunning, your thoughts will be led astray from a sincere and pure devotion to Christ.*

Here we are being warned that the devil is going to use the same method on us that he used on Eve. That method will be to get us to doubt the Word of God and put us on a slippery slide of doubt leading to unbelief. There's no doubt the devil has used this method in today's world to get generations of people to doubt God's Word in Genesis because of the false teaching of evolution and millions of years. Sadly, this has put many young people on a slippery slide of unbelief regarding God's Word greatly contributing to the majority walking away from the church. Don't succumb to the devil's method and doubt God's Word because of what fallible scientists may claim.

Also note that the devil deliberately misquoted God's Word to make God sound unfair. The devil claimed God said to not eat of *any* tree in the garden. But God said Adam and Eve could eat from all the trees except one. The devil gets people today to misquote the Word of God to make it sound like it can't be true. Make sure you check everything anyone claims God Word says by studying the actual words in the Bible carefully and in context.

I've often wondered if the temptation of Adam and Eve to be their own gods stems from the devil's own problem of pride and wanting to be God. When the angel who became the devil was created, he would have had to accept by faith that God created him. As he is the *father of lies*, maybe he rejected that God created him and believed he evolved and could evolve to be God. Even though it would seem that the angels saw God create humans, so maybe the devil wanted Adam and Eve to believe they could evolve to be someone higher than they were. Could this be why most human beings are so eager to accept man's evolutionary ideas to try to explain life?

You Will Not Surely Die

And the woman said to the serpent, "We may eat of the fruit of the trees in the garden, but God said, 'You shall not eat of the fruit of the tree that is in the midst of the garden, neither shall you touch it, lest you die'" (Genesis 3:2–3).

I believe Eve had already started to succumb to doubting God's Word because she misquotes what God actually said. Now the instruction that they could eat from all the trees except one was given directly by God to Adam, not to Eve (*And the LORD God **commanded the man**, saying, "You may surely eat of every tree of the garden, but of the tree of the knowledge of good and evil you shall not eat, for in the day that you eat of* it you shall surely die [Genesis 2:16–17], emphasis added). Presumably, Adam told Eve what God had said. Adam, being a free agent (not a puppet as we previously discussed), may have also told Eve not to even touch the tree. So the devil's method began to work on Eve. However, she did correctly state that God warned they would die.

> But the serpent said to the woman, "You will not surely die. For God knows that when you eat of it your eyes will be opened, and you will be like God, knowing good and evil" (Genesis 3:4–5).

The serpent now directly lies to Eve when he says they won't die if they eat from that tree. In John 8:44 we're told this about the devil: *When he lies, it is consistent with his character; for he is a liar and the father of lies* (NLT). In many ways, the devil uses people today to tell lies about God. That's why we need to study God's Word carefully and judge what we hear and read against what God clearly states:

> *Do your best to present yourself to God as one approved, a worker who has no need to be ashamed, rightly handling the word of truth* (2 Timothy 2:15).

You Will Be Like God

The devil tells Eve if they eat the fruit (from the tree of the knowledge of good and evil), then they *will be like God, knowing good and evil*. Basically, the temptation was that they could be their own god and they could decide what is good and what is evil for themselves. But only God, who knows everything, who has infinite power to be infinitely good, can do that. As we continue to read God's Word, we find Adam did take the fruit and sin entered the human race, so all humans have that sin nature. An aspect of the sin nature is we all want to be our own gods and want to decide for ourselves what is "truth" or "good." This also means human beings will have the propensity to want to believe man's fallible word over God's Word. We even see this with Christians today who take man's false ideas about evolution and millions of years and add that to the Bible. That's one of the reasons, as we studied Genesis 1, I emphasized what it means that God is infinite.

The more people in our world reject God's Word and become their own god, the more we will see moral relativism permeate our cultures. And that's exactly what we are seeing as issues like abortion, gay "marriage," LGBTQIA+ movement, transgenderism, pedophilia, polygamy, polyamory, and other evils increasingly infect our cultures. As I've stated before, Judges 21:25 really is an apt description of such a situation where we are told that people do what is right in their own eyes when there's no authority to tell them what is right and wrong.

Look to God's Word

So when the woman saw that the tree was good for food, and that it was a delight to the eyes, and that the tree was to be desired to make one wise, she took of its fruit and ate, and she also gave some to her husband who was with her, and he ate (Genesis 3:6).

Note that the woman looked at the fruit and it was *a delight to the eyes*. Now the text also tells us Adam was with her. They should have looked to their Creator and His Word about not eating from the tree. Instead, they looked at the fruit and interpreted it the way the devil wanted instead of the way God had explained. Think about it — this is the same problem we have today. The majority of people interpret the evidence around them based on man's ideas, not on the foundation of the Word of God. For example, think about the origins issue. The majority of people look at the living creatures, and the fossils, and try to interpret them within the framework of evolution and millions of years. But if you look to God's Word as the foundation for your thinking, then the biblical worldview founded on the written Word of God will give a totally different interpretation of the same evidence. We all have this propensity to look at the evidence around us using man-centered glasses, looking with our own eyes, instead of putting on biblical glasses to see the evidence through God's "eyes," so to speak.

He Was with Her

Now consider this: *and she also gave some to her husband who was with her*! Adam may have been watching the whole time the serpent was lying to Eve and tempting her to sin. Tragically, Adam didn't try to step in and warn Eve. Adam was given the instruction from God not to eat from that tree, and yet he didn't remind Eve what God had said. Adam didn't try to tell Eve or the devil that what was said contradicted God's Word.

Quote and Obey God's Word

In the New Testament, the devil tried to tempt the Lord Jesus. However, Jesus quoted God's Word to reject what the devil stated. The devil even used God's Word incorrectly. Read the passage and take note of how Jesus answered the devil. This is what Adam should have done to reject the devil's temptation — quote and obey God's Word. And it's what we should be doing when people try to get us to reinterpret God's Word.

> And the tempter came and said to him, "If you are the Son of God, command these stones to become loaves of bread." But he answered, "It is written, 'Man shall not live by bread alone, but by every word that comes from the mouth of God.'"

> Then the devil took him to the holy city and set him on the pinnacle of the temple and said to him, "If you are the Son of God, throw yourself down, for it is written, 'He will command his angels concerning you,' and 'On their hands they will bear you up, lest you strike your foot against a stone.'" Jesus said to him, "Again it is written, 'You shall not put the LORD your God to the test.'"

> Again, the devil took him to a very high mountain and showed him all the kingdoms of the world and their glory. And he said to him, "All these I will give you, if you will fall down and worship me." Then Jesus said to him, "Be gone, Satan! For it is written, 'You shall worship the LORD your God and him only shall you serve'" (Matthew 4:3–10).

We need to make sure that we know God's Word so we are not led astray by the temptations of the devil:

I have stored up your word in my heart, that I might not sin against you (Psalm 119:11).

The Saddest Day of All Time

Adam ate the fruit. I call this "the saddest day of all time." When Adam ate the fruit, he disobeyed God. He rebelled against what God had clearly told him not to do. This act of rebellion is called sin. Now, with Adam's choice, sin entered the human race. We call this original sin — it's the origin of sin. As we are all descendants of Adam, who was the head of the human race, we also have this sin nature. Adam failed the test God gave him by disobeying God's clear instruction. That's why the Bible tells us that:

For all have sinned and fall short of the glory of God (Romans 3:23).

Because Adam fell into sin, every human being (each one a descendant of Adam) would now have this sin nature.

Their Eyes Were Opened

Then the eyes of both were opened, and they knew that they were naked. And they sewed fig leaves together and made themselves loincloths (Genesis 3:7).

Now Adam and Eve had a problem. They were finite beings who had sinned against God. The perfect free will they had when God gave them the test was gone. Now their very nature (and ours as descendants of them) was the opposite of good. In fact, God's Word explains our sin nature this way:

The heart is deceitful above all things, and desperately sick; who can understand it? (Jeremiah 17:9).

None is righteous, no, not one; no one understands; no one seeks for God. All have turned aside; together they have become worthless; no one does good, not even one (Romans 3:10–12).

Suddenly Adam and Eve realized something. They were commanded to "be fruitful and multiply and fill the earth" (Genesis 1:28), but they now became aware of their nakedness and recognized all their descendants would be tainted with this sin nature. They were ashamed. They realized the curse of sin and death would be upon all their descendants, *as one trespass led to condemnation for all men* (Romans 5:18).

Now Adam and Eve tried to take away their shame and guilt by making coverings for themselves from fig leaves. But sinful humans can't take away that sin. Only God can do that. Adam and Eve making garments for themselves to cover their sin would not work:

> *We have all become like one who is unclean, and all our righteous deeds are like a polluted garment* (Isaiah 64:6).

Only God can take away our sin. What God did, as recorded in Genesis 3:21, when He gave garments of skin to Adam and Eve, was a promise of the coming solution to the sin problem. We will discuss this in detail when we get to that verse, but we need to understand that when humans try to be righteous to take away sin, our righteousness is like a *polluted garment*, or as the King James Version of the Bible puts it, *as filthy rags*. We will learn how the coverings God made for Adam and Eve would symbolize how it is only God's righteousness that can deal with our sin:

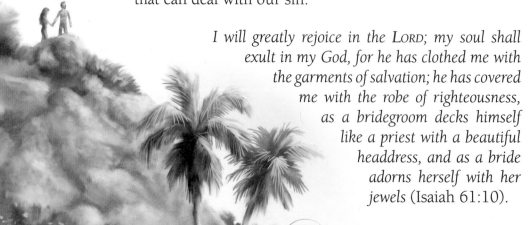

> *I will greatly rejoice in the LORD; my soul shall exult in my God, for he has clothed me with the garments of salvation; he has covered me with the robe of righteousness, as a bridegroom decks himself like a priest with a beautiful headdress, and as a bride adorns herself with her jewels* (Isaiah 61:10).

The First Theophany

And they heard the sound of the LORD God walking in the garden in the cool of the day, and the man and his wife hid themselves from the presence of the LORD God among the trees of the garden. But the LORD God called to the man and said to him, "Where are you?" And he said, "I heard the sound of you in the garden, and I was afraid, because I was naked, and I hid myself." He said, "Who told you that you were naked? Have you eaten of the tree of which I commanded you not to eat?" The man said, "The woman whom you gave to be with me, she gave me fruit of the tree, and I ate." Then the LORD God said to the woman, "What is this that you have done?" The woman said, "The serpent deceived me, and I ate" (Genesis 3:8–13).

The word "theophany" is used for when God appears in human form. There are a number of instances of this in Scripture (e.g., Genesis 18:1–3; Genesis 3:24–30; Judges 13:3–6, etc.). Genesis 3:8 (*they heard the sound of the LORD God walking in the garden*) is understood by many scholars to imply that God appeared in physical form. If so, this would be the first of all theophanies where Jesus used the human form to appear to people. When He did this, He knew that one day He would step into history to take on human flesh, the Godman Jesus, when He was born of a woman, so He could die for our sin.

How Long Were They in the Garden?

We don't know how long Adam and Eve were in the garden before they sinned. If they had waited very long, they would have been sinning against God by not being fruitful (they didn't conceive a child until after they were removed from the garden). Keep in mind, since they were created with perfect bodies, it would not have taken long for Eve to conceive. So, the time between creation and the Fall must have been short.

It's interesting to note that Archbishop Ussher, in his famous history book *The Annals of the World*, suggests that Adam sinned on the tenth day of the first month, which is the Day of Atonement

(Leviticus 23:27). The Day of Atonement presumably represents the first sacrifice, which God made by killing animals (from which He made coats of skins as stated in Genesis 3:21) to cover Adam and Eve's sin. Ussher's reasons for choosing this date do make sense. However, we can't be certain of the exact date or length of time prior to the Fall. I do believe this time was not that long though. I'm sure the devil didn't want Adam and Eve to learn to trust God so he would have wanted to tempt them very quickly after he himself fell (which would have been sometime after creation week).

God didn't need to ask Adam and Eve if they had disobeyed Him. He obviously asked them so they would admit what they did and be repentant. However, they were not repentant at all. This is a reminder to us that all humans have the same sin nature, and we don't want to admit we're sinners. Note that Adam blamed God and the woman! Think of how bad it was that Adam actually blamed his Creator for his sin (*the woman whom you gave to be with me*). And then he blamed his wife, Eve. But, remember, Adam was the one given the instruction not to eat from this tree, and Adam was with Eve as he watched her take the fruit and he said and did nothing! After Adam blamed her, the woman then blamed the serpent. Adam and Eve didn't want to take responsibility for what they had done. Humans today still don't want to take responsibility for their sins. We are just like Adam and Eve.

As we go on, we find that God then judged the serpent, the woman, and the man. But in judgment, God provided a means of salvation, as we will see.

God Speaks to the Serpent

The LORD God said to the serpent, "Because you have done this, cursed are you above all livestock and above all beasts of the field; on your belly you shall go, and dust you shall eat all the days of your life. I will put enmity between you and the woman, and between your offspring and her offspring; he shall bruise your head, and you shall bruise his heel" (Genesis 3:14–15).

We do not know exactly what the animal that the devil used to tempt Eve looked like (it's often portrayed as a snake-like creature). Some people think it had legs before it was cursed, but we are not told that. God doesn't question the serpent as He did man, because in the animal there would be no sense of sin. God questioned Adam and Eve because of His care for their salvation. But remember, they didn't admit their sin and weren't repentant. Even so, God cared for them (and all of us) so much, He provided a means of salvation in Jesus Christ.

The serpent (whatever it was) had a special judgment from God. Now the whole animal creation suffers from the effects of Adam's sin as we read in Romans 8:20–21. This had nothing to do with the curse pronounced on the serpent. The whole creation was made for man who was given dominion over it. This included dominion over the animals that were created to benefit man. So the whole creation had to share the consequences of man's sin, because the whole creation was made for man and under his dominion. But there was a specific judgment, a curse, that came upon the serpent for having been involved in the temptation of the woman, putting itself above humans, not under them as God had ordained. It's important to note that in Genesis 9:5 and Exodus 21:28–29 God ordered that any beast which injured a man was to be put to death. Leviticus 20:15–16 is another example of when a beast is to be put to death for being involved in unnatural behavior.

God's Judgment on the Serpent

The judgment on the serpent, *on your belly you shall go, and dust you shall eat,* certainly changed how it moved. Moving on the belly and eating dust (not for food, obviously) meant it will be looked upon as detestable.

But when God is speaking to the serpent, He is also speaking to the devil who used the serpent. So what is being stated in the curse on the serpent, in a figurative or symbolic sense, also applies to the devil. Therefore, the devil would also be looked upon as detestable. And even though the creation is waiting for a restoration to the perfect state before the Fall (Romans 8:21), God said the judgment on the serpent would be for *all the days of your life*. Applying this to the devil means there is no deliverance (or redemption) for him. He will remain detestable and under judgment for eternity. This is even implied in Isaiah 65:25 when referring to some future state, we read, *and dust shall be the serpent's food*. This is an obvious reference back to Genesis 3:14 and an allusion to the eternal judgment of *that ancient serpent, who is the devil and Satan* (Revelation 20:2).

The Protoevangelium

Genesis 3:15 is one of the most extraordinary verses in the Bible: *I will put enmity between you and the woman, and between your offspring and her offspring; he shall bruise your head, and you shall bruise his heel.* Church fathers called this verse the *"protoevangelium."* This means it's the first time the gospel is preached in God's Word. It is the first time God promises the Savior, the Lord Jesus, who would come as the "Seed," who would be bruised (crucified) but who would bruise (or "crush" as some translations put it) Satan's head. As God judged the serpent, the woman, and the man, at the same time He promised a Savior for the human family.

This verse is also telling us there will now be an ongoing war. It's a war between good and evil. It's a war between God's Word and man's word. It's a war between those who are godly and those who are not. It's a war between the devil and his angels, against Adam's family. It's a war that's ongoing until Jesus returns. However, this verse tells us that as part of this war the seed of the woman (which also points to Jesus) will be wounded (bruise his heel) but the serpent (the devil) will be crushed (bruise his head). This we believe is a direct reference to Christ's victory on the Cross in defeating the devil and paying the penalty for sin and the judgment of death. Also the *seed of the woman* is referring to the fact that the one who would *bruise the head* of the serpent comes from the woman. This, I believe, is a reference to the virgin birth. Everywhere else in Scripture, Adam's family tree is traced through the seed of the man.

Yes, Genesis 3:15 is a marvelous verse that sums up the spiritual war raging around us and God's provision of salvation in Jesus Christ.

God's Judgment on the Woman

God speaks to the woman:

> *To the woman he said, "I will surely multiply your pain in childbearing; in pain you shall bring forth children. Your desire shall be contrary to your husband, but he shall rule over you"* (Genesis 3:16).

God's judgment on the woman includes pain in childbirth. This includes not only the physical pain of pregnancy and childbirth, but the emotional pain of losing unborn children in what today we call miscarriages or stillbirths, along with the pain of infertility. It's interesting to note that animals don't seem to have nearly as much pain in childbirth as humans do. That's because they weren't cursed as the woman was (although they, like us, live in a broken world, so complications do arise).

The second part of the curse concerns the marriage relationship, specifically the spheres of responsibility for a husband and wife. What's clear is that, because of sin, the marriage relationship is now distorted.

What it means specifically is debated. Later, in Genesis 4, we will see the same Hebrew phrase, "your desire shall be," being used in regard to sin wanting to rule over Cain. A number of commentators understand this to mean that the marriage relationship is now cursed with conflict, which includes the wife trying to usurp her husband's God-given authority as the head of the family (for instance, as we see in the feminist movement) and the husband lording his authority over the wife in an unkind, harsh, or even despotic way. (Ephesians teaches a husband is to love his wife as Christ loves the church.) Here's the basic concept: because of sin, the marriage relationship will be distorted. Because of sin, the roles have been reversed — the woman will want to take over the man's role and the husband will want to rule despotically over the wife. This is a reminder that Satan always takes what God has done and tries to pervert it.

God's Judgment on the Man

God speaks to the man:

> And to Adam he said, "Because you have listened to the voice of your wife and have eaten of the tree of which I commanded you, 'You shall not eat of it,' cursed is the ground because of you; in pain you shall eat of it all the days of your life; thorns and thistles it shall bring forth for you; and you shall eat the plants of the field. By the sweat of your face you shall eat bread, till you return to the ground, for out of it you were taken; for you are dust, and to dust you shall return" (Genesis 3:17–19).

Adam was the one given the specific instruction by God, and he is the federal head of the human race. That's why Adam is blamed for sin and death entering the world. Eve was deceived, but Adam gets the blame for sin:

> Adam was not deceived, but the woman was deceived and became a transgressor (1 Timothy 2:14).

> Therefore, just as sin came into the world through one man, and death through sin, and so death spread to all men because all sinned (Romans 5:12).

So, because of Adam's sin, God then judged as follows:

1. *The ground is now cursed.* The ground would not yield food for man as it did in the perfect world. Plants would not grow well in a cursed ground. In today's world, we even see areas that are barren and where plants can't grow.

2. *Thorns and thistles will now plague the world.* Thorns and all sorts of weeds would now cause man problems. It's interesting to note that in the fossil record there are many examples of fossil thorns which evolutionists claim are millions of years old. However, thorns didn't come into existence until after sin and the curse. This is yet another reason Christians can't accept the idea that the fossil record (including the fossil thorns) was laid down millions of years before man sinned. Every time we weed our gardens, we need to be reminded that we sinned in Adam, and that's why we now have problems.

3. *It will now be very hard work to get the ground to yield food.* When God created Adam and Eve, He made the garden for them filled with trees loaded with fruit for food. Adam was to till the garden to look after it. But it wasn't hard work. Now, because of sin, man would have to work extra hard to be able to grow the plants needed for food. It would be wearisome work now. And because the ground was cursed and there were now thorns and weeds, this work would be so much harder.

4. *Man would now physically die.* God warned Adam they would die if he disobeyed God's directive not to eat of that one tree. When Adam sinned, he and Eve were immediately cut off from the perfect relationship they had with their Creator. They instantly died spiritually. But the penalty wasn't just spiritual death — physical death also resulted from sin. God makes it clear in His curse on Adam that physical death would now happen when He says they were made from dust and would return to dust. Adam and Eve didn't instantly die physically, but their bodies started to die (Adam died when he was 930 years old). As I stated earlier, some Christians who believe in evolution claim God evolved Adam and Eve from ape-like creatures. However, the Bible makes it clear that Adam was made from dust and Eve from Adam's side. Some people claim the "dust" represents the supposed ape-like creature that became Adam. But God said

Adam and Eve would now return to dust, not to some sort of ape-like creature!

Mother of All the Living

The man called his wife's name Eve, because she was the mother of all living (Genesis 3:20).

Eve means "life." Adam had previously called her "woman," and now he names her Eve. He knew that from Eve would come the first children and eventually the one promised in Genesis 3:15 to be our Savior.

First Corinthians 15:45 tells us that Adam was the first man, and here we are told Eve was "the mother of all living." Thus, there was only one man and one woman to begin the human race. There were no other people, just two. All humans belong to Adam's race. That's why all are sinners and in need of salvation. Even though death was the penalty for sin, Adam and Eve didn't immediately die physically. Thus, they could propagate the human race as commanded in Genesis 1:28. They certainly died spiritually (separation from God) immediately when they sinned, but Adam didn't die physically until he was 930 years old (Genesis 5:5), even though their bodies would have started to die immediately when God pronounced the sentence of death upon the human race (Genesis 3:19).

The Origin of Clothing

And the LORD God made for Adam and for his wife garments of skins and clothed them (Genesis 3:21).

There is so much we could say about this verse. Let me summarize all the points first, and then we will discuss each one in detail:

1. This is the origin of clothing and the problem with humans and nakedness.

2. This is the first death and the first shedding of blood (death of animals).

3. This is the origin of the sacrificial system.

4. This is a promise of the Messiah.

Animals don't wear clothes, but humans do. Because God gave clothes as a result of sin, it means it's important for humans to wear clothes, as sin distorts nakedness. Women, in particular, need to understand that certain styles of clothing (or lack thereof) can put a stumbling block in a man's way in regard to attraction because of the sin of lust. This means it's important to have a standard of clothing that takes this into account.

We Can't Cover Our Sin

Now Adam and Eve had clothed themselves in fig leaves (Genesis 3:7), but God clothed them with animal skins. Adam and Eve, as sinners, couldn't cover their sin. And a covering of plants wasn't going to work anyway. When God clothed them in animal skins, this showed them that God was the only one who could provide the way for their sin to be taken away. God must have killed an animal(s), shedding their blood, to obtain these skins. As mentioned earlier, I wonder if the

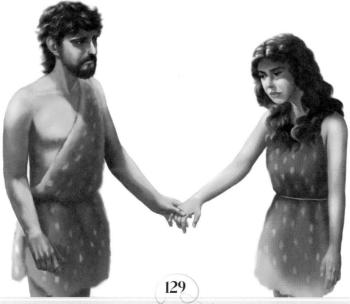

animals God killed were sheep. Remember, Jesus is called the lamb of God (John 1:29). This was the first blood sacrifice as a covering for their sin, a picture of what was to come in Jesus Christ, *the Lamb of God, who takes away the sin of the world* (John 1:29). We know the Israelites sacrificed animals over and over again. This was the origin of the sacrificial system, as God tells us that there had to be the shedding of blood for the forgiveness of sin (Hebrews 9:22). As death was the penalty for sin, there had to be the giving of life to pay sin's penalty. Consider these two verses:

> *Indeed, under the law almost everything is purified with blood, and without the shedding of blood there is no forgiveness of sins* (Hebrews 9:22).

> *For the life of the flesh is in the blood, and I have given it for you on the altar to make atonement for your souls, for it is the blood that makes atonement by the life* (Leviticus 17:11).

Now atonement means a payment must be made for sin so we can be reconciled to God. There has to be atonement for our sin. But an animal's skin only covered Adam and Eve, it didn't take away their sin. This is really a picture of the fact that someone would come to shed blood and give His life to take away our sin. Of course, that one is Jesus. The shedding of blood and the death of an animal can't take away our sin. Humans are not just animals — we are made in God's image. No animal was made in God's image. Only a human — but it would have to be a perfect human — could pay the penalty for our sin. God's Word makes this clear:

> *For it is impossible for the blood of bulls and goats to take away sins* (Hebrews 10:4).

A man brought sin and death into the world, so a man would need to pay the penalty for sin. But a sinner can't pay the penalty for sin, only a perfect man can. As all humans are descendants of Adam and Eve, one of them needs to pay the penalty for sin. But everyone is a sinner: *for all have sinned and fall short of the glory of God* (Romans 3:23). But

God already had a solution in the person of His Son, who would step into history taking on human flesh to become the perfect man — the Godman Jesus.

Christ's Death – Predetermined by God

Think about the fact that, as God killed these animals to cover Adam and Eve, He knew that this would happen to the Son of God one day. In fact, He knew this before He had even created the universe, before there was time. God had predetermined that the Son of God would become a sacrifice for sin so that those who received the gift of salvation could be saved for eternity.

Acts 2:23 states: *this Jesus, delivered up according to the definite plan and foreknowledge of God, you crucified and killed by the hands of lawless men.*

Revelation 13:8 states: *All who dwell on the earth will worship him, whose names have not been written in the Book of Life of the Lamb slain from the foundation of the world* (NKJV).

And think about this: before the universe was created, before time existed, before man was created, God knew that we (in Adam) would sin. He knew we would rebel against our Creator. And in the wisdom and love of God, in eternity, He predetermined a plan so that we could receive a free gift of salvation. In eternity, God planned for the Son of God to step into history to provide the ultimate sacrifice — the sinless Son of God would suffer sin's penalty of death and be raised from the dead, thus providing a way of salvation. Hebrews 10:10 declares: *By that will we have been sanctified through the offering of the body of Jesus Christ once for all.*

As you think about the fact that in eternity, God had predetermined the Son of God would become a man to die for our sins, also contemplate these things as I have mentioned before:

1. When God created the heavenly bodies on day four of creation *for signs and for seasons and for days and years* (Genesis 1:14),

He knew that one of the signs would be for the time the Son of God would become a man, born of a virgin in a town called Bethlehem.

2. When God made the trees (and all plants) on the third day of creation (Genesis 1:11), He knew that a tree would one day be used for the most evil event of history: when wicked men would crucify the Son of God. And yet, by God's foreknowledge and predetermined plan, this event would occur for the salvation of souls.

3. When God made the land animals on day six (Genesis 1:24), He knew that He would soon sacrifice at least one of those animals because of our sin in Adam — and He knew He had predetermined that this would one day happen to the Son of God, so we could receive the free gift of salvation.

4. When God cursed the ground and caused thorns and thistles to grow because of sin (Genesis 3:18), contemplate the fact that God knew that one day, thorns would be used to pierce the brow of His Son as He hung on that tree paying the penalty for our sin. *And they clothed him in a purple cloak, and twisting together a crown of thorns, they put it on him* (Mark 15:17).

Doesn't this all make you to want to fall on your knees and worship our Creator, praise Him, and continually thank Him for the . . . *lamb slain from the foundation of the world*?

And for those of you who have not received the free gift of salvation, God's Word tells you: *if you confess with your mouth that Jesus is* LORD *and believe in your heart that God raised him from the dead, you will be saved* (Romans 10:9).

So Genesis 3:21 really points to the fact that God's Son would come as the babe in a manger to die for our sin.

Other Implications from This Text

Three additional points.

1. None of this makes sense if one believes that the fossil layers were laid down over millions of years. If there was the shedding of blood for millions of years before sin, then *without the shedding of blood there is no forgiveness of sins* (Hebrews 9:22) would make no sense. No — death, bloodshed, and disease is a consequence of sin. There's no way believing in millions of years for the fossil record can fit with God's Word. As we will discuss later, most of the fossil record is the graveyard of the Flood of Noah's day, not the graveyard of supposed millions of years of evolution!

2. The Bible makes it clear there are fallen angels. The question people often ask is, why is it that God had a plan of salvation for humans, but not for angels. This is a mystery, but I give you what one of my favorite preachers of all time, Dr. Martin Lloyd Jones, one of the great expositional preachers of the 20th century, suggested for our consideration. His sermons are available online, free to listen to from the Martin Lloyd Jones Trust. In his sermon entitled "The Fall," Dr. Jones stated:

   Nowhere in the Bible do we read the fallen angels will be redeemed. Salvation is only for man. Why? The angels fell as men fell, so why shouldn't there be salvation for angels as well as for men? In the case of men, the temptation and the fall came from the outside. When Satan fell, he fell because of something within. The temptation did not come to Satan from outside himself. It was something that happened within, but what it was we don't know. And is it possible, I wonder that God in his infinite grace and kindness has drawn that distinction, because man was subjected to this subtilty, this beguiling, this malign influence, this angelic power of this fallen angel, God has had mercy and compassion and pity upon men and has provided for him a way of salvation. He has not done so in the case of the angels.[1]

3. Understanding the gospel rules out the possibility of some alien race on a planet somewhere in the universe.

Secularists are desperate to find life in outer space, as they believe that would provide evidence that life can evolve in different locations, given the supposed right conditions! The search for extraterrestrial life is really driven by man's rebellion against God in a desperate attempt to supposedly prove evolution!

According to the secular, evolutionary worldview there must be other inhabited worlds out there. Secularists cannot allow earth to be special or unique — that's a biblical idea (Isaiah 45:18). If life evolved here, it simply must have evolved elsewhere they believe.

The Bible, in sharp contrast to the secular worldview, teaches that earth was specially created, that it is unique and the focus of God's attention (Isaiah 66:1; Psalm 115:16). Life did not evolve but was specially created by God, as Genesis clearly teaches. Christians certainly shouldn't expect alien life to be cropping up across the universe.

Now the Bible doesn't say whether or not there is animal or plant life in outer space. I certainly suspect not. The earth was created for human life. And the sun and moon were created for signs and our seasons — and to declare the glory of God. *The heavens are the Lord's heavens, but the earth he has given to the children of man* (Psalm 115:16).

I do believe there can't be other intelligent beings in outer space because of the meaning of the gospel. The Bible makes it clear that Adam's sin affected the whole universe. This means that any aliens would also be affected by Adam's sin, but because they are not Adam's descendants, they can't have salvation. One day, the whole universe will be judged by fire, and there will be a new heavens and earth. God's Son stepped into history to be Jesus Christ, the "Godman," to be our relative, and to be the perfect sacrifice for sin — the Savior of mankind.

---

1. https://www.mljtrust.org/search/?name=&q=the+fall.

Jesus did not become the "GodKlingon" or the "GodMartian"! Only descendants of Adam can be saved. God's Son remains the "Godman" as our Savior. In fact, the Bible makes it clear that we see the Father through the Son (and we see the Son through His Word). To suggest that aliens could respond to the gospel is just totally wrong.

An understanding of the gospel makes it clear that salvation through Christ is only for the Adamic race — human beings who are all descendants of Adam.

Many secularists want to discover alien life, hoping that aliens can answer the deepest questions of life: "Where did we come from?" and "What is the purpose and meaning of life?" But such people are ignoring the revelation from the infinite God behind the whole universe. The Creator has told us where we came from: *In the beginning God created the heavens and the earth* (Genesis 1:1; Nehemiah 9:6). And He told us what life's purpose is: *Fear God and keep His commandments* (Ecclesiastes 12:13).

The answers to life's questions will not be found in imaginary aliens but in the revelation of the Creator through the Bible and His Son, Jesus Christ, who came to die on a Cross to redeem mankind from sin and death that our ancestor, Adam, introduced.

We need to be proclaiming the authority of God's Word from the very first verse — even on the subject of alien life!

Banished from the Garden

Then the LORD God said, "Behold, the man has become like one of us in knowing good and evil. Now, lest he reach out his hand and take also of the tree of life and eat, and live forever —" therefore the LORD God sent him out from the garden of Eden to work the ground from which he was taken. He drove out the man, and at the east of the garden of Eden he placed the cherubim and a flaming sword that turned every way to guard the way to the tree of life (Genesis 3:22–24).

Now remember that the devil told Eve that if they ate of the fruit of the tree of the knowledge of good and evil, they would be like God, knowing good and evil (Genesis 3:5). But the devil lied. Think about what has happened now because of sin: they were cut off from God spiritually, they felt shame, they saw God kill animals to clothe them in animal skins, and now they were banished from the garden where they lived.

The Tree of Life

God had placed two special trees in the garden — the tree of the knowledge of good and evil, and the tree of life. They were real trees, but each had a symbolic meaning. If Adam and Eve ate from the tree of the knowledge of good and evil, they would die. It wasn't the fruit that caused them to die, but the fact is they disobeyed God and God had decreed that if they ate of this tree they would die. So God, who never goes back on His Word, judged them with death. God had decreed the other special tree was the Tree of Life. I don't believe there was anything "magical" about the fruit of the tree if someone ate it to enable them to live forever. But because God had said this was the Tree of Life, if Adam and Eve had access to it, then they would be able to live forever. But God didn't want them living forever in their sinful state, so He denied them access to this tree by driving Adam and Eve out of the garden.

Now instead of looking after the garden, which provided fruit for them to nourish their bodies, they would have to work hard to till the ground to get it to yield food for them. They and their descendants would have to face up to what sin had done to them, to their relationship with God, and to the world. This must have greatly saddened Adam and Eve, but they must also have been encouraged that God had promised a Savior. We don't know how much they understood about the sacrificial system, but presumably God explained it to them, as we know Cain and Abel knew about the need for such a system as we will discuss soon.

When God banned us from paradise on earth (living in the garden with access to the Tree of Life), He was being merciful to us so we wouldn't live forever in that miserable, sinful state separated from God. He wants us to be in heaven with Him, which is a paradise without sin.

Genesis 3:23–24 says that God drove Adam and Eve out of the garden and had angels, specifically cherubim, guard the way with a flaming sword to stop anyone from getting back into the garden. In Scripture, cherubim are always closely associated with the throne of God. So maybe there was a special presence of God at that place. Later on, we read about the ark of the covenant in the tabernacle and temple, having sculptures of cherubim over the mercy seat. This was where blood was sprinkled by the high priest once a year to atone for sin. What a reminder that the only way back to a perfect relationship with God is through the shedding of blood. In other words, the only way we can have access to the tree of life is through what the Lord Jesus Christ did on the Cross.

Now we also read about the Tree of Life in Revelation 22:1–2:

> *Then the angel showed me the river of the water of life, bright as crystal, flowing from the throne of God and of the Lamb through the middle of the street of the city; also, on either side of the river, the tree of life with its twelve kinds of fruit, yielding its fruit each month. The leaves of the tree were for the healing of the nations.*

So the Tree of Life grows in the New Jerusalem (called the city of God), and only those whose names are written in the Lamb's Book of Life will be allowed in to have access to it.

> *And I saw no temple in the city, for its temple is the LORD God the Almighty and the Lamb. And the city has no need of sun or moon to shine on it, for the glory of God gives it light, and its lamp is the Lamb. By its light will the nations walk, and the kings of the earth will bring their glory into it, and its gates will never be shut by day— and there will be no night there. They will bring into it the glory and*

the honor of the nations. But nothing unclean will ever enter it, nor anyone who does what is detestable or false, but only those who are written in the Lamb's book of life (Revelation 21:22–27).

This also reminds us of what Jesus said:

Jesus said to him, "I am the way, and the truth, and the life. No one comes to the Father except through me" (John 14:6).

When Was the Fall?

One question we discussed earlier was in regard to how long Adam and Eve lived in the garden. I stated I didn't believe it was very long at all. Let's consider more on this topic. Adam and Eve were told to be fruitful and multiply. Now, in Romans 5:12 we're reminded that every human being is born in sin:

Therefore, just as sin came into the world through one man, and death through sin, and so death spread to all men because all sinned.

Looking back at the creation week, Adam and Eve couldn't have sinned on day six (the day Adam and the woman were created), since God declared that everything was "very good." Otherwise, sin would be "very good." Day seven is also unlikely, since God sanctified that day. Therefore, the Fall likely happened soon after this.

I previously mentioned that Archbishop Ussher in his *The Annals of the World* suggests that Adam sinned on the tenth day of the first month in Ussher's chronology, which is the Day of Atonement (Leviticus 16:29). The Day of Atonement presumably represents the first sacrifice, which God made by killing animals (from which He made coats of skins in Genesis 3:21, to cover Adam and Eve's sin). Ussher's reasons for choosing this date make sense. However, we can't be certain of the exact date or length of time prior to the Fall beyond the points established above.

However, Adam and Eve would not have conceived any children before they fell, as all humans have been born in sin. Based on female reproductive physiology, I suggest it had to be less than a month, as Eve could have conceived within a month. It makes sense their time in the garden was short — maybe as short as Ussher suggests.

Now we come to Genesis 4 as history unfolds for us the account of Adam and Eve now living in a fallen world.

Chapter 10

Genesis 4

Genesis 4:1

Now Adam knew Eve his wife, and she conceived and bore Cain, saying, "I have gotten a man with the help of the LORD" (Genesis 4:1).

It appears that this is the first child Eve conceived. We can't be absolutely sure about that, but most Bible commentators believe it's most likely Cain was the first. Eve was obviously excited about this male child. Maybe she even thought he would be the deliverer (the Savior). Maybe she was just expressing excitement that she could procreate as God had commanded.

Three Boys: Cain, Abel, and Seth

And again, she bore his brother Abel. Now Abel was a keeper of sheep, and Cain a worker of the ground (Genesis 4:2).

Some believe Abel was the second child. But we don't know that this was so. We read in Genesis 5:4 that Adam had *other sons and daughters.* It's interesting that the Jewish historian Josephus wrote, "The number of Adam's children, as says the old tradition, was thirty-three sons and twenty-three daughters."[1] Now that's just Jewish tradition, so we don't know for sure how many children Adam and Eve had, but it certainly could have been as many as this tradition indicates.

---

1. F. Josephus, *The Complete Works of Josephus,* translated by W. Whiston (Grand Rapids, MI; Kregel Publications, 1981), 27.

Only three of Adam and Eve's children receive specific mention, though: Cain, Abel, and Seth. Now the lineage leading to Jesus comes through Seth, so we can see why he is specifically mentioned. Also, Abel is held up as a great example of faith in Hebrews 11, and Cain's sinful behavior is given to us as a warning in Hebrews 11, 1 John 3:12, and Jude 11.

Abel, a Keeper of Sheep

Since God didn't give the instruction for humans to eat animals until after the flood in Genesis 9:3, why was Abel a keeper of sheep? One reason could be for clothing, and another for the purpose of sacrifice. It seems logical to assume that God explained the sacrificial system to Adam and Eve, and they explained this to their children. After all, we read in Genesis 4:4 that, *Abel also brought of the firstborn of his flock and of their fat portions.* Now the law given to Moses specifically requires the sacrifice (or redemption) of the firstborn of livestock (Exodus 13:2, 34:19) and specifies the inclusion and significance of the fat (Leviticus 3:9–10, 16, 4:19–20, 25–26). So it seems likely God had given specific instructions concerning the blood sacrifice that Abel was following.

Cain, a Tiller of the Ground

Cain was a tiller of the ground, so he may have been farming fruits, vegetables, and grains. As God gave specific instructions to Adam and Eve in Genesis 1:29 to eat plants, it would make sense that they would have farmed various plant foods.

> In the course of time Cain brought to the LORD an offering of the fruit of the ground, and Abel also brought of the firstborn of his flock and of their fat portions. And the LORD had regard for Abel and his offering, but for Cain and his offering he had no regard. So Cain was very angry, and his face fell (Genesis 4:3–5).

The big question here is why was Cain's offering rejected? One suggestion is that Cain's offering was not a blood sacrifice, which is required for atonement (forgiveness of sin). It is true that God gave the Israelites instructions for grain offerings, but those offerings had nothing to do with the remission of sins. From reading Leviticus 2, and other passages, it appears the main purpose of the grain offering was for worship, and acknowledgment of God's provision of life and of the various needs of the Israelites. In other words, such offerings were to give praise to God for His supply of their "daily bread." The grain offerings certainly were not for atonement.

As it seems Cain and Abel would have had an understanding of the importance of a blood sacrifice for the remission of sin, it seems reasonable to suggest Cain did not bring such a sacrifice as he should have. He could have traded grains, fruits etc. with his brother for such a sacrifice.

From what we read in the New Testament, Cain's offering was rejected because his works were evil:

> By faith Abel offered to God a more acceptable sacrifice than Cain, through which he was commended as righteous, God commending him by accepting his gifts. And through his faith, though he died, he still speaks (Hebrews 11:4).

> For this is the message that you have heard from the beginning, that we should love one another. We should not be like Cain, who was of the evil one and murdered his brother. And why did he murder him? Because his own deeds were evil and his brother's righteous (1 John 3:11–12).

> Woe to them! For they walked in the way of Cain and abandoned themselves for the sake of gain to Balaam's error and perished in Korah's rebellion (Jude 1:11).

The great Bible expositor John Gill in his commentary of Genesis stated, "The superior excellency of Abel's sacrifice to Cain's, lay both in the matter, and in the manner of it; the one was offered heartily to the LORD, the other only in show; the one was offered in faith, the other not."[2] So Gill is saying it was both Cain's heart, as well as what he offered. What deeds of Cain's were evil though? Did he do evil things even before the offering he made, and he didn't have a repentant heart? That's certainly possible. Was the bringing of a grain offering, instead of a blood sacrifice, an evil deed? We certainly read in the next verses that Cain was envious and welled up with anger to such a state he committed murder! Personally, I take the position John Gill does, that Cain brought the wrong offering because he had a rebellious heart.

Regardless, this is a reminder for all of us to ensure we do things the way God instructs us, and to examine our hearts to make sure we are not filled with envy or anger that could lead to horrible sinful actions.

In the next verses of Genesis 5, we read that Cain kills Abel. Do we know when this happened?

Before we move on to the next verses, we need to look at the phrase at the beginning of Genesis 4:3, *in the course of time*. How long after Cain was born did this situation with Abel occur? We find out in Genesis 5 that Eve had a son, Seth, when Adam was 130 years old, that she saw as a replacement for Abel. It's certainly possible that this situation between Cain and Abel could have been about 130 years after Adam was created. During that time, many of those other sons and daughters may have been born, so by then there could have been quite a number of family members present. This helps us understand Genesis 5:14 in regard to who Cain was frightened might kill him because he murdered his brother.

Sin Is Crouching at the Door

The LORD said to Cain, "Why are you angry, and why has your face fallen? If you do well, will you not be accepted? And if you do not do well, sin is crouching at the door. Its desire is contrary to you, but you must rule over it."

2. John Gill, *An Exposition of the First Book of Moses, Called Genesis* (London, England: Aaron Ward Publisher, 1763–1766). Reprinted by Particular Baptist Press, Springfield, Missouri, 2010, p. 126.

Cain spoke to Abel his brother. And when they were in the field, Cain rose up against his brother Abel and killed him (Genesis 4:6–8).

God obviously knew Cain's heart. However, He asked Cain those questions to give him the opportunity to confess and repent. God also warns that in a sense, sin is crouching, ready to take over his life, but that Cain needs to stop this and not let his sin nature get the better of him. Just for interest, this is the first time the word "sin" is used in the Bible.

Cain did not confess or repent of his sin concerning his attitude and evil works. He let sin get the better of him and killed his brother Abel. This is the first recorded murder in the Bible. In a way, this battle between Cain and Abel represents the battle spoken of in Genesis 3:15 between the seed of the serpent and the seed of the woman. Perhaps the devil thought by getting Cain to kill Abel, that this would stop the promise given in Genesis 3:15 regarding the fact that the seed of the woman would overcome the devil. We know that Jesus overcame the devil when He died and rose again. There are other events recorded in history where the devil tries to stop the seed of the woman: killing the children at the time of Moses (Exodus 1), Herod killing the children after Jesus was born as the babe in a manager (Matthew 2).

What Have You Done?

Then the LORD said to Cain, "Where is Abel your brother?" He said, "I do not know; am I my brother's keeper?" And the LORD said, "What have you done? The voice of your brother's blood is crying to me from the ground. And now you are cursed from the ground, which has opened its mouth to receive your brother's blood from your hand. When you work the ground, it shall no longer yield to you its strength. You shall be a fugitive and a wanderer on the earth (Genesis 4:9–12).

God knew what Cain had done. But by asking Cain, God again is giving Cain an opportunity to confess and repent. Instead, Cain answers in a very insolent way which, again, shows the sinful attitude of his heart, and his attitude of rebellion toward the Creator God. Cain lied, which is a reminder to us of what we read in John 8:44:

> You are of your father the devil, and your will is to do your father's desires. He was a murderer from the beginning, and does not stand in the truth, because there is no truth in him. When he lies, he speaks out of his own character, for he is a liar and the father of lies.

Now when God speaks of Abel's blood which soaked into the ground, this is actually the first use of the word "blood" in the Bible. God then begins His judgment on Cain.

1. God specifically judges the ground that Cain will till to grow food. God had already cursed the ground in Genesis 3:17, but now there was an extra judgment regarding Cain and the earth. As a result of the curse in Genesis 3:17, we know that man has to till the earth for food and deal with weeds, pests, problems of drought, and so on. But now, whenever Cain tried to till the earth, it would be much more difficult and wouldn't be as productive as it would for anyone else. This means Cain would struggle with this for the rest of his life.

2. Cain would be a wanderer. In other words, because of what he had done he would not be able to stay in one place very long. This could be because he would keep looking for land that would yield food for him. It could also be because people (his close family) would know what he had done and so because of fear, he would be continually moving to keep away from them. Regardless, it's a reminder to us that God judges sin. Yes, He is a God of grace and mercy. He even gave Cain opportunity to repent, but sadly, Cain was unrepentant. But always remember:

… *and be sure your sin will find you out* (Numbers 32:23).

The Mark of Cain

Cain said to the LORD, "My punishment is greater than I can bear.

*Behold, you have driven me today away from the ground, and from
your face I shall be hidden. I shall be a fugitive and a wanderer on
the earth, and whoever finds me will kill me." Then the LORD said to
him, "Not so! If anyone kills Cain, vengeance shall be taken on him
sevenfold." And the LORD put a mark on Cain, lest any who found
him should attack him* (Genesis 4:13–15).

Cain now complains about his punishment. Once again, there does
not seem to be any indication Cain was sorry for what he did, but only
sorry he was caught and was being judged. No wonder we are warned
in the New Testament about Cain (e.g., Jude 11). Think about it. Cain
murdered his brother Abel, and now he was complaining about the
judgment God had decided for his actions. Even though he had killed
his brother, he was worried someone would kill him! However, God
decreed that Cain would not be killed. In fact, as a warning, God said
if someone were to kill Cain then they and seven generations of their
family would be judged because of that. Now that's a stern warning!

Many people have written about what it means that God "put a mark
on Cain." Some claim the Hebrew word translated "mark" is better
translated "sign" and that God gave some sort of sign for Cain (maybe
some sort of miracle) to reassure him that He would not allow anyone
who met him to kill him. Some think the "mark" was intended for
others so they wouldn't kill Cain. We are unsure of what this "mark"
was, but it's purpose (to protect Cain from being killed by others)
seems clear.

This seems perplexing. After all, in Genesis 9:6, after the Flood, God
said:

*Whoever sheds the blood of man, by man shall his blood be shed, for
God made man in his own image* (Genesis 9:6).

This verse is where God sets up capital punishment (the death penalty) for murder and, by extension, also sets the foundation for civil
government. But then why did God not require that of Cain? Well,
maybe because God had not specifically given that instruction yet.
There's no indication in God's Word that there was any civil law at this

stage for the restriction of crime. Also, maybe God wanted people to see the miserable life Cain had to lead as a warning to them not to be like Cain.

Also, we learn in Scripture that the role of the state is to maintain law and order, so any death penalty judgment would be up to the state. At the time of Abel's murder, there would have been quite a number of fairly close family members. As discussed earlier, there could have been close to 130 years from the creation of Adam to when Cain killed Abel. As Adam and Eve had many sons and daughters (Genesis 5:4), there could have been a significant number of family members by this time. Now in Deuteronomy 21, concerning the death penalty, family was excluded from the execution of the law. It could be that God was also protecting the family unit as He would do when giving the law to the Israelites. The protection of Cain may not have been so much for Cain as a person, but for the protection of the family unit.

But God is the righteous judge, and as Abraham said:

> *Shall not the Judge of all the earth do what is just?* (Genesis 18:25).

Cain Builds a City

> *Then Cain went away from the presence of the LORD and settled in the land of Nod, east of Eden. Cain knew his wife, and she conceived and bore Enoch. When he built a city, he called the name of the city after the name of his son, Enoch* (Genesis 4:16–17).

We now will get some details concerning the history of Cain and certain of his descendants. After this, we then read a history of Seth and his descendants. When we compare the two lines, we will see a great contrast between the descendants of Cain (who were very worldly) and the descendants of Seth who called on the name of the LORD.

As part of Cain's judgment was that he would be a wanderer ("a fugitive and a vagabond"), maybe Cain determined this wouldn't happen and so he would build a city (the first city mentioned in the Bible) and settle down. However, it is interesting that the city is called Enoch after his son. Maybe Cain didn't stay in this city but moved on, perhaps out of fear of what people might do to him because he killed Abel. After all, since God said Cain would be a "fugitive" and "vagabond," then that would definitely happen.

Cain's Wife – Who Was She?

The text states that "Cain knew his wife." This seems to indicate he was already married and therefore he was probably married at the time he killed Abel.

But who was Cain's wife?

The simple answer is that Cain married his sister or another close relation, like a niece. This answer may sound revolting for those of us who grew up in societies that have attached a stigma to such an idea, but if we start from Scripture, the answer is clear.

First Corinthians 15:45 tells us that Adam was "the first man." Genesis 3:20 states that Eve "was the mother of all the living" (NASB), and Genesis 5:4 reveals that Adam and Eve "had other sons and daughters" (besides Cain, Abel, and Seth).

There were no other people on earth as some have claimed. God did not create other people groups from which Cain chose a wife, as we are all made of one blood (Acts 17:26). If He had made others, these people would not have been able to be saved from their sins, since only descendants of Adam can be saved — that's why it was so important for Jesus to be Adam's descendant.

Doesn't the Bible forbid marriage between close relations? It does, but the laws against marrying family members were initially given as part of the Mosaic covenant, approximately 2,500 years after God created Adam and Eve. Due in part to genetic mistakes, these laws were necessary to help protect offspring from mutations shared by both parents.

But isn't that incest? In today's world, this would be called incest. But originally there would have been no problem with it. Looking back through history, the closer we get to Adam and Eve, the fewer genetic mistakes people would have, so it would have been safer for close relatives to marry and have children. There are a number of sins that would be called incest today, but originally, close relations marrying was not sin.

Christians who have a problem with this answer need to remember that Noah's grandchildren must have married brothers, sisters, or first cousins — there were no other people (1 Peter 3:20; Genesis 7:7). Abraham married his half-sister (Genesis 20:2, 12); Isaac married Rebekah, the daughter of his cousin Bethuel (Genesis 24:15, 67); and Jacob married his cousins Leah and Rachel. Clearly, the Bible does not forbid the marriage of close relatives until the time of Moses.

When we start from Scripture, it is easy to see who Cain's wife was. God's Word has the answer to this question and so many others like it; we just need to trust what He has revealed.

The Line of Cain

To Enoch was born Irad, and Irad fathered Mehujael, and Mehujael fathered Methushael, and Methushael fathered Lamech. And Lamech took two wives. The name of the one was Adah, and the name of the other Zillah. Adah bore Jabal; he was the father of those who dwell in tents and have livestock. His brother's name was Jubal; he was the father of all those who play the lyre and pipe. Zillah also bore Tubal-cain; he was the forger of all instruments of bronze and iron. The sister of Tubal-cain was Naamah (Genesis 4:18–22).

As we now follow more of the line of Cain, we find out fascinating details about these Cainites. What do we learn from these five verses?

1. The first recorded instance of polygamy is when Lamech took two wives. This ignores that God created and designed marriage in Genesis 2:24 as to be between one man (male) and one woman (female). Here we find Lamech in rebellion against

what God ordained in regard to marriage.

2. Jabal invented tents, presumably associated with raising live-stock. Such tents would enable people to move with their live-stock to better pastures, or once pastures had been consumed by the animals.

3. Jubal invented stringed and wind instruments. He must have been quite a genius to do this. One could imagine people then using such instruments for all sorts of entertainment. And if people did not worship God as they should have, they no doubt used music for pleasure and evil purposes.

4. Tubal-cain invented processes to produce bronze and iron and taught people to make all sorts of items. Perhaps he taught them how to make items that could even be used for violence in killing people, particularly as we find out in Genesis 6 how violent and wicked the people had become at the time of Noah.

So within 7 generations, we now have people inventing quite sophisticated technology. This reminds us that humans are very intelligent and certainly didn't evolve over millions of years. Even after the Flood, people developed advanced technology fairly quickly, as evidenced by archaeological research. In the first generation of children, we have Abel keeping sheep, and by the seventh generation, we have their children inventing tents and livestock management, metallurgy, and musical instruments. Man has always been highly intelligent. The Cainitic civilization obviously grew to great heights with inventive technology.

We don't know why Naamah is specifically mentioned. Her name apparently means fair and beautiful. But it is interesting that many scholars believe that some of the heathen gods (such as Venus, Apollo, Vulcan, etc.) are based on the lives of these pre-Flood people. No doubt stories about such people were handed down from those who survived the Flood on the Ark.

A Double Murder

Lamech said to his wives: "Adah and Zillah, hear my voice; you wives of Lamech, listen to what I say: I have killed a man for wounding me, a young man for striking me. If Cain's revenge is sevenfold, then Lamech's is seventy-sevenfold (Genesis 4:23–24).

Lamech here appears to be gloating to his two wives that he killed two men. It seems he is also using what God said to Cain (that if anyone killed him, there would be a sevenfold revenge — interpreted by some to mean that God would judge them for seven generations), to then threaten a much greater judgment for anyone who tried to kill him. From what we read about Lamech, we can deduce that he was in rebellion against God, and a violent and prideful man. No doubt this influence impacted his children (Jabal, Jubal, and Tubal-cain) in regard to how they would live in the world, using their intelligence to create sophisticated items used for evil, pleasure, violence, etc.

This then ends the details about the line of Cain. Maybe God wanted us to understand how this seemingly ungodly line contrasted to the descendants of Seth. And perhaps all this is to help us understand how the world's population could become so corrupt by the time of Noah, as no doubt those who promoted evil impacted others. As 1 Corinthians 15:33 warns, *Do not be deceived: Bad company ruins good morals.*

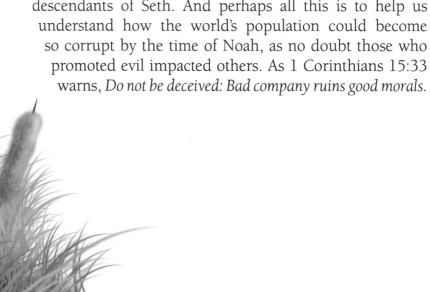

The Line of Seth

And Adam knew his wife again, and she bore a son and called his name Seth, for she said, "God has appointed for me another offspring instead of Abel, for Cain killed him." To Seth also a son was born, and he called his name Enosh. At that time people began to call upon the name of the LORD *(Genesis 4:25–26).*

Now we begin to read the record of Adam through the line of Seth. Notice that we don't read about an emphasis on human accomplishments or people boasting (like Lamech). The first thing we read about the descendants of Seth is that *"people began to call upon the name of the* LORD."

Remember, God promised in Genesis 3:15 that the seed of the woman would come to defeat the seed of the serpent (the devil). It's obvious from what we read in Genesis 4 that the seed of the woman wouldn't come through the Cainites (the line of Cain) but through the line of Seth.

Eve saw Seth as a replacement for Abel who was killed by Cain. Seth was born when Adam was 130 years old (Genesis 5:3). Because Eve knew how wicked Cain was, and Abel had been killed, it's possible she saw Seth as fulfilling God's promise in regard to the seed of the woman. When Seth was 105 years old, he had a son, Enosh (Genesis 5:6). This is when we read that *"people began to call upon the name of the* LORD." This seems to mean that there was more of a public worship by those in Seth's line now that there would have been quite a number of people. Also, maybe they called themselves this, meaning they were sons of God (acknowledging God as their Creator), to contrast with the Cainites who were really sons of men (glorying in their human accomplishments).

We now move into the line of the promised seed as it is traced through Seth.

Chapter 11

Genesis 5

The Book of the Generations of Adam

Genesis 5:1-2

This is the book of the generations of Adam. When God created man, he made him in the likeness of God. Male and female he created them, and he blessed them and named them Man when they were created (Genesis 5:1–2).

Chapter five begins with "This is the book of the generations of Adam." The word "book" means a written record. Could it be possible that Adam actually recorded history in written form, that was handed down to Noah and eventually to Moses? It certainly is possible. Sadly, many people have been impacted by the evolutionary worldview that teaches man evolved from some primitive creature to eventually be able to communicate with language, and eventually invent writing. Because of that, even many Christians don't think of the possibility that Adam could write.

However, God's record in the Bible makes it clear that man could use language and speak right from the beginning. So why couldn't Adam know how to write? He was highly intelligent, after all. And remember, Adam was different from all of us. As the passage states, *he made him in the likeness of God.* Only Adam was created directly by God, to be fully mature, made in God's image, and ready to communicate immediately. In Genesis 5:3 we read that Adam had a son, Seth, who was "in his own likeness, after his image." Seth was born as a child and was born as a sinner (*all have sinned* [Romans 3:23]) because his father Adam had sinned. Seth was born with the innate ability for language but would have had to learn the language as he grew up —just as we do today. But Adam and Eve didn't have to do that. They were made directly as mature human beings.

It's also interesting to note that Genesis 2:4 states, *These are the generations of the heavens and the earth when they were created, in the day that the LORD God made the earth and the heavens.* The history of the universe and all life, including the creation of Adam and Eve, would have had to be relayed by God Himself. It would make sense that He told this to Adam.

After reading *This is the book of the generations of Adam,* which would refer to the history Adam possibly wrote, we then read:

> *These are the generations of Noah.*
>
> *These are the generations of the sons of Noah, Shem, Ham, and Japheth.*
>
> *These are the generations of Shem.* (Genesis 6:9, 10:1, 11:10)

It is possible then that the next section was recorded by Noah, then Noah's sons, and so on.

And it is very possible that Noah took such writings that had been handed down from Adam, on the Ark, so eventually Moses would compile the Book of Genesis under the inspiration of God. We don't know for sure, but this is certainly very possible.

Now note that Genesis 5:2 states, *male and female he created them.* This is reinforcing the fact that God stated in Genesis 1:27 that He made only two genders of humans, male and female — Adam and Eve. This is reinforced throughout Scripture including when Jesus as the Godman said God made man *male and female* in Matthew 19:4 and Mark 10:6. The scientific study of human chromosomes confirms there are only two genders of humans. But we must also keep in mind that because of sin, now there can be mistakes (mutations) in human chromosomes that can cause lots of different problems for humans. We certainly need to be sympathetic to people with such problems and help them understand how our sin has negatively affected things. Nonetheless, this doesn't in any way change the fact that God created human beings with only two genders — male and female.

The text also says *and named them Man* (Genesis 5:2). The term "man" in the Bible is often used in the context of mankind, or the human race. "Adam" and "man" are both translated from the same Hebrew word. The context of the passage determines if it means one man, Adam, or mankind in general.

And He Died

When Adam had lived 130 years, he fathered a son in his own likeness, after his image, and named him Seth. The days of Adam after he fathered Seth were 800 years; and he had other sons and daughters. Thus all the days that Adam lived were 930 years, and he died (Genesis 5:3–5).

In the previous section, I discussed what it meant that Seth was a "son in his own likeness." Many people skip over Genesis 5:4 without thinking about the fact that Adam and Eve had children (sons and daughters) other than Cain, Abel, and Seth. I also discussed this in a previous section when we dealt with who Cain's wife was.

Now Adam lived for 930 years. We find out that the patriarchs (heads of families — men who were fathers of the human race) before the Flood lived for what we today would call very long ages. After the Flood, people's length of life began to drop until we get to around 70 on average. We don't know why people's ages dropped so rapidly after the Flood. There are many possibilities, including possible biological and environmental changes. But I think that God ensured man's life span would be shortened to bring us face-to-face with our own mortality. We will read soon how people became so wicked that God judged the world with a global Flood. Because of man's sinful heart, I often wonder if God shortened our lives to make us realize how important it is to think about our eternity and not just the short, almost insignificant time we spend on earth. It's a reminder of how vital it is that each of us have trusted in Jesus Christ for salvation.

For those who say the creation days were long periods of time (even millions of years), then as stated earlier, it doesn't make sense that Adam was made on day six, and lived through day seven of the creation week, and then died at 930.

The last part of Genesis 5:5 reads...*and he died.*

As you read Genesis 5, what a reminder that God judged sin with death. As Hebrews 9:27 states:

> *And just as it is appointed for man to die once, and after that comes judgment.*
>
> *Thus all the days that Adam lived were 930 years,* **and he died.**
>
> *Thus all the days of Seth were 912 years,* **and he died.**
>
> *Thus all the days of Enosh were 905 years,* **and he died.**
>
> *Thus all the days of Kenan were 910 years,* **and he died.**
>
> *Thus all the days of Mahalalel were 895 years,* **and he died.**
>
> *Thus all the days of Jared were 962 years,* **and he died.**
>
> *Thus all the days of Methuselah were 969 years,* **and he died.**
>
> *Thus all the days of Lamech were 777 years,* **and he died.**
>
> (Genesis 5:5, 8, 11, 14, 17, 20, 27, 31; emphasis added)

And then after the Flood we read:

> *All the days of Noah were 950 years, **and he died*** (Genesis 9:29;
> emphasis added).

What a reminder this is that everyone will die and meet their Creator.
No human being can ultimately stop people dying, which is why it is
so important that everyone ensure they have repented of their sin and
received the free gift of salvation in Jesus:

> *If we confess our sins, he is faithful and just to forgive us our sins and
> to cleanse us from all unrighteousness* (1 John 1:9).

> *…because, if you confess with your mouth that Jesus is* Lord *and
> believe in your heart that God raised him from the dead, you will be
> saved* (Romans 10:9).

I remember meeting someone once who told me he invited his friend
who was a non-Christian to church. When the friend said he would
come, this person called his pastor to tell him and insisted the pastor
give a strong message about salvation. The friend came to church, and
at the beginning of the service the pastor read his passage for the day
which happened to be the genealogies in Genesis 5. The person who
invited his friend was angry. He told me he was mumbling under his
breath as to why the pastor would choose such a boring passage which
just had genealogies. But after the service, this friend committed his
life to the Lord. The person who invited him asked what had led him
in that direction. The friend said he kept hearing the words "and he
died" over and over again as the passage was read. He realized he was
going to die and needed to do something about where he would spend
eternity, and he received the free gift of salvation.

Now, as you read through this section of Genesis 5, I want you to be
thinking about what is stated in Jude 1:14, *Enoch, the seventh from
Adam.* In other words, there are no gaps in these genealogies. We are
told when people were born and when people died. Such genealogies
enable us to add up the years throughout Scripture back to Adam.
As we do that and then add in the years from when Jesus became the

babe in a manger in Bethlehem until now, we get a total of about 6,000 years. There is no way anyone can fit millions of years into the Bible.

When Seth had lived 105 years, he fathered Enosh. Seth lived after he fathered Enosh 807 years and had other sons and daughters. Thus all the days of Seth were 912 years, and he died.

When Enosh had lived 90 years, he fathered Kenan. Enosh lived after he fathered Kenan 815 years and had other sons and daughters. Thus all the days of Enosh were 905 years, and he died.

When Kenan had lived 70 years, he fathered Mahalalel. Kenan lived after he fathered Mahalalel 840 years and had other sons and daughters. Thus all the days of Kenan were 910 years, and he died.

When Mahalalel had lived 65 years, he fathered Jared. Mahalalel lived after he fathered Jared 830 years and had other sons and daughters. Thus all the days of Mahalalel were 895 years, and he died.

When Jared had lived 162 years, he fathered Enoch. Jared lived after he fathered Enoch 800 years and had other sons and daughters. Thus all the days of Jared were 962 years, and he died (Genesis 5:6–20).

Enoch Walked with God

When Enoch had lived 65 years, he fathered Methuselah. Enoch walked with God after he fathered Methuselah 300 years and had other sons and daughters. Thus all the days of Enoch were 365 years. Enoch walked with God, and he was not, for God took him (Genesis 5:21–24).

Can you imagine a man like Enoch, who so loved God and was so close to Him, that God, who has a right to do whatever He determines, gave him an exception (the only other exception being Elijah in 2 Kings 2:11), and took him to heaven without dying. What a man of God he must have been. Oh, that each one of us could attain to a fraction of the relationship Enoch must have had with his Creator!

Enoch is also one of two of the pre-Flood patriarchs (the other being Lamech, father of Noah) who gave prophesies that are recorded in Scripture. In Jude 1:14, Jude states, *It was also about these that Enoch, the seventh from Adam, prophesied, saying, "Behold, the* LORD *comes with ten thousands of his holy ones."*

We don't know where Jude obtained this prophecy, though apparently it was well-known in Jewish tradition. As it is in Scripture, God, through the inspiration of the Holy Spirit, moved Jude to write this down as a true prophecy Enoch made. No doubt Enoch saw the wickedness increasing on the earth, and he was warning people that one day God would come back in judgment. Even back then, before the Flood, Enoch was prophesying about the second coming of Jesus — before Jesus had even come the first time as a babe in a manger. This is also a reminder of how long-suffering God is. As we read in 2 Peter 3:9, *The* LORD *is not slow to fulfill his promise as some count slowness, but is patient toward you, not wishing that any should perish, but that all should reach repentance.*

A Very Old Man

When Methuselah had lived 187 years, he fathered Lamech. Methuselah lived after he fathered Lamech 782 years and had other sons and daughters. Thus all the days of Methuselah were 969 years, and he died.

When Lamech had lived 182 years, he fathered a son and called his name Noah, saying, "Out of the ground that the LORD *has cursed, this one shall bring us relief from our work and from the painful toil of our hands." Lamech lived after he fathered Noah 595 years and had other sons and daughters. Thus all the days of Lamech were 777 years, and he died* (Genesis 5:25–31).

Enoch was the father of Methuselah, who, as we read in the next verse, was the longest living person recorded in history. There is some debate among scholars, but some believe the name Methuselah means "man of the spear," but others say it means "when he dies, it shall be sent." Because we don't know for sure, it's best not to make much of this. But we can learn some interesting things from the life of Methuselah.

If you match up the ages of the patriarchs, Methuselah died the same year as the Flood. See the chart on the following page.

Though some may mistakenly think Methuselah died in the Flood, this is highly unlikely. Methuselah was raised by a godly parent (Enoch) who walked with God and pleased God so that God took him away without death as we discussed, and Methuselah's grandson, Noah, was righteous. It seems likely, therefore, that Methuselah followed the LORD. In fact, Methuselah may perhaps have helped Noah in the construction phase of the ark. But his death likely preceded the Flood.

Some have suggested that Methuselah died immediately before the Flood. Whether this is true or not, we cannot be certain. God's instruction for Noah and his family to board the Ark seven days in advance was for several reasons (Genesis 7:1, 4, 10). Obviously, one reason was to complete the final phase of loading the animals (Genesis 7:2–9), and a second was a final test of faith for Noah and his family, the final boarding being on the seventh day (Genesis 7:11–16).

But keep in mind that it was common for prominent people to be honored with designated times of mourning after they passed (e.g., Genesis 27:41, 50:4; Deuteronomy 34:8; 2 Samuel 11:27). However, there were surely many who had mourning periods that are simply not mentioned in the Bible. In light of this, others have suggested that these seven days were also a mourning period for Methuselah. Whether this is true or not, we cannot be certain, but it would make a good "cap" to the life of Methuselah.

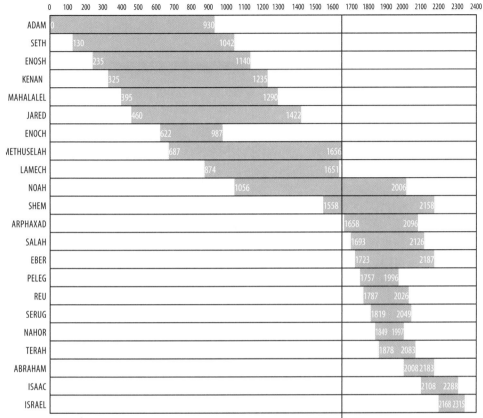

YEARS AFTER CREATION

	0	100	200	300	400	500	600	700	800	900	1000	1100	1200	1300	1400	1500	1600	1700	1800	1900	2000	2100	2200	2300	2400
ADAM	0									930															
SETH		130									1042														
ENOSH			235								1140														
KENAN				325								1235													
MAHALALEL					395							1290													
JARED					460									1422											
ENOCH							622		987																
METHUSELAH							687										1656								
LAMECH									874								1651								
NOAH											1056										2006				
SHEM																1558						2158			
ARPHAXAD																		1658			2096				
SALAH																		1693				2126			
EBER																		1723				2187			
PELEG																		1757		1996					
REU																		1787			2026				
SERUG																			1819		2049				
NAHOR																			1849	1997					
TERAH																			1878			2083			
ABRAHAM																					2008	2183			
ISAAC																						2108	2288		
ISRAEL																							2168	2315	

FLOOD 1656

With the passing of Methuselah, and the recent passing of Lamech, we pause to realize that there were not many righteous people left on earth. After all, fewer than ten people were saved on the Ark.

Consider Abraham's discussion with the LORD over the destruction of Sodom (Genesis 18:26–32). Abraham did not proceed to fewer than ten righteous people when pleading for Sodom. He may have believed that judgment would come if there were fewer than ten — perhaps a reflection of his knowledge of the Flood and that for eight God didn't stop His judgment. Methuselah and Lamech had recently died, and this left eight. So, judgment was coming, but the LORD also prepared a means of salvation for Noah and his family on the Ark, just as He did by sending the angels to rescue Lot and his family from Sodom.

Now note that Lamech made a prophecy concerning Noah: *Out of the ground that the Lord has cursed, this one shall bring us relief from our work and from the painful toil of our hands* (Genesis 5:29). We cannot be sure as to what this meant. There are Jewish traditions that Noah invented all sorts of farming equipment to help people in tilling the land. That may be so, but we can't be sure. Others say it is a prophecy that Noah would do something that would help overcome the evil in the world — the building of the Ark for the salvation of the righteous people. It certainly seems Lamech knew from God that his son Noah was set aside to do something special for the Lord.

By the way, this is a totally different Lamech to the one in the line of Cain. Just as people today will use the same names as others for their children, this obviously was the case back at that time. We also see there was an Enoch in the line from Cain, but a totally different Enoch to the one in the line from Seth.

Introducing Noah

Chapter five ends by telling us:

> *After Noah was 500 years old, Noah fathered Shem, Ham, and Japheth* (Genesis 5:32).

These four people played a very important part in human history. Noah was called by God to build a great ship because God was going to judge the wicked world with a catastrophic Flood. Only Noah and these three sons and their wives survived that great Flood. The three sons of Noah and their wives gave rise to all the people who have ever lived on earth since the Flood.

Chapter 12

Genesis 6

Genesis chapter 6 begins with context of the wickedness of this pre-Flood world.

Genesis 6:1-8

When man began to multiply on the face of the land and daughters were born to them, the sons of God saw that the daughters of man were attractive. And they took as their wives any they chose. Then the LORD said, "My Spirit shall not abide in man forever, for he is flesh: his days shall be 120 years." The Nephilim were on the earth in those days, and also afterward, when the sons of God came in to the daughters of man and they bore children to them. These were the mighty men who were of old, the men of renown. The LORD saw that the wickedness of man was great in the earth, and that every intention of the thoughts of his heart was only evil continually. And the LORD regretted that he had made man on the earth, and it grieved him to his heart. So the LORD said, "I will blot out man whom I have created from the face of the land, man and animals and creeping things and birds of the heavens, for I am sorry that I have made them." But Noah found favor in the eyes of the LORD (Genesis 6:1–8).

The Battle Continues

In Genesis chapter 3, a battle began between God's Word and man's word. It's portrayed throughout Scripture as a battle between light and darkness, those who gather and those who scatter, those for Christ and those against, those on the broad way and those on the narrow way, those who build their house on the sand and those who build on the rock.

At the beginning of history, we see this battle intensify as we read about the descendants of Cain versus the descendants of Seth. But we must remember that all humans are sinful, and as such, sin is crouching at the door of all of us as it was for Cain: *And if you do not do well, sin is crouching at the door. Its desire is contrary to you, but you must rule over it* (Genesis 4:7). Sadly, Cain did not rule over it and much evil resulted. As God's Word teaches us, *and people loved the darkness rather than the light because their works were evil* (John 3:19). And we read in Jeremiah 17:9, *The heart is deceitful above all things, and desperately sick; who can understand it?*

After tracing the line of Cain and their worldliness, and then the line of Seth and those that called upon the name of the LORD (Genesis 4:24), we now come to a climax in the history of the world about 1,656 years after creation (the date we calculated based on Ussher's work in *The Annals of Word History*). To me it is a climax of the battle between good and evil in the pre-Flood world, and we see evil seeming to win and destroy almost everyone. But God, after much patience, acts in judgment and deals with the rampant wickedness. As we read: *…because they formerly did not obey, when God's patience waited in the days of Noah, while the ark was being prepared, in which a few, that is, eight persons, were brought safely through water* (1 Peter 3:20).

This is a reminder for us that as we see evil taking over our present-day culture, and evil seeming to win out over good, God will, at some stage, step in and deal with that evil.

Who Were the Nephilim?

Genesis 6:1–4 has been a much-debated passage. Christian scholars have taken a number of different positions on what these verses mean. As this section doesn't impinge on any major doctrines, the ministry of Answers in Genesis doesn't take an official position on the identity of the Nephilim, but speakers and researchers have their own personally preferred positions. The position I personally lean toward is given below, as I have done my best to negotiate through these verses, including reading many different scholars' commentaries on these verses. Remember, God has put these verses in Scripture for our learning, so there must be an important reason for them to be included.

The context of these verses is to relay the extent to which wickedness had come to prevail on the earth. One of the ways this happened has something to do with people marrying. I like to take as straightforward an interpretation as possible without trying to complicate things (e.g., Proverbs 8:8-9, 2 Corinthians 4:2).

It seems to me the simplest explanation is that the line of Seth (which could have been referred to as "sons of God" because they were godly and called upon the name of the LORD) started marrying the line of Cain (the "daughters of men" — women who were beautiful but ungodly). Such mixing of spiritual light and darkness destroys families. We see a warning of this with the godly Israelites entering into ungodly Canaan, e.g., Deuteronomy 7:1–4, 1 Kings 11:2. In the New Testament, we are also warned in 2 Corinthians 6:14: *Do not be unequally yoked with unbelievers. For what partnership has righteousness with lawlessness? Or what fellowship has light with darkness?*

Because of the sin nature of every human being, such mixing could easily lead to increasing ungodliness. As an example, that was the case of wise and godly King Solomon who was led into idolatry and sin by his pagan wives (1 Kings 11:1–11; Nehemiah 13:26). Therefore, God judged him. That should be a stern warning for us to ensure we obey God's rules in regard to marriage and the training of children.

Associated with all this is the mention of Nephilim. We read, *The Nephilim were on the earth in those days, and also afterward, when the sons of God came in to the daughters of man and they bore children to them. These were the mighty men who were of old, the men of renown* (Genesis 6:4).

Who were the *Nephilim*? Certainly, the description may imply that they were of great stature (perhaps giants in the build of their bodies), greatly feared, and well known, presumably for extreme wickedness. Perhaps they were certain individuals of the offspring resulting from this mixing of "the sons of God" and the "daughters of man" who became extremely evil. An interesting point concerning the *Nephilim* is the phrase, *and also afterward.* It seems this is referring to after the Flood, as *Nephilim* are mentioned once again in Numbers 13:33 (though it is spelled differently in Hebrew): *And there we saw the Nephilim (the sons of Anak, who come from the Nephilim), and we seemed to ourselves like grasshoppers, and so we seemed to them.* The *Nephilim* in Numbers 13 were indeed giant in stature as the text indicates.

Regardless of the position one takes on understanding these particular verses, it is certainly a warning from God as to what happens when sin is allowed to rule over us. It's a reminder to make sure we raise up godly generations who call upon the name of the LORD and have boldness and courage to stand for God and His Word without compromise. All the way through Scripture we read of examples where the people of God compromised God's Word with the pagan beliefs of the nations around them and it destroyed them, and God judged them for it. We also see examples where the people of God married ungodly people and it destroyed families. This has been a problem since the beginning. It's another reminder to know God's Word, obey what He instructs us to do, and be aware of how sin is crouching at the door for each one of us to destroy us.

120 Years?

Now what does the phrase, *his days shall be 120 years* mean?

These 120 years are a countdown to the Flood. In other words, mankind's violence had reached its peak and God declared that 120 years was the "drop dead" date for mankind who is a mortal being (Genesis 6:3–7). Even in stating this, God was being patient, as He allowed people another 120 years to turn from their wicked ways.

Some people think the 120 years refers to how long Noah took to build the Ark. However, consider the following information.

Noah's son, Shem, had his first son two years after the Flood, when he was 100 (Genesis 11:10). This means that Shem was around 97 or 98 years old when the Flood came, and was 98 when he came off the Ark. Now we are told Noah was 500 when he had Shem, Ham, and Japheth and 600 years old when the Flood began. The order usually represents oldest to youngest. We don't know exactly when each of the sons were born, but it does mean that Noah was not building the Ark for 120 years.

When God finally gave Noah instructions to build the Ark, it was not at the beginning of the 120-year countdown. God told Noah that *he, his wife, and his three sons and their wives* (Genesis 6:14–18) would go aboard the Ark at this same time.

Although the Bible is silent on the exact timing, it is reasonable to assume that some time elapsed for the three sons to grow up and find wives. I would be most comfortable giving a range of anywhere from 55 to 75 years for the building of the Ark.

So if we think about this logically and tabulate it:

Years until the Flood	Event	Bible Reference
120	Countdown to the Flood begins	Genesis 6:3
100	Noah had Japheth, the first of his sons, when he was 500 years old	Genesis 5:32, 10:21
98	Noah had Shem who was 100 two years after the Flood	Genesis 11:10
? Perhaps 95 or 96 the same time between Japheth and Shem	Ham was the youngest one born to Noah and was aboard the Ark, so he was born prior to the Flood	Genesis 9:24, 7:13
? Perhaps 20–40 years for all of the sons to be raised and find a wife	Each son was old enough to be married before construction on the Ark began	Genesis 6:18
~ 55–75 years (estimate)	Noah was told to build the Ark, for he, his wife, his sons, and his sons' wives would be aboard the Ark	Genesis 6:18
Ark Completed		
?	Gather food and put it aboard the Ark	Genesis 6:21
7 days	Loading the Ark	Genesis 7:1–4
0	Noah was 600 when the floodwaters came on the earth	Genesis 7:6

We would end up with a tentative range of about 55 to 75 years for a reasonable *maximum* time to build the Ark. Of course, it could be much less than this depending on the age that Noah's sons took wives. And Noah could easily have hired people to work for him, even if they scoffed at him for building such a ship.

Consider that the Ark was completed *prior* to loading the animals that the LORD brought to Noah (Genesis 7:1–4) and that they had to take time to gather food and store it aboard the Ark (Genesis 6:21). So carefully considering the text, we can conclude that the construction of the Ark did not involve the 120 years mentioned in Genesis 6:3 but probably 75 years at the most.

Now some people believe the 120 years referred to man's lifespan after Noah's Flood. But, just because men began to live shorter lives after the Flood does not prove that God set a limit on man's life span. The fact is some still lived well beyond 120 years until the time of Moses. So God would have been wrong had this declaration been about life spans being 120 years.

The Lord Regretted That He Had Made Man

The LORD saw that the wickedness of man was great in the earth, and that every intention of the thoughts of his heart was only evil continually. And the LORD regretted that he had made man on the earth, and it grieved him to his heart. So the LORD said, "I will blot out man whom I have created from the face of the land, man and animals and creeping things and birds of the heavens, for I am sorry that I have made them." But Noah found favor in the eyes of the LORD (Genesis 6:5–8).

God's Word now explains how great the wickedness of man had become. Except for Noah, no one did anything good. Everything people did was evil. We look at our Western culture today and see evils like abortion and sexual perverseness in all sorts of ways, but I don't believe this is as bad as what it must have been in Noah's day. There are millions of Christians throughout the Western world today, but in Noah's day all but Noah (and presumably his family that went on the ark with him) had rebelled against God.

But what does it mean that the LORD "regretted," or as some translations put it "repented," that He made man? God doesn't change as we read in Malachi 3:6: *For I the LORD do not change.* But because people changed things in becoming so evil in their actions, God then changed the course of His providence (the way in which He, in His wisdom, care, and infinite love, directs all things in the universe). Because God is holy and without sin, then because He doesn't change, He has to judge man's sin.

An opposite type of situation occurred at the time of Jonah. God had said He was going to judge the people of Nineveh. But then, after Jonah's preaching, the people truly repented. So we read, *When God saw what they did, how they turned from their evil way, God relented of the disaster that he had said he would do to them, and he did not do it* (Jonah 3:10). God changed His direction because the people changed. When there is true repentance, God forgives.

Mankind Blotted Out

Because of the wickedness, God said he would "blot out" man from the face of the earth. Think of names in a book being blotted out. There would be utter destruction of man from the earth. It's interesting that there has been virtually no evidence of the pre-Flood civilization found in the fossil record. Such a civilization has been blotted out of the book of creation so to speak. Also, because the animals were made for man's use and benefit, and man was given dominion over them, they too were to be blotted out except for the representatives of each kind to be taken on the Ark. We all need to understand the gravity of man's sin and what this has done to creation. As we look on the fallen world with so much death, disease, and suffering, we should be reminded that our sin did that, and fall on our knees before a holy God in repentance. When we look at the fossil record (most of it is the graveyard of the Flood of Noah's day), we should grieve at the horribleness of the havoc man's sin has wrought on the earth.

Noah Found Favor

But, now, as you read Genesis 6:8 again, stop and ponder the words: *But Noah found favor in the eyes of the LORD.*

Twice Ezekiel mentions Noah as one of the three most righteous men in history:

> *...even if these three men, Noah, Daniel, and Job, were in it, they would deliver but their own lives by their righteousness, declares the LORD GOD. . . . even if Noah, Daniel, and Job were in it, as I live, declares the LORD GOD, they would deliver neither son nor daughter. They would deliver but their own lives by their righteousness* (Ezekiel 14:14, 20).

In Hebrews chapter 11, what I call the "Godly Hall of Fame," Noah is specifically mentioned for his faith in God. In fact, at the beginning of the verse it states, *By faith*, and then at the end of the verse we are told again that what he did came *by faith*. What a man of faith he was.

> *By faith Noah, being warned by God concerning events as yet unseen, in reverent fear constructed an ark for the saving of his household. By this he condemned the world and became an heir of the righteousness that comes by faith* (Hebrews 11:7).

Peter also mentions Noah in regard to him being a preacher of righteousness:

> *...if he did not spare the ancient world, but preserved Noah, a herald of righteousness, with seven others, when he brought a flood upon the world of the ungodly* (2 Peter 2:5).

There are more statements about Noah as we read through chapter 6 concerning his faith and obedience. I often ponder what it must have been like for Noah. The whole world (except those who went with him on the Ark) was in total rebellion against God. Yet Noah was a preacher of righteousness. We don't know exactly what he did in those days. Did he preach to people like street preachers do today? Did he verbally warn them of the coming judgment? Just by his obedience in building the Ark, he was preaching to the world. Because of

how evil people were, it must surely have been stressful for Noah and his family living at that time. Maybe we get an inkling when we read about Lot: *and if he rescued righteous Lot, greatly distressed by the sensual conduct of the wicked (for as that righteous man lived among them day after day, he was tormenting his righteous soul over their lawless deeds that he saw and heard (2 Peter 2:7–8).*

God must have specially protected Noah and his family. Would we have the courage to be like Noah and obey God in the midst of a world where everyone else except our immediate family was against God? I don't think I can even imagine the faith Noah must have had. But as we look at our world today, we need to be thinking about Noah and be reminded to stand boldly for God.

The Generations of Noah

Now we come to what might be Noah's signature for the history he recorded, as this is then taken on by his sons.

> *These are the generations of Noah. Noah was a righteous man, blameless in his generation. Noah walked with God. And Noah had three sons, Shem, Ham, and Japheth (Genesis 6:9–10).*

Only three sons of Noah are mentioned: Shem, Ham, and Japheth. The Bible does not say if Noah had any children before he was 500 years old. We are only told about these three sons who went on the Ark with him.

What's a Cubit?

> *Now the earth was corrupt in God's sight, and the earth was filled with violence. And God saw the earth, and behold, it was corrupt, for all flesh had corrupted their way on the earth. And God said to Noah, "I have determined to make an end of all flesh, for the earth is filled with violence through them. Behold, I will destroy them with the earth. Make yourself an ark of gopher wood. Make rooms in the ark, and cover it inside and out with pitch. This is how you are to*

make it: the length of the ark 300 cubits, its breadth 50 cubits, and its height 30 cubits. Make a roof for the ark, and finish it to a cubit above, and set the door of the ark in its side. Make it with lower, second, and third decks (Genesis 6:11–16).

Again, we are told how corrupt the earth is, so God instructed Noah to build a great ship, the Ark.

God tells us the dimensions of Noah's Ark in cubits, so we need to understand what a cubit is.

Unlike the measure of cubits, we either use a metric (e.g., decimal-based like centimeters, meters, kilometers, liters) or English/Imperial/US Customary system of units (e.g., often fraction-based like inches, feet, miles, gallons). So while the Bible tells us that the length of Noah's Ark was 300 cubits, its width 50 cubits, and its height 30 cubits, we must first ask, "How long is a cubit?"

The answer, however, is not so precise, because ancient people groups assigned different lengths to the term "cubit" (Hebrew word אמה [*ammah*]), the primary unit of measure in the Old Testament. This unit of measure was also used for the Ark of the Covenant (Exodus 25:10), the altar (Exodus 38:1), Goliath (1 Samuel 17:4), and Solomon's temple (1 Kings 6:2).

The length of a cubit was based on the distance from the elbow to the fingertips, so it varied between different ancient groups of people. See the following chart of samples from Egypt, Babylon, and ancient Israel.

Culture	Inches (Centimeters)
Hebrew (short)	17.5 (44.5)
Egyptian	17.6 (44.7)
Common (short)	18 (45.7)
Babylonian (long)	19.8 (50.3)
Hebrew (long)	20.4 (51.8)
Egyptian (long)	20.6 (52.3)

When Noah came off the Ark, naturally it was his cubit measurement that existed — the one he had used to construct the Ark. Unfortunately, the exact length of this cubit is unknown. After the nations were divided years later at the

Tower of Babel, different cultures (people groups) adopted different sized cubits. So it requires some logical guesswork (based on historical research) to reconstruct the most likely length of the cubit Noah used.

Since the Babel dispersion was so soon after the Flood, it is reasonable to assume that builders of that time were still using the cubit that Noah used. Moreover, we would expect that the people who settled near Babel would have retained or remained close to the cubit used by Noah. Yet cubits from that region (the ancient Near East) are generally either a common (short) or a long cubit. Which one is most likely to have come from Noah?

In large-scale construction projects, ancient civilizations typically used the long cubit (about 19.8–20.6 inches [52 cm]). The Bible offers some input in 2 Chronicles 3:3, which reveals that Solomon used an older (long) cubit in construction of the temple.

Most archaeological finds in Israel are not as ancient as Solomon. More modern finds consistently reveal the use of a short cubit, such as confirmed by archaeologists while measuring Hezekiah's tunnel. However, in Ezekiel's vision, an angel used "a cubit plus a handbreadth," an unmistakable definition for the long cubit (Ezekiel 43:13). The long cubit appears to be the preferred standard of measurement. Perhaps this matter did not escape Solomon's notice either.

The cubit length Noah used is uncertain. It was most likely one of the long cubits (about 19.8–20.6 inches). If so, the Ark was actually bigger than the size described in most books today (prior to the opening of the Ark Encounter in Northern Kentucky, USA), which usually use the short cubit of 18 inches.

Using the shorter cubit (18 inches), Noah's Ark would have been about 450 feet (137 meters) by 75 feet (22.9 meters) by 45 feet (13.7 meters).

Using the longer cubit of about 20.4 inches, Noah's Ark would have been about 510 feet (155 meters) long by 85 feet (25.9 meters) wide by 51 feet (15.5 meters) tall. These are the dimensions used in the construction of the life-size Ark for the Ark Encounter Christian-themed attraction in Kentucky. Again, the longer (older) cubit is to be preferred, so Noah's vessel was likely about this length, give or take a little.

What Was Gopher Wood?

The Ark was to be made of gopher wood, consisting of nests (rooms/cages for the animals) with three decks, and inside and out to be covered in pitch.

"Gopher" is not named for the animal of the same name; it is simply a transcription of the Hebrew word גֹּפֶר. And since the term appears only one time in Scripture, we cannot look at other contexts to help us identify it. Since the Bible does not provide enough information for us to make such a determination, we simply have no way of knowing what gopher wood is today. It is likely safe to assume that gopher wood was identifiable when Moses wrote Genesis; otherwise, both he and his audience would not have understood what the term meant. But whether this kind of tree is still around today is unknown. Some people think the name (gopher wood) might refer to a process to make wood harder, like laminating or burying, as the Chinese once did to harden teak. But we just don't know.

What Was the Pitch?

The word "pitch" is translated from a Hebrew word that basically means "to cover." Now this word is the one used for "atonement" such as in Leviticus 17:11. So in a sense we could say that just as the blood of the lamb provides a perfect atonement for our souls, so this pitch was a perfect covering for the Ark to keep the waters of judgment out.

Some people ask how Noah could make pitch. Today, a lot of pitch is made by heating coal. But if most of the coal deposits are from plants being laid down during the Flood, how could Noah produce pitch? Well, pitch-making was a well-known industry in Europe during the age of great wooden ships. Resin was collected from pine trees and boiled in great pots, and powdered charcoal was added to this. The pitch resulting from this process was then used to waterproof modern ships. Now we don't know if this is how Noah made pitch, but he didn't need coal or oil to make this substance.

What Did the Ark Look Like?

We need to understand the meaning of the Hebrew words used for "rooms," "pitch," and "roof" ("window" in some translations).

The Hebrew word translated as "rooms" is usually rendered "nests"; "pitch" would normally be called "covering"; and "window" (roof) would be "noon light." Using these more typical and literal meanings, the Ark would be described something like this:

> The *tebah* (ark) was made from gopher wood, it had nests inside, and it was covered with a pitch-like substance inside and out. It was 300 cubits long, 50 cubits wide, and 30 cubits high. It had a noon light that ended a cubit upward and above, it had one door in the side, and there were three decks.

The Bible leaves the details regarding the shape of the Ark wide open — anything from a rectangular box with hard right angles and no curvature at all, to a ship-like form. Box-like has the largest carrying capacity, but a ship-like design would be safer and more comfortable in heavy seas. We aren't given the details, and maybe Noah had ship-building experience and knew how to make such a vessel seaworthy. After all, as technology advanced, surely people would work out how to build vessels to travel on the waters of the seas surrounding the continent. Who knows, but maybe God ensured Noah worked as a shipbuilder to have the experience necessary to build the Ark.

The word "ark" in Hebrew is the obscure term *tebah*, a word that appears only one other time when it describes the basket that carried baby Moses (Exodus 2:3). One was a huge, wooden ship and the other a tiny, reed basket. Both floated, both preserved life, and both were covered; but the similarity ends there. If the word implied anything about shape, it would be "an Egyptian basket-like shape," typically rounded. More likely, however, *tebah* means something else, like "lifeboat."

Three Firsts

For behold, I will bring a flood of waters upon the earth to destroy all flesh in which is the breath of life under heaven. Everything that is on the earth shall die. But I will establish my covenant with you, and you shall come into the ark, you, your sons, your wife, and your sons' wives with you. And of every living thing of all flesh, you shall bring two of every sort into the ark to keep them alive with you. They shall be male and female. Of the birds according to their kinds, and of the animals according to their kinds, of every creeping thing of the ground, according to its kind, two of every sort shall come in to you to keep them alive. Also take with you every sort of food that is eaten, and store it up. It shall serve as food for you and for them." Noah did this; he did all that God commanded him (Genesis 6:17–22).

There are three firsts in this passage.

1. This is the first time we learn that God is going to send a flood as a judgment because of man's wickedness. We certainly knew something was coming regarding water, as Noah was told to build this great ship.

2. This is the first time the Hebrew word translated "flood" appears. It appears only one other time, in Psalm 29:10. This flood was going to be unique, different from other floods. The word has the meaning of a mighty flood resulting in destruction. Even in the New Testament, the word for the flood of Noah's day is used only of this flood. It was to be a unique flood — different from any other flood in history. This flood would destroy all mankind (except those on the Ark) and all land-dwelling, air-breathing animals (except those on the Ark).

As we read in the next chapter, this was to be a global flood covering the entire globe.

3. This is also the first time we read about a "covenant." The actual details of this covenant would be given later in Genesis 9:9–17. This covenant involved the promise to save Noah's family and the animals that accompanied him on the Ark so they could begin again in the new world after the Flood.

In verse 20, Noah is told that the representatives of the animal kinds to be saved on the Ark would come to him. In other words, Noah didn't have to go out and gather the animals, God would bring them to the Ark. And remember from our discussion of the third day in the creation week that there was one continent before the Flood. Australia, as a continent, didn't exist before the Flood, so Noah didn't have to worry about how the kangaroo kind would get to the ark! So God, who created the animals, ensured that those animals He selected from each kind would get to the Ark for this journey.

We are told here that a pair of each kind of land-dwelling, air-breathing animal would come to the Ark. In Genesis 7:2–3, we read additional information that for the flying creatures and what are called the "clean animals" there would be seven pairs.

Enough Room on the Ark?

Now Noah was commanded to take two of every kind of land-dwelling, air-breathing animal on the Ark with him. And seven pairs of some.

A lot of people still say that there would not have been enough room for all the species of animals in the world today to fit on the Ark, but Noah did not have to take all the species. In fact, the vast majority of species did not have to get on the Ark. God told Noah he would only be taking air-breathing, land-dwelling animals on the Ark. That means that none of the sea creatures needed to go. Also, keep in mind the average size of a land animal is actually not that large. Further, God said Noah would take members of every "kind" (Genesis 6:20).

As we've discussed, kinds are not the same as species. Most kinds consist of dozens or more species. Answers in Genesis asked scientists to do a large-scale study to determine what the kinds that were on the Ark would have been. For most land animals, as stated earlier, the kind level is probably about the family level of modern classification, which is a grouping of similar animals, such as cats like lions, tigers, leopards, cheetahs, jaguars, etc. that can be documented to be interrelated through breeding.

In determining how many animals were on the Ark, creation scientists assumed a worst-case scenario. In other words, if they weren't sure if two animals were of the same kind, they assumed they were different kinds. For example, in bats they made every family its own kind, even though some of the families could probably be grouped together.

In this "worst case scenario" view, Answers in Genesis believes that there were slightly less than 7,000 animals on the Ark, representing slightly less than 1,400 kinds. Some more recent studies show that all that were needed may be as few as 2,000–3,000 animals from as few as 1,000 kinds. There was plenty of room on the Ark.

Only One Door

In Genesis 6:16 we read that Noah was to build one door in the side of the Ark. In some fascinating ways, Noah's Ark displays similarities to Jesus Christ.

In December, Christians specially celebrate a singular moment in history, when God sent His only Son to save a sinful world.

By entering the Ark, Noah ensured the physical survival of himself and his family. When we enter into saving faith through Jesus (John 10:9), we ensure our spiritual survival through eternal life with Christ.

When the destruction of the world loomed, God called out to Noah: *"Go . . . into the ark"* (Genesis 7:1). God was with Noah and his family throughout that frightening year-long ordeal and protected and presumably comforted them. When we receive Jesus as our Savior, God, in the person of the Holy Spirit, comforts and protects us.

The Ark had only one door through which Noah had to enter in order to be saved from the Flood. Likewise, salvation in Christ has only one door. We enter it by faith in Jesus's once-and-for-all-time sacrificial death on the Cross and His bodily Resurrection three days later.

> *I am the door. If anyone enters by me, he will be saved and will go in and out and find pasture* (John 10:9).

Finally, after Noah entered the Ark, God Himself closed the door (Genesis 7:16). Those people outside who chose not to enter the Ark's door were left to face the destructive force of the Flood. Today, we have only this one life to enter Christ's door of salvation. I pray everyone reading this has done that, and if not would stop right now and repent of sin and trust Christ for salvation.

> *...because, if you confess with your mouth that Jesus is* Lord *and believe in your heart that God raised him from the dead, you will be saved* (Romans 10:9).

The theologian John Gill in his commentary on Genesis states:

> Noah: was a type of Christ, the builder of his church the ark was a figure of, and the pilot of it through the tempestuous sea of this world, and the provider of all good things for it, for the sustenance of it, and of those who are in it.[1]

Before we move to Genesis chapter 7, I want us to ponder the last verse of Genesis 6:

> *Noah did this; he did all that God commanded him* (Genesis 6:22).

Noah was a man of great faith (as Hebrews 11 records), and also a

---

1. John Gill, *An Exposition of the First Book of Moses, Called Genesis* (London, England: Aaron Ward Publisher, 1763–1766). Reprinted by Particular Baptist Press, Springfield, Missouri, 2010, p. 126.

man of total obedience to God. Nowhere do we read that Noah questioned God or even complained in any way. Again, in Genesis 7:5 we read, *And Noah did all that the* Lord *had commanded him.* Noah had such a close relationship with God. In fact, God's Word records seven times when God spoke directly to Noah in Genesis 6:13, 7:1, 8:15, 9:1, 8, 12, 17.

I often think about Noah, this godly man, living in a wicked world, yet he had such a close walk with God, such faith, such obedience to everything God instructed him to do. How does our walk with God, and our faith and our obedience to God's Word measure up?

Chapter 13

Genesis 7

Genesis 7:1

Then the LORD said to Noah, "Go into the ark, you and all your household, for I have seen that you are righteous before me in this generation."

Go Into the Ark

I love this verse of Scripture. The Hebrew word translated "Go" means to "enter in," or "come in." God invited Noah and his family into the Ark. What a beautiful picture of salvation this is. There was one door in the side of the Ark, which is a picture of Jesus, who is the one door through whom we go to be saved. Noah's Ark is a picture of salvation for those who enter through the door. There are many passages of Scripture that apply here, such as:

Come to me, all who labor and are heavy laden, and I will give you rest (Matthew 11:28).

Truly, truly, I say to you, whoever hears my word and believes him who sent me has eternal life. He does not come into judgment but has passed from death to life (John 5:24).

My sheep hear my voice, and I know them, and they follow me. I give them eternal life, and they will never perish, and no one will snatch them out of my hand (John 10:27–28).

Noah had faith and trusted in God and believed God's Word and obeyed Him. Noah and his family were invited into the Ark to be saved from the coming judgment.

This reminds us that Jesus invites us to be saved as Matthew 11:28 states. God's Word states, *For by grace you have been saved through faith. And this is not your own doing; it is the gift of God* (Ephesians 2:8). It is God who saves us. God instructed Noah to build the Ark. God invited Noah into the Ark. In Genesis 7:5 we read that Noah did all that God told him to do. God tells us that *If we confess our sins, he is faithful and just to forgive us our sins and to cleanse us from all unrighteousness* (1 John 1:9). We are to be like Noah and do what God has told us to do. We must repent of our sin and trust Him for salvation. When we do this and obey His voice and enter through the door (Jesus), we will be saved for eternity — saved from the eternal judgment to come for those who refuse God's gift and don't go through the door.

Clean and Unclean

Take with you seven pairs of all clean animals, the male and his mate, and a pair of the animals that are not clean, the male and his mate, and seven pairs of the birds of the heavens also, male and female, to keep their offspring alive on the face of all the earth (Genesis 7:2–3).

As we've discussed before, God sent representatives of each kind of land-dwelling, air-breathing animals to go into the Ark. A pair of what are called the unclean and seven pairs of the clean and the birds. The clean animals include those that are very closely associated with man (e.g., cattle, sheep, etc.).

The Flood Is Coming

"For in seven days I will send rain on the earth forty days and forty nights, and every living thing that I have made I will blot out from the face of the ground." And Noah did all that the LORD had commanded him (Genesis 7:4–5).

Now think about it. In Genesis 6:3, God gave a warning that in 120 years the judgment would come. Now the Ark was ready, and the animals had been sent to the Ark. Put yourself in Noah and his family's place. Would you be wondering when this Flood is going to come? What if they weren't on the Ark when it started? How would they know when to be on board? Obviously, they must have known the time was close because the animals had arrived. Then God tells Noah that in seven days the Flood would come. Now they knew the actual day they needed to be on the Ark. One wonders if Noah and any of his family shared this with the people of that day as an even further warning of what was about to happen. But regardless, God knew only eight people would be on that Ark.

God again states He is going to blot out land-dwelling animal life and man. This was going to be a Flood of cataclysmic proportions.

Note again that Noah did everything God commanded him to do. A man of obedience to his Creator.

They Went into the Ark

Noah was six hundred years old when the flood of waters came upon the earth. And Noah and his sons and his wife and his sons' wives with him went into the ark to escape the waters of the flood. Of clean animals, and of animals that are not clean, and of birds, and of everything that creeps on the ground, two and two, male and female, went into the ark with Noah, as God had commanded Noah (Genesis 7:6–9).

If Noah's sons were writing this record of history, they made a specific point of noting Noah's age, perhaps to mark a new era. This would mark the time the population of the whole world would be reduced to eight as they get ready for the new world after the Flood.

The land animals of each kind went into the Ark by pairs. One pair of the unclean and seven pairs of the clean animals and birds. Note the specific phrase, "male and female," to make sure we understood God was preparing for animals to reproduce after the Flood so they could once again increase in numbers over the earth.

Again we read that the land animal kinds and Noah and his family were on the Ark. God is ensuring we understand that what He promised concerning saving each kind of land animal and Noah's family happened as He had said it would.

Water from Above and Below

And after seven days the waters of the flood came upon the earth.

In the six hundredth year of Noah's life, in the second month, on the seventeenth day of the month, on that day all the fountains of the great deep burst forth, and the windows of the heavens were opened. And rain fell upon the earth forty days and forty nights (Genesis 7:10–12).

What God says is true. After the seven-day warning, the Flood began as God said it would. The waters of the Flood came from two sources. Water came from above in the form of torrential rain, and water came from underneath the earth's crust as the fountains of the deep were broken open. Exactly how God accomplished all this we are not told. Many have speculated on how it could have occurred with earthquakes, an asteroid hit, and so on. But what we do know for sure is that it happened.

Why does the text specifically state that the windows of heaven were opened and it rained for 40 days and 40 nights? Well, later on in Genesis 8:2, we read that 150 days after the Flood began, the fountains of the deep and the windows of heaven were stopped. This means it did continue to rain after the first 40 days and nights. What is the 40 days and nights referring to then?

I suggest two ideas:

1. The rain continued after the first 40 days and nights but not as intensely as it did for the first 40 days and nights.

2. During the first 40 days, the floodwaters increased until they covered the earth and the Ark was lifted up. At the end of the 40 days the highest places on the earth were covered by around 25 feet of water. However, I don't believe the Himalayas, for example, were covered by 25 feet of water, as I don't believe our modern-day mountains existed at that time, as discussed earlier. The mountains weren't as high before the Flood.

Delivered from an Evil Age

On the very same day Noah and his sons, Shem and Ham and Japheth, and Noah's wife and the three wives of his sons with them entered the ark, they and every beast, according to its kind, and all the livestock according to their kinds, and every creeping thing that creeps on the earth, according to its kind, and every bird, according to its kind, every winged creature. They went into the ark with Noah, two and two of all flesh in which there was the breath of life. And those that entered, male and female of all flesh, went in as God had commanded him. And the LORD shut him in (Genesis 7:13–16).

Once again God reminds us of the faithfulness of Noah as he and his family obeyed God in building the Ark and going into the Ark through the one door to be saved. Also, we are reminded that each land-dwelling, air-breathing animal kind was represented on the Ark with male and female so that they could reproduce in the new world after the Flood. In a way, this is also a picture of salvation in that God was taking those who went through the door to be saved from the evil world to a new world. When we are saved by God's grace, having gone through the door (the LORD Jesus) to be saved, God's Word tells us in

Galatians 1:4, *who gave himself for our sins to deliver us from the present evil age, according to the will of our God and Father.* Noah and his family were delivered from that evil age.

Can you imagine being on the Ark and wondering how long the door was going to be closed? Here we have a real nugget we could spend a long time discussing. We are told that God shut the door. When He shut the door, then the judgment of the Flood came. As discussed earlier, Jesus is our ark of salvation. He is the "door": *I am the door. If anyone enters by me, he will be saved and will go in and out and find pasture* (John 10:9). Right now, that "door" is open. And since Jesus died on the Cross and rose again, that "door" has continued to remain open for 2,000 years. That seems like a long time to us, but it's not to God. As we read in 2 Peter 3:8–9:

> …*that with the* Lord *one day is as a thousand years, and a thousand years as one day. The* Lord *is not slow to fulfill his promise as some count slowness, but is patient toward you, not wishing that any should perish, but that all should reach repentance.*

God was also patient with the people of Noah's day. He gave 120 years of warning. Also, while Noah was building the Ark this was a warning to the people of that day that judgment was coming. In 1 Peter 3:20 we read:

> *God's patience waited in the days of Noah, while the ark was being prepared, in which a few, that is, eight persons, were brought safely through water.*

Only eight people survived the Flood of Noah's day. The Bible makes it clear that no other people on the earth survived the Flood.

Now one day, God will once again shut the "door" so only those in the ark of salvation will be saved, and the rest will be judged. This "door" shuts in two ways:

1. When a person dies: *And just as it is appointed for man to die once, and after that comes judgment* (Hebrews 9:27).

2. When Jesus returns to judge the earth and universe with fire and make a new heavens and earth: *But by the same word the heavens and earth that now exist are stored up for fire, being kept until the day of judgment and destruction of the ungodly. . . . But the day of the LORD will come like a thief, and then the heavens will pass away with a roar, and the heavenly bodies will be burned up and dissolved, and the earth and the works that are done on it will be exposed. . . . But according to his promise we are waiting for new heavens and a new earth in which righteousness dwells* (2 Peter 3:7, 10, 13).

> *For this we declare to you by a word from the LORD, that we who are alive, who are left until the coming of the LORD, will not precede those who have fallen asleep. For the LORD himself will descend from heaven with a cry of command, with the voice of an archangel, and with the sound of the trumpet of God. And the dead in Christ will rise first. Then we who are alive, who are left, will be caught up together with them in the clouds to meet the LORD in the air, and so we will always be with the LORD* (1 Thessalonians 4:15–17).

What a reminder to make sure we have gone through the "door" to be saved. Stop right now and ponder that — it is more important than anything else, as this determines where you will spend eternity.

Even the Mountains Were Covered

The flood continued forty days on the earth. The waters increased and bore up the ark, and it rose high above the earth. The waters prevailed and increased greatly on the earth, and the ark floated on the face of the waters. And the waters prevailed so mightily on the earth that all the high mountains under the whole heaven were covered. The waters prevailed above the mountains, covering them fifteen cubits deep (Genesis 7:17–20).

So the first 40 days and 40 nights of rain and water from the fountains of the deep covered the earth with water and the Ark was lifted up. In verse 20 we are told the waters rose about 25 feet (15 cubits) above the mountains. Now, as I mentioned, the water didn't rise above today's mountains, as they have been formed as a result of tectonic activity during the Flood. The water arose above the mountains of the pre-Flood world, which was a very different world to the one today. As stated earlier, originally there would have been one continent which was divided up into the continents we have today because of the geologic processes of this catastrophic Flood.

When you read the words in verse 19 that *the waters prevailed so mightily on the earth that all the high mountains under the whole heaven were covered*, one can only conclude that this wasn't just a local flood as some Christians who believe in millions of years for the fossil record have tried to claim. No, this was a global, worldwide, entire earth-covering Flood. This was a major cataclysmic event. And to reinforce how destructive it was, God gives us a detailed description in the next four verses.

Only 8 Survived

And all flesh died that moved on the earth, birds, livestock, beasts, all swarming creatures that swarm on the earth, and all mankind. Everything on the dry land in whose nostrils was the breath of life died. He blotted out every living thing that was on the face of the ground, man and animals and creeping things and birds of the heavens. They were blotted out from the earth. Only Noah was left, and those who were with him in the ark (Genesis 7:21–23).

There's no doubt all land-dwelling animals, and all people, on the entire earth were blotted out. This was a global (the entire globe, not just part of it) Flood. Only eight people on the entire earth (and perhaps there were millions, or even billions, of people at that time) were left.

Dark and Dreary

And the waters prevailed on the earth 150 days (Genesis 7:24).

Can you imagine being in this Ark now for 5 months? The whole time it was probably dark outside because of ash in the atmosphere from volcanic upheavals, and the continuous rain from dark clouds. It was probably very difficult to even distinguish day from night. There's no indication God spoke to Noah during this time. Noah and his family were only human, so I'm sure they wondered what was going to happen. Noah trusted God, so I'm sure he reminded his family over and over again to have faith. And then, the situation changed dramatically.

Chapter 14

Genesis 8

Genesis 8:1-2

But God remembered Noah and all the beasts and all the livestock that were with him in the ark. And God made a wind blow over the earth, and the waters subsided. The fountains of the deep and the windows of the heavens were closed, the rain from the heavens was restrained (Genesis 8:1–2).

Now God had not forgotten Noah. God can't forget anything as He is the infinite Creator God. He knows everything. In Colossians 2:3, we read of Jesus (who is God, our Creator) *in whom are hidden all the treasures of wisdom and knowledge.*

God knew that He had made a covenant with Noah and the animals to preserve Noah's family and the land animal kinds for the world after the Flood (Genesis 6:17–19). And as part of fulfilling that promise, God now sent a wind over the earth, presumably to help dry up the waters, and He also stopped the rain and the water coming from the fountains of the deep. So now the water would start to go down. As a result of this, perhaps Noah and his family saw some light from the sun for the first time in five months.

The Mountains Rose and the Valleys Sank

…and the waters receded from the earth continually. At the end of 150 days the waters had abated, and in the seventh month, on the

seventeenth day of the month, the ark came to rest on the mountains of Ararat. And the waters continued to abate until the tenth month; in the tenth month, on the first day of the month, the tops of the mountains were seen (Genesis 8:3–5).

Many scholars believe Psalm 104 is relating aspects of what happened as a result of the Flood:

You covered it with the deep as with a garment; the waters stood above the mountains. At your rebuke they fled; at the sound of your thunder they took to flight. The mountains rose, the valleys sank down to the place that you appointed for them. You set a boundary that they may not pass, so that they might not again cover the earth (Psalm 104:6–9).

Because verse 9 states that the water would not again cover the earth, scholars believe this section has to be a reference to the Flood, as God promised in Genesis 9:15 there would never be such a global flood again. Now note as we read this section from Psalm 104 that it states, "the mountains rose, the valleys sank." This seems to indicate mountain building was a result of the Flood. So the suggestion is that as the waters started to go down, mountains and valleys that didn't exist in the pre-Flood world started to form. This means fossil-bearing layers of sediment were being raised up, explaining why we find marine fossils on the top of mountains like the Himalayas, for example.

Actually, if one were to level out the entire surface of the land on the earth today, there's enough water on the surface of the earth to cover it to a depth of about two miles. So there is plenty of water to flood the whole earth. It makes sense that God raised up the mountains at the end of the Flood as part of the movement of the crust as the previous singular continent broke up into different continents.

Where Did the Ark Land?

After the 150 days, as the waters started to recede, the Ark came to rest on the mountains of Ararat. Note that the text does not say "Mount Ararat." It landed on the range of mountains that includes Mount

Ararat. Creation geologists don't believe the Ark could have landed on what we today call Mount Ararat, as this mountain was formed at the end of the Flood due to volcanic activity forming certain mountains, including Mount Ararat. Obviously, as Moses (inspired by God) compiled the text of Genesis, he would have used names in the post-Flood world that people would be familiar with to understand where these events occurred. But we really don't know the exact location of where the Ark landed, except it was in the area we today call the mountains of Ararat. This area included mountain ranges in Eastern Turkey and likely extended farther east into Armenia.

Have We Found the Ark?

There have been many claims that the Ark, or pieces of the Ark, have been found, but every claim lacks credible evidence. Most creation geologists reject these claims. Certainly, such a find would probably be the greatest archaeological discovery of our time. But do we really need to find Noah's Ark? Does it matter?

Well, there is already overwhelming evidence confirming the Flood of Noah's day — the massive fossil record over the majority of the earth's surface. This record exhibits evidence of a watery catastrophe consistent with the global flood account as recorded in Genesis 6–9. But despite all this overwhelming evidence, the majority of people, including the majority of scientists, reject the global flood of Noah's day as a real event in history.

Why do the majority reject this evidence? The simple answer is that it's a spiritual issue. Because of their sinful hearts, those who reject God's Word don't want to accept the account of the Flood. In 2 Peter 3, we read that in the last days people will willingly reject the account of creation, the Flood, and the coming judgment by fire.

> For they deliberately overlook this fact . . . the earth was formed out of water and through water by the word of God, and . . . the world that then existed was deluged with water and perished. But by the same word the heavens and earth that now exist are stored up for fire (2 Peter 3:5–7).

I've had atheists tell me that if we can show them evidence for the Flood and creation they will believe. But no matter what evidence these people are shown, they reinterpret it within their evolutionary secular worldview because of their sinful hearts.

The spiritual nature of this battle over evidence can be seen in the biblical account of Jesus raising Lazarus from the dead. The chief priests wanted to kill Lazarus to get rid of the evidence because they refused to acknowledge that Jesus was the Son of God.

In Luke 16 we have an account of a rich man and a man called Lazarus.

Both had died. The rich man was in a place of torment whereas Lazarus was with Abraham. The rich man wanted Abraham to send Lazarus back to warn his five brothers about the place of torment after death.

> But Abraham said, "They have Moses and the Prophets; let them hear them." And he said, "No, father Abraham, but if someone goes to them from the dead, they will repent." He said to him, "If they do not hear Moses and the Prophets, neither will they be convinced if someone should rise from the dead" (Luke 16:29–31).

Now it's true that evidence is important. Jesus said to the Jews, *"If I am not doing the works of my Father, then do not believe me; but if I do them, even though you do not believe me, believe the works, that you may know and understand that the Father is in me and I am in the Father"* (John 10:37–38). Jesus gave people the evidence of His divine nature by His works. But most still did not believe He was the Messiah because of the spiritual state of their hearts.

Moses gave Pharaoh evidence that God was telling him to take the Israelites out of Egypt. But Pharaoh kept rejecting the evidence. The spiritual nature of the battle is seen in the biblical account when Pharaoh "hardened his heart" (Exodus 8:32) and refused to accept the evidence. But we are also told that God hardened Pharaoh's heart (Exodus 7:3, 10:20, 14:4). It's God that opens people's hearts to the truth, which is why it's important to understand that *"faith comes from hearing, and hearing through the word of Christ"* (Romans 10:17).

Yes, we need to give answers for what we believe as we're instructed in 1 Peter 3:15. And we also need to point people to the Word of God. Our responsibility is to do all we can to convince people of the truth, using whatever evidence we can, but always point them to the Word of God, as only God opens people's hearts to believe in Him.

> For by grace you have been saved through faith. And this is not your own doing; it is the gift of God (Ephesians 2:8).

Does it matter if we find Noah's Ark? No, it doesn't. God has already allowed us to find all the evidence we need that confirms the Flood.

God has given everyone enough evidence that He is the Creator. If they don't believe, they are without excuse (Romans 1:20).

A Timeline of the Flood

Now at around 224 days (the tenth month) after the Flood began, the mountaintops were seen. The waters were going down and mountains were rising up.

> At the end of forty days Noah opened the window of the ark that he had made and sent forth a raven. It went to and fro until the waters were dried up from the earth. Then he sent forth a dove from him, to see if the waters had subsided from the face of the ground. But the dove found no place to set her foot, and she returned to him to the ark, for the waters were still on the face of the whole earth. So he put out his hand and took her and brought her into the ark with him. He waited another seven days, and again he sent forth the dove out of the ark. And the dove came back to him in the evening, and behold, in her mouth was a freshly plucked olive leaf. So Noah knew that the waters had subsided from the earth. Then he waited another seven days and sent forth the dove, and she did not return to him anymore.
>
> In the six hundred and first year, in the first month, the first day of the month, the waters were dried from off the earth. And Noah removed the covering of the ark and looked, and behold, the face of the ground was dry. In the second month, on the twenty-seventh day of the month, the earth had dried out (Genesis 8:6–14).

The best way to understand all of the events of the Flood is to summarize it all in a timeline. Bodie Hodge, a speaker and writer with Answers in Genesis, has written an excellent timeline of the Flood events that I reproduce on the following page.

Timeline (days)	Duration	Month/Day	Description	Bible Reference
0	Initial reference point	600th year of Noah's life: 2nd month, 17th day of the month	The fountains of the great deep broke apart and the windows of heaven were opened; it began to rain. This happened on the seventeenth day of the second month. Noah actually entered the Ark seven days prior to this.	Genesis 7:11
40	40 days and nights	3rd month, 27th day of the month	Rain fell for 40 days, and then water covered the earth's highest places (at that time) by over ~20 feet (15 cubits) and began the stage of flooding until the next milestone.	Genesis 7:11–12, Genesis 7:17–20
150	150 days (including the initial 40 days)	7th month, 17th day of the month	The water rose to its highest level (covering the whole earth) sometime between the 40th and 150th day, and the end of these 150 days was the seventeenth day of the seventh month. The Ark rested on the mountains of Ararat. On the 150th day, the springs of the great deep were shut off, and the rain from above ceased, and the water began continually receding.	Genesis 7:24–8:5
150 + 74 = 224	74 days	10th month, 1st day of the month	The tops of the mountains became visible on the tenth month, first day.	Genesis 8:5
224 + 40 = 264	40 days	11th month, 11th day of the month	After 40 more days, Noah sent out a raven.	Genesis 8:6
264 + 7 = 271	7 days	11th month, 18th day of the month	The dove was sent out seven days after the raven. It had no resting place and returned to Noah.	Genesis 8:6–12

Timeline (days)	Duration	Month/Day	Description	Bible Reference
271 + 7 = 278	7 days	11th month, 25th day of the month	After seven more days, Noah sent out the dove again. It returned again but this time with an olive leaf in its beak.	Genesis 8:10–11
278 + 7 = 285	7 days	12th month, 2nd day of the month	After seven more days, Noah sent out the dove again, and it did not return.	Genesis 8:12
314	29 days	601st year of Noah's life: 1st month, 1st day of the month	Noah removed the cover of the Ark on the first day of the first month. The surface of the earth was dried up, and Noah could verify this to the extent of what he could see.	Genesis 8:13
370 (371 if counting the first day and last day as full days)	56 days	2nd month, 27th day of the month	The earth was dry, and God commanded Noah's family and the animals to come out of the Ark. From the first day of the year during the daylight portion there were 29.5 more days left in the month plus 26.5 more days left in the second month until the exit.	Genesis 8:14–17, Genesis 7:11

Now the floodwaters were abated, and the land was dry. The entire event was approximately one year long. I'm sure after being cooped up in a wooden ship with all those animals, Noah and his family couldn't wait to get out of the Ark.

Noah Sends Out Birds

The last time God spoke to Noah was when He told Noah to enter the Ark with his family. God doesn't speak again until the next verse (Genesis 8:15). But note that Noah didn't just sit back and wait for God to tell him what he should do. Noah's family must have been busy looking after the animals during the time they were on the Ark. At the appropriate time, Noah opened a window and sent out a raven and a dove. Noah saw that the earth was dry and so was ready for them to get off the Ark. God always expects us to do what we can do — that's our responsibility. We do whatever is humanly possible, but trust God to guide and direct us, and trust God to do what is not humanly possible when that is needed.

"Go Out from the Ark"

Then God said to Noah, "Go out from the ark, you and your wife, and your sons and your sons' wives with you. Bring out with you every living thing that is with you of all flesh — birds and animals and every creeping thing that creeps on the earth — that they may swarm on the earth, and be fruitful and multiply on the earth." So Noah went out, and his sons and his wife and his sons' wives with him. Every beast, every creeping thing, and every bird, everything that moves on the earth, went out by families from the ark (Genesis 8:15–19).

Now God spoke to Noah (whether in a dream, a vision, or in some other way we are not told) to tell him to leave the ark with his family and with all the land animal kinds that had been preserved. God said the animals were to "swarm" on the earth, which means they would reproduce after their kind. God also told Noah to be "fruitful and multiply." In other words, have children so the population of the world would increase once again.

When Noah came out of the Ark, he would have been walking on earth which contained the remains of billions of animals and plants that were buried by the Flood. Many of these remains were turned into fossils. Most of the fossil record is actually the graveyard of the Flood, not the graveyard of millions of years as evolutionists claim. As I love to say, if there really was a worldwide flood, you would find billions of dead things buried in rock layers, laid down by water all over the earth.

When we think about the fossil record, we need to remember that God judged the wicked world of Noah's day, and He is going to judge again, but next time by fire. Noah's Flood was a major event in history forming most of the fossil record, causing the one continent to be broken up into the continents we see today, and causing massive mountain building and volcanic activity. As well as that, the human population and land animal kinds populations had a massive reset as those that were on the Ark began to reproduce after the Flood to once again fill the earth with humans and animals.

Creation scientists also believe the Flood of Noah's day generated an ice age that climaxed a few hundred years after the Flood. Because of warm oceans from tectonic movements and volcanic action resulting in a lot of evaporation, and dust in the atmosphere from volcanoes producing a cooling effect, this would have created conditions for snow and ice to form and cause the onset of a massive ice age. During this time, ocean levels would have been lowered, forming land bridges around the world in various places that enabled animals and people to move out into different places (such as Australia).

Noah Brings Glory to God

Then Noah built an altar to the LORD and took some of every clean animal and some of every clean bird and offered burnt offerings on the altar. And when the LORD smelled the pleasing aroma, the LORD said in his heart, "I will never again curse the ground because of man, for the intention of man's heart is evil from his youth. Neither will I ever again strike down every living creature as I have done" (Genesis 8:20–21).

Notice that the first thing Noah did was for the glory of God. He didn't build a house first. He built an altar first. He put God first. I'll never forget my mother drumming into us as children, "God first, others second, yourselves last." Even when I was taught the LORD's prayer as a child, I was taught to note how it started as Jesus taught us how to pray:

> Our Father which art in heaven, Hallowed be thy name …(Matthew 6:9, KJV, the translation that I learned this passage in as a child).

Yes, this prayer starts with giving glory to God before asking for our daily bread. We need to be like Noah and put God first in all we do.

Noah, of course, understood the sacrificial system that God set up in the garden as we discussed in Genesis 3:21. He used what were called the "clean animals" for sacrifice. Remember, there were seven pairs of each kind of clean animal on the Ark, so using some for sacrifice didn't affect this kind reproducing its kind. God was very pleased with Noah's action and sacrifice.

God's Merciful Promise

God said He would never again curse the ground, as the intention of man's heart from his youth is evil. God cursed the ground in Genesis 3:17 because of man's sin. God had just flooded the entire earth because of the wickedness of man. God knows that all humans are sinners, and that is not going to change while we live in these bodies on this earth. The prophet Jeremiah reminds us of how sinful human hearts are when he states in Jeremiah 17:9, *The heart is deceitful above all things, and desperately sick.*

Even destroying the earth with a Flood in judgment could not change man's sinful heart. What a reminder that the only way we can be changed is through the blood of the LORD Jesus Christ.

> *In him we have redemption through his blood, the forgiveness of our*

trespasses, according to the riches of his grace (Ephesians 1:7).

And there is salvation in no one else, for there is no other name under heaven given among men by which we must be saved (Acts 4:12).

God also promised He would never again destroy all the land animals as He did at this time (except those saved on the Ark). God certainly has judged places, liked Sodom and Gomorrah, since the Flood. But never another global judgment like the Flood. There will be a final global judgment by fire when God makes a new heavens and earth and puts an end to this sin-cursed creation.

…waiting for and hastening the coming of the day of God, because of which the heavens will be set on fire and dissolved, and the heavenly bodies will melt as they burn! But according to his promise we are waiting for new heavens and a new earth in which righteousness dwells (2 Peter 3:12–13).

Another Merciful Promise

While the earth remains, seedtime and harvest, cold and heat, summer and winter, day and night, shall not cease (Genesis 8:22).

God then promises that until the final judgment, and while the earth remains, that seasons will continue and day and night will continue. During that first 40 days and 40 nights of the Flood, as I stated earlier, it was probably difficult to even discern the difference between day and night. And during the entire Flood, which lasted over a year, there was probably no sense of the different seasons. So it seems that this is also a part of the promise to Noah that God will not judge like this again — at least until the final judgment.

This promise of God is also something for us to take note of in our day. There are various politicians and others who claim that because of supposed man-made climate change, that man is going to destroy the earth in a few years if things don't change. But as Christians, we can know for sure that is not going to happen. There will always be seasons and day and night until God destroys the earth with the final judgment by fire. It's a reminder to fear God and not man.

> *It is better to take refuge in the* Lord *than to trust in man* (Psalm 118:8).

Chapter 15

Genesis 9

Genesis 9:1-4

And God blessed Noah and his sons and said to them, "Be fruitful and multiply and fill the earth. The fear of you and the dread of you shall be upon every beast of the earth and upon every bird of the heavens, upon everything that creeps on the ground and all the fish of the sea. Into your hand they are delivered. Every moving thing that lives shall be food for you. And as I gave you the green plants, I give you everything. But you shall not eat flesh with its life, that is, its blood.

Fill the Earth

As God told Adam and Eve, He now instructed Noah and his family to be fruitful and multiply so the population would increase and fill the earth. When God told Adam and Eve to fill the earth in Genesis 1:28, this was before sin. Some people have asked what would have happened if Adam hadn't sinned and then the earth was filled with people — what then? Well, first of all, God knew Adam would sin so He knew death would enter the world. Secondly, we need to recognize God is the infinite, sovereign Creator. And as Mary was told by the angel, *For nothing will be impossible with God* (Luke 1:37). Just because we think something is a problem doesn't mean there's not a solution, it just means we don't know what the solution is because we are not God!

A Different Dominion

In Genesis 9:2 we now read that once again God gives man dominion over the animals ("into your hand they are delivered"), but with a difference. Now the animals would generally be fearful of man. Now Adam and Eve were originally given dominion over all the animal groups in Genesis 1:26. But this was in a perfect world where there was no death, disease, suffering, or anger. All was at peace. Remember, God brought animals to Adam to name. There was perfect harmony between man and the animals. However, with Noah, things are different now, as the animals would fear man.

A Different Diet

Further, in Genesis 9:3, God changes man's diet to allow the eating of animals. Originally, as we read in Genesis 1:29–30, Adam and Eve and the animals were vegetarian. There was no death in the world before sin. Now in Genesis 9:3, God tells Noah that just as He originally gave plants to eat, now He gives all things. So from that time on humans could eat animals as well as plants. There were no restrictions on which animals man could eat until specific restrictions given to the Israelites in Leviticus.

Genesis 9:4 gives an instruction that is for all people. This was reiterated for the Israelites in Leviticus, but it has never been revoked for man in general. We read, *But you shall not eat flesh with its life, that is, its blood.*

Some commentators say that this had a couple of meanings. First, animals were to be killed before they were eaten. The Israelites were given laws to stop cruelty to animals.

But the main meaning is something very important.

Note the emphasis, *with its life*. Life is associated with blood. In Hebrews 9:22 we are told:

without the shedding of blood there is no forgiveness of sins.

The explanation is given in detail in Leviticus 17:11–12:

For the life of the flesh is in the blood, and I have given it for you on the altar to make atonement for your souls, for it is the blood that makes atonement by the life. Therefore I have said to the people of Israel, No person among you shall eat blood, neither shall any stranger who sojourns among you eat blood.

The blood represents the life that was given by God. Man can eat the body of the animal, but the blood, which represents life, belongs solely to the LORD. The life of the animal sacrificed was accepted for the life of the sinner. The blood made atonement for the soul, and so should never be looked upon as just something common. The blood must be poured out before the LORD.

God's Gives the Death Penalty

And for your lifeblood I will require a reckoning: from every beast I will require it and from man. From his fellow man I will require a reckoning for the life of man.

Whoever sheds the blood of man, by man shall his blood be shed, for God made man in his own image (Genesis 9:5–6).

The penalty for murder is given here: death for death. In fact, the use of the word "require" is a judicial term; God is judge. The foundations for civil government are being set up. A major role of government is to maintain law and order. Recall back to when Cain killed his brother Abel, as the Bible does not give any indication there was a civil law set up at that stage. It's also important to understand that these judicial statements that God gives in Genesis 9 are for all humans while on this earth. They have never been revoked.

There are two aspects to this passage.

1. If an animal kills a human, the animal is to be killed. We do need to abide by this. It was also spelled out to the Israelites as part of their civil law as a nation:

When an ox gores a man or a woman to death, the ox shall be stoned, and its flesh shall not be eaten, but the owner of the ox shall not be liable (Exodus 21:28).

Even in our present world, if an animal kills a human, usually that animal (if caught) is put to death.

2. The authority for capital punishment for murder is given. The willful taking of a human life must be punished. This obviously implies that laws were to be set up to maintain law and order and punish those who commit crimes. For the Israelites as a nation, capital punishment was enacted, not just for murder, but for other sins as well. However, capital punishment for murder was given to mankind as part of the civil law for governing human activities, and this has never been revoked. There also has to be a way of ensuring a crime has truly been committed.

In Deuteronomy, we read how the Israelites were to establish guilt:

On the evidence of two witnesses or of three witnesses the one who is to die shall be put to death; a person shall not be put to death on the evidence of one witness (Deuteronomy 17:6).

Now this principle is also reiterated for all of us in the New Testament in a number of passages such as:

Every charge must be established by the evidence of two or three witnesses (2 Corinthians 13:1).

Some people have claimed that God has been inconsistent in applying the death penalty. After all, David and the woman at the well should have been put to death according to the Mosaic law. But God also says He is a forgiving God when people come in true repentance. Recall that God had decreed He was going to kill the people at Nineveh, but the people truly repented and so God didn't carry out His death penalty against them. The same is true of David and the woman at the well. David committed murder and adultery, and the woman at the well had committed fornication and adultery. Because David and the woman Jesus spoke to were truly repentant, God forgave them. Of course, sin is not without consequences as we see what happened to David and Bathsheba's child as a result of David's adultery.

Check out 1 Timothy 4:3–4, Acts 15:19–20, Romans 13:4, and Acts 25:11. The eating of meat, abstaining from eating blood, and obeying the government in regard to law and order are all reaffirmed. This was teaching Christians that such things were not just a part of the Jewish law but were given by God for all.

Now one more very important point needs to be made from this passage. Why did God give these requirements for when an animal kills a human, or a human commits murder? God states, *for God made man in his own image.* No animal was made in God's image, only humans. Another important reason for us to teach our children and others that, unlike how the world classifies humans, humans are not a part of the animal kingdom. Humans are different from animals. Yes, we are mammals, but we are made in God's image.

Think about how the above then should be applied to issues like abortion and euthanasia. In both instances, there is a deliberate action of taking a human life. Our lives are not our own so we may not end them whenever we want to or end the lives of others whenever we want to. Our lives belong to God, and therefore we must leave it to Him as to when we die. If we in any way hasten our own deaths or the deaths of others, we are accountable to God for that. But at the same time, I always like to remind people that God is a forgiving God if we come in true repentance.

But what about the killing of people during a war? In the Old Testament, we read of many wars including wars where God instructed the Israelites to go and do battle with evil people. We live in a sin-cursed world, and so sadly there will be forces of evil that need to be stopped. As a result of such wars, there can be much bloodshed as many people are killed. It's obvious that killing during such a war is not sinful in itself. It's not murder. But people need to decide for themselves as a matter of one's conscience as to what they should do in regard to being involved in military conflict. As Ecclesiastes 3:1–8 states:

> *For everything there is a season, and a time for every matter under heaven: a time to be born, and a time to die; a time to plant, and a time to pluck up what is planted; a time to kill, and a time to heal; a time to break down, and a time to build up; a time to weep, and a time to laugh; a time to mourn, and a time to dance; a time to cast away stones, and a time to gather stones together; a time to embrace, and a time to refrain from embracing; a time to seek, and a time to lose; a time to keep, and a time to cast away; a time to tear, and a time to sew; a time to keep silence, and a time to speak; a time to love, and a time to hate; a time for war, and a time for peace.*

A great way to end this section is to take note of what we are told in Romans 13:1–5:

> *Let every person be subject to the governing authorities. For there is no authority except from God, and those that exist have been instituted by God. Therefore whoever resists the authorities resists what God has appointed, and those who resist will incur judgment. For rulers are not a terror to good conduct, but to bad. Would you have no fear of the one who is in authority? Then do what is good, and you will receive his approval, for he is God's servant for your good. But if you do wrong, be afraid, for he does not bear the sword in vain. For he is the servant of God, an avenger who carries out God's wrath on the wrongdoer. Therefore one must be in subjection, not only to avoid God's wrath but also for the sake of conscience.*

Life Producing Life

And you, be fruitful and multiply, increase greatly on the earth and multiply in it (Genesis 9:7).

Right after the section with the death of humans by animals or willful acts of other humans, God tells Noah and his family to be fruitful and multiply. Maybe God is reminding them of all the violence and killing before the Flood because of man's sin nature. So now, after the Flood,

God sets up civil government with laws in regard to the killing of humans. It's as if God is saying that, instead of thinking about killing, place an emphasis on life producing life.

An Unconditional Covenant

Then God said to Noah and to his sons with him, "Behold, I establish my covenant with you and your offspring after you, and with every living creature that is with you, the birds, the livestock, and every beast of the earth with you, as many as came out of the ark; it is for every beast of the earth. I establish my covenant with you, that never again shall all flesh be cut off by the waters of the flood, and never again shall there be a flood to destroy the earth." And God said, "This is the sign of the covenant that I make between me and you and every living creature that is with you, for all future generations: I have set my bow in the cloud, and it shall be a sign of the covenant between me and the earth. When I bring clouds over the earth and the bow is seen in the clouds, I will remember my covenant that is between me and you and every living creature of all flesh. And the waters shall never again become a flood to destroy all flesh. When the bow is in the clouds, I will see it and remember the everlasting covenant between God and every living creature of all flesh that is on the earth." God said to Noah, "This is the sign of the covenant that I have established between me and all flesh that is on the earth (Genesis 9:8–17).

This is the first time the word "covenant" is used in the Bible. It means a promise or binding relationship. Sometimes God made conditional promises, conditioned on people's obedience. Other times He made unconditional promises, which means once God has decreed them, they don't change. Here in Genesis 9, God makes an unconditional promise to the animals and man. This means this promise cannot be broken. He promises to never send another flood like that one that had occurred. Now there have been lots of local floods since that time, so if God's promise is true (which it is), then God must be referring to something other than a local flood. And, of course, He is. He is referring to the global Flood of Noah's day. He promises to never again send such a global event to wipe out all land animals and all humans (except those saved on the Ark).

God then says that from then on the rainbow is to be seen as a sign of this covenant. Whenever we see a rainbow, we will be reminded that God will keep His promise and there never will be another global flood. It's also interesting to note that a rainbow is associated with God's throne:

> And he who sat there had the appearance of jasper and carnelian, and around the throne was a rainbow that had the appearance of an emerald (Revelation 4:3).

Ham, the Father of Canaan

The sons of Noah who went forth from the ark were Shem, Ham, and Japheth. (Ham was the father of Canaan.) These three were the sons of Noah, and from these the people of the whole earth were dispersed (Genesis 9:18–19).

All humans today are descendants of either Shem, Ham, Japheth, or a mixture, depending on what happened in history. But once again we understand there is only one race of humans — the human race. All humans are descendants of Noah and back to Adam. There are no different races of humans biologically.

Why though is Ham singled out as *Ham . . . the father of Canaan?* As we continue, we find out about an event which displayed the hearts of Noah's sons. And sadly, we see the effects of the sin nature as Ham seemed to find pleasure in Noah's sin of drunkenness as he went to his brothers rather than covering his father's shame. Something was amiss in Ham's heart. Perhaps because he had seen his father Noah as such a righteous man, he gloried in pointing out Noah also showed his sin nature. As mentioned, Ham was the father of Canaan who gave rise to the Canaanites, some of the most wicked people to live on earth (e.g., the people of Sodom and Gomorrah were Canaanites). It would seem that as a consequence of the problem Ham had with sin, his son Canaan also was impacted. And often when there is sin in one generation, one usually finds, as a consequence, that sin is in the next generation to an even greater extent if it's not dealt with. Because of the order of the sons of Ham listed in Genesis 10:6, it is likely that Canaan was the youngest son. It's also true that over time, it's easy for parents to become complacent with the younger kids because of how difficult it is to train up children, each of whom has a sin nature.

This diagram helps us see that the descendants of Canaan were ones described in the Bible as very wicked.

Noah Shem Japheth **Ham** Cush Mizraim Phut **Canaan** **Sidon his firstborn and Heth**	Genesis 9:18
the Jebusites, the Amorites, the Girgashites, the Hivites, the Arkites, the Sinites, the Arvadites the Zemarites, and the Hamathites. Afterward the clans of the Canaanites dispersed. And the territory of the Canaanites extended from Sidon in the direction of Gerar as far as Gaza, and in the direction of Sodom, Gomorrah, Admah, and Zeboiim, as far as Lasha.	Genesis 10:15–19

Noah's Sin

Noah began to be a man of the soil, and he planted a vineyard. He drank of the wine and became drunk and lay uncovered in his tent. And Ham, the father of Canaan, saw the nakedness of his father and told his two brothers outside. Then Shem and Japheth took a garment, laid it on both their shoulders, and walked backward and covered the nakedness of their father. Their faces were turned backward, and they did not see their father's nakedness (Genesis 9:20–23).

We are not told a lot of details about this event, so we don't know exactly why Noah drank too much wine and ended up drunk — and drunkenness is a sin: *And do not get drunk with wine, for that is debauchery, but be filled with the Spirit* (Ephesians 5:18). As a result of becoming drunk, he ended up naked. Ham saw this nakedness, and it appears from all that happened that Ham did not have the right heart attitude.

As I stated earlier, Ham may have gloried in the fact that his wonderful, godly dad also had defects because of sin. God's Word doesn't hide the defects of even the greatest of God's people to help us understand every one of us has a sin problem. None of us are above the effects of sin in our lives. Remember Cain, and how sin got the better of him leading to evil consequences, seemingly for generations.

Shem and Japheth showed great respect for their father in their action in looking away and covering their father. The fact that Ham didn't act the same way shows that Ham had a problem. This now sets the scene for what happened next.

"Cursed be Canaan"

When Noah awoke from his wine and knew what his youngest son had done to him, he said, "Cursed be Canaan; a servant of servants shall he be to his brothers" (Genesis 9:24–25).

Why does Canaan, the youngest son of Ham, get singled out? Wasn't it Ham who told his brothers about his father's drunkenness and nakedness? Well, in the order Noah's sons are listed, Shem, Ham and Japheth, Ham was in the middle, so Japheth was the youngest. Now, remember, Canaan was Ham's youngest son. Also this word "son" in Hebrew can also mean "grandson."

Therefore, it seems that what this verse is telling us is that "Noah awoke from his wine and knew what his youngest son [grandson Canaan] had done to him." This is substantiated by the fact that Noah doesn't say "cursed be Ham," but *cursed be Canaan*. We could surmise that Canaan saw his grandfather's nakedness and drunkenness. We don't know exactly what Canaan did, but it must have been quite sinful. Canaan would have gone and told his father Ham who then went to his two brothers Shem and Japheth.

Note that there is no such thing as a "curse of Ham," even though such has been falsely taught in a number of churches. The supposed "curse of Ham" has even been used in regard to skin shade. Such is nonsense and this false teaching needs to be stopped.

So what does it mean for Canaan that a *servant of servants shall he be to his brothers*? This is difficult for us to understand, and many great Bible expositors give varied interpretations. As this "curse" is directed at Canaan specifically, and we know the descendants of Canaan were very wicked people, then it makes sense to consider what happened to these descendants. We find they became slaves to pagan gods and involved in idolatry and child sacrifice. We know that Shem's descendants (the Israelites) conquered Canaanite cities (like Jericho and Ai) and killed and enslaved them. But we are also reminded that the Rahab in Joshua 6:25, is probably the same Rahab in the lineage leading to Jesus (as the Godman) in Matthew 1:25. Now the Israelites were told not to marry the pagan Canaanites. But it seems the Rahab of Jericho stopped being a Canaanite spiritually and became an Israelite spiritually, believing in the true God. Then she was free to marry an Israelite. Even those in wicked cultures can be saved by the grace of God.

When Noah pronounced the curse on Canaan, no doubt he was prophesying by God's Holy Spirit as to what would become of Canaan's descendants. What a warning to all parents not to raise up a Canaan but to raise up children in the nurture and admonition of the Lord (Ephesians 6:4).

Shem and Japheth Blessed

Noah also prophesied about Shem and Japheth.

> He also said, "Blessed be the Lord, the God of Shem; and let Canaan be his servant. May God enlarge Japheth, and let him dwell in the tents of Shem, and let Canaan be his servant" (Genesis 9:26–27).

What does this prophetic message mean? Many scholars have suggested various interpretations. The simplest understanding seems to be this:

Through Shem would come the line of Abraham, giving rise to God's chosen people the Israelites, through whom would come the Scriptures (. . . *the Jews were entrusted with the oracles of God* [Romans 3:2]), and the seed of the woman (the promised Messiah, Jesus Christ). This would be a blessing to Japheth's descendants, in fact to all people. Canaan's descendants, because of wickedness, would conflict with the descendants of Shem and Japheth.

It's interesting that Noah's prophetic word includes Shem, Japheth, and Canaan, but not specifically Ham. There are many ideas as to why this is so, but we can't be totally sure. Generally speaking, though (there are exceptions, of course), Shem's descendants have been dominated by zealousness for monotheism (even if many do not worship the true God), the Japhetites used science and philosophy and developed great cultures such as the Romans and Greeks, and the Hamites (think of the Egyptians, Sumerians, etc.) were phenomenal pioneers in opening up the world for settlement, farming, and industrial advancements (technology).

The Patriarchs Met

Now we come to the last two verses of Genesis 9, and the conclusion of the record of Noah's life.

After the flood Noah lived 350 years. All the days of Noah were 950 years, and he died (Genesis 9:28–29).

If we take the genealogies of Genesis 11 as written, Noah would have lived until after the Tower of Babel event and even up to close to when Abraham was born. It seems difficult to imagine, but Abraham could have spoken to Shem (Noah's son), who surely talked to his great-grandfather Methuselah, who in turn could have spoken to Adam, the first man, directly. Although the Bible never records that Adam and Methuselah or Abraham and Shem met, that possibility is likely. Consider the other patriarchs that could have talked to one another in the chart in chapter 11 (page 162).

Everyone today shares the same lineage from Adam to Noah, since only Noah's family survived the Flood. After the Flood, Noah's three sons and wives populated the earth. The list of men record Shem's line to Abraham, Isaac, and Jacob, who is also called Israel. Israel had 12 sons, and through his son Judah, the Bible traces the genealogy of Jesus Christ (Luke 3:23–38).

Noah and Adam

As we finish Genesis chapter 9, I wanted to bring together some interesting parallels between Adam and Noah as something interesting to think about.

Adam was the head of the human race.

Noah was the head of the human race after the Flood.

Both Adam and Noah are ancestors of all the people in the present world.

Adam was told to be fruitful and multiply and have dominion over the animals.

Noah (and his family) was told to be fruitful and multiply and have dominion over the animals.

Adam sinned by eating the forbidden fruit.

Noah sinned (drunkenness) by drinking wine made from a fruit.

Adam saw his nakedness after sinning.

Noah's sin resulted in nakedness.

God gave a covering for Adam's sin (coats of skins).

Noah was provided with a covering for his nakedness by his two sons.

God judged Adam's actions with a curse and promised a Savior.

Noah's actions resulted in a curse and also promise of a spiritual blessing through Shem.

Chapter 16

Genesis 10

Genesis 10 gives a detailed account of genealogies as the descendants of the three sons of Noah spread out around the world from the Tower of Babel, forming many different nations. Of course, it is ultimately only the line of Shem that can be traced from the present with precision, because this is the line from which the seed of the woman, the Messiah, would come and for which much detail is given in the Bible.

Genesis 10 and 11 should be viewed in a similar way to Genesis 1 and 2. Genesis 1 gave a chronological overview of the creation week, whereas Genesis 2 focused on certain details, specifically the creation of man and woman on the sixth day. Genesis 10 is an overview of the descendants of Noah's three sons who then moved away from each other according to their family groups and languages. Genesis 11 gives us the detailed account of the event (the Tower of Babel and confusion of languages) that caused this dispersion.

Before you read Genesis 10, I have selected a few specific lines to comment on.

1. *each with his own language, by their clans, in their nations* (Genesis 10:5).

   This enables us to understand what happened after the dispersion from the Tower of Babel which we read about in Genesis 11. Each group had their own language because of the event of Genesis 11.

2. *Cush fathered Nimrod; he was the first on earth to be a mighty man. He was a mighty hunter before the LORD. Therefore it is said, "Like Nimrod a mighty hunter before the LORD." The beginning of his kingdom was Babel, Erech, Accad, and Calneh, in the land of Shinar. From that land he went into Assyria and built Nineveh, Rehoboth-Ir, Calah, and Resen between Nineveh and Calah; that is the great city. Egypt fathered Ludim, Anamim, Lehabim, Naphtuhim, Pathrusim, Casluhim (from whom the Philistines came), and Caphtorim (Genesis 10:8–14).*

It seems Nimrod became a mighty hunter of wild animals, and that led him to be possibly some sort of tyrant in persuading people to obey him. You will notice that it includes Babel as the beginning of his kingdom. This was obviously after the Tower of Babel event, as Genesis 10 is post-dispersion. Presumably he took over Babel after the judgment event. To find out more about Nimrod and why many people mistakenly believe he led the Tower of Babel event, see Appendix 3.

3. *To Eber were born two sons: the name of the one was Peleg, for in his days the earth was divided (Genesis 10:25).*

Some people have tried to insist that this is a reference to the division of continents because it says the "earth was divided" — supposedly plate tectonics. But if the continents were splitting up at the time, it would have caused catastrophic upheaval and destroyed everything. In context, Peleg is given that name because the population was being divided up because of the Tower of Babel event. In other words, this is a reference to the dispersion because of what happened in Genesis 11.

Now read through Genesis 10 and get a sense of the tremendous detail here concerning the dispersion of people after the Flood and after the Tower of Babel. For more detail, check out Appendices 1 and 2 which show that many names from cultures we are familiar with can be traced back to various people listed in Genesis 10.

How Many Languages?

These are the generations of the sons of Noah, Shem, Ham, and Japheth. Sons were born to them after the flood. The sons of Japheth: Gomer, Magog, Madai, Javan, Tubal, Meshech, and Tiras. The sons of Gomer: Ashkenaz, Riphath, and Togarmah. The sons of Javan: Elishah, Tarshish, Kittim, and Dodanim. From these the coastland peoples spread in their lands, each with his own language, by their clans, in their nations.

The sons of Ham: Cush, Egypt, Put, and Canaan. The sons of Cush: Seba, Havilah, Sabtah, Raamah, and Sabteca. The sons of Raamah: Sheba and Dedan. Cush fathered Nimrod; he was the first on earth to be a mighty man. He was a mighty hunter before the LORD. Therefore it is said, "Like Nimrod a mighty hunter before the LORD." The beginning of his kingdom was Babel, Erech, Accad, and Calneh, in the land of Shinar. From that land he went into Assyria and built Nineveh, Rehoboth-Ir, Calah, and Resen between Nineveh and Calah; that is the great city. Egypt fathered Ludim, Anamim, Lehabim, Naphtuhim, Pathrusim, Casluhim (from whom the Philistines came), and Caphtorim.

Canaan fathered Sidon his firstborn and Heth, and the Jebusites, the Amorites, the Girgashites, the Hivites, the Arkites, the Sinites, the Arvadites, the Zemarites, and the Hamathites. Afterward the clans of the Canaanites dispersed. And the territory of the Canaanites extended from Sidon in the direction of Gerar as far as Gaza, and in the direction of Sodom, Gomorrah, Admah, and Zeboiim, as far as Lasha. These are the sons of Ham, by their clans, their languages, their lands, and their nations.

To Shem also, the father of all the children of Eber, the elder brother of Japheth, children were born. The sons of Shem: Elam, Asshur, Arpachshad, Lud, and Aram. The sons of Aram: Uz, Hul, Gether, and Mash. Arpachshad fathered Shelah; and Shelah fathered Eber. To Eber were born two sons: the name of the one was Peleg, for in his days the earth was divided, and his brother's name was Joktan. Joktan fathered Almodad, Sheleph, Hazarmaveth, Jerah, Hadoram,

Uzal, Diklah, Obal, Abimael, Sheba, Ophir, Havilah, and Jobab; all these were the sons of Joktan. The territory in which they lived extended from Mesha in the direction of Sephar to the hill country of the east. These are the sons of Shem, by their clans, their languages, their lands, and their nations.

These are the clans of the sons of Noah, according to their genealogies, in their nations, and from these the nations spread abroad on the earth after the flood (Genesis 10:1–32).

When you summarize the above, it would appear there were possibly 70 languages involved (each group having their own language as stated in the text). Thus, it seems when God confused their language at the Tower of Babel, this resulted in 70 language groups that became the foundation for the hundreds of languages (and dialects) we find in today's world.

Genesis 10
By their clans, their languages, their lands, and their nations

1. Gomer	20. Sheba	39. Arkite	58. Almodad
2. Ashkenaz	21. Dedan	40. Sinite	59. Sheleph
3. Riphath	22. Sabtechah	41. Arvadite	60. Hazarmaveth
4. Togarmah	23. Nimrod	42. Zemarite	61. Jerah
5. Magog	24. Mizraim	43. Hamathite	62. Hadoram
6. Madai	25. Ludim	44. Put	63. Uzal
7. Javan	26. Anamim	45. Aram	64. Diklah
8. Elishah	27. Lehabim	46. Uz	65. Obal
9. Tarshish	28. Naphtuhim	47. Hul	66. Abimael
10. Kittim	29. Pathrusim	48. Gether	67. Sheba
11. Dodanim	30. Casluhim	49. Mash	68. Ophir
12. Tubal	31. Caphtorim	50. Elam	69. Havilah
13. Meshech	32. Canaan	51. Asshur	70. Jobab
14. Tiras	33. Sidon	52. Lud	
15. Cush	34. Heth	53. Arphaxad	
16. Seba	35. Jebusite	54. Salah	
17. Havilah	36. Amorite	55. Eber	
18. Sabtah	37. Girgashite	56. Peleg	
19. Raamah	38. Hivite	57. Joktan	

Now we get to the detail of what caused this dispersion as we come to Genesis 11.

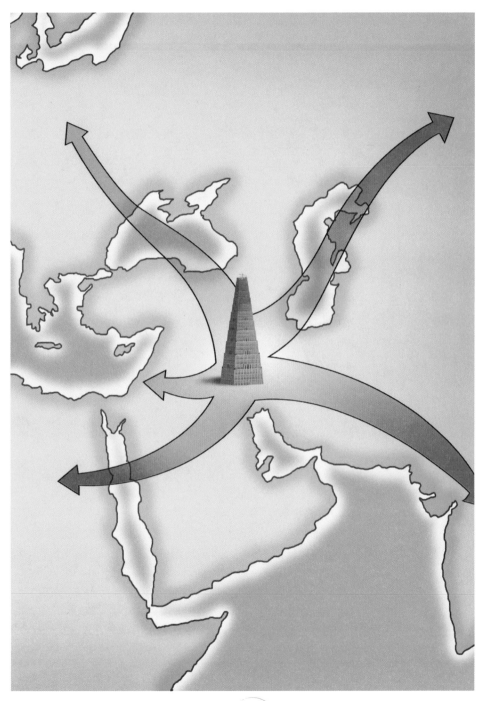

Chapter 17

Genesis 11

Genesis 11:1-4

Now the whole earth had one language and the same words. And as people migrated from the east, they found a plain in the land of Shinar and settled there. And they said to one another, "Come, let us make bricks, and burn them thoroughly." And they had brick for stone, and bitumen for mortar. Then they said, "Come, let us build ourselves a city and a tower with its top in the heavens, and let us make a name for ourselves, lest we be dispersed over the face of the whole earth."

Using Ussher's chronology, we date the Flood at 2348 B.C., and the event of Babel at 2242 B.C. This would mean the Babel event occurred about 100 years after the Flood. By then (based on the lists in Genesis 10 and assuming reasonably large families), there could have been 1,000 people by this time.

Major Dates According to Ussher

Major event	Date
Creation	4004 B.C.
Global Flood	2348 B.C.
Tower of Babel	2242 B.C.
Call of Abraham	1922 B.C.
Time of the Judges (Moses was first)	1491 B.C. (God appeared to Moses in the burning bush)
Time of the Kings (Saul was the first)	1095 B.C.
Split Kingdom	975 B.C.
Christ Was Born	~4 B.C.

God had told Noah's family to be fruitful and multiply and fill the earth. By the time of Babel, people decided they didn't want to be dispersed over the earth. So they gathered together to build a city with a great tower. There seems to be a lot of evidence that many of the pagan religions over the years had their origin at the Tower of Babel. Sadly, from their own human pride and self-centeredness they were intent on defying God's decree to fill the earth. It was as if they were shaking their fist at God and saying, "We can do whatever we want to do." How quickly they must have forgotten the judgment God had meted out at the Flood because of man's wickedness. What happened at Babel must have been very wicked, because God stepped into history again to judge man for rebellion.

Nothing They Do Will be Impossible

And the LORD came down to see the city and the tower, which the children of man had built. And the LORD said, "Behold, they are one people, and they have all one language, and this is only the beginning of what they will do. And nothing that they propose to do will now be impossible for them. Come, let us go down and there confuse their language, so that they may not understand one another's speech." So the LORD dispersed them from there over the face of all the earth, and they left off building the city. Therefore its name was called Babel, because there the Lord *confused the language of all the earth. And from there the* Lord *dispersed them over the face of all the earth* (Genesis 11:5–9).

And nothing that they propose to do will now be impossible for them. God saw the seed of growing evil and knew what this would result in. Remember, by the time of the Flood, the whole world, except for Noah and his family, had rebelled. And now, only a hundred years after the judgment of the Flood, it seems most of the whole world was plotting rebellion again. There may have been some who didn't participate in the Babel event. Some have suggested Shem's descendants weren't involved. We can't know for sure. The text doesn't give us any indication that some people weren't involved.

The people at this time spoke one language. We don't know what the language was. Some suggest it could have been Hebrew. If writings from Adam and others were handed down to Noah to eventually reach Moses, it would make sense it would be in a language Moses could understand. But this is speculation that can't be proved.

When God confused their languages, we believe it's possible up to 70 different language groups were formed as discussed in Genesis 10.

Different People Groups Form

The event of the Tower of Babel also resulted in different people groups forming, eventually with distinct characteristics such as skin shade, hair color, eye color, etc., because of the phenomenal genetic diversity God created when He made Adam and Eve.

Here is a summary of the human race from Adam through Noah and the Tower of Babel to help us understand why there are different people groups with distinguishing characteristics.

We know from Scripture that Adam and Eve were the first two people. Their descendants filled the earth. The world's population was reduced to eight during the Flood of Noah. From these eight individuals have come all the tribes and nations. Because there was a common language and everybody lived in the same general vicinity, barriers that may have prevented their descendants from freely intermarrying weren't as great as they are today. Then in Genesis 11 we read of the rebellion at the Tower of Babel. God judged this rebellion by giving each family group a different language. This made it impossible for the groups to understand each other, and so they split apart, each extended family going its own way, and finding a different place to live. The result was that the people were scattered over the earth. Because of the new language and geographic barriers, the groups no longer freely mixed with other groups (at least for a time), and the result was a splitting of the gene pool. Different cultures formed, with certain features becoming predominant within each group. The characteristics of each became more and more prominent as new generations of children were born. If we were to travel back in time to Babel, and mix up the people into completely different family groups, then people groups with completely different characteristics might result.

A correct understanding of the history of the human race then enables us to know how to deal with racism.

We live at a time when we hear accusations of prejudice and racism almost on a daily basis.

Prejudice is still alive. Why? Well, because racism is a consequence of sin in a fallen world infused with evolutionary thinking. The consequences of racism on a personal and social level are huge.

But what do we do about it? What do you do about it? Here are three very practical and personal application points from chapter five of my book coauthored with Dr. Charles Ware, *One Race, One Blood*. Like any true biblical conviction, these actions should start from a changed heart and a changed understanding about what is real and true.

We Need to Do Away with "Race"

First, I would propose that we do away with using the term "race" when discussing the different groups of people in the world. *The Bible is clear (and science confirms) that there's only one race: the human race (Adam's race).* The idea of "race" is rooted in the thinking of the early evolutionists, even well before Darwin. We all need to treat every human being as our relative. We are of one blood (Acts 17:26). All of us are equal in value before our Creator God. Any descendant of Adam can be saved, because our mutual relative by blood (Jesus Christ) died and rose again. This is why we are commanded to preach the gospel to all people groups and nations.

We Need to be Reprogrammed

Here's something you might find hard to accept: in the U.S. culture, we are racially programmed, particularly in regard to the skin color issue. Because of our culture's racist roots, because of the way the world thinks, because of the influence of Darwinian thinking, we have been programmed to look at the exterior rather than the interior of a person, and to make broad judgments based on what we see. Had we not been programmed that way in this culture, we wouldn't see the differences as we do. Different cultures are programmed in different ways. Our biases and prejudices show themselves in different ways, but in every case it is the world and our sinfulness (rather than science and the Bible) that drives our personal racism. I realize those are very strong words. You might struggle to agree with me. But the fact is, it's true. We just go through our days making all sorts of assumptions and judgment calls based on outward appearances of skin tone, facial features, size, height, etc. It's very hard to see through the programming because it seems to be such a natural part of the way we think. No one likes to admit it, but the consequences are too serious to ignore. We've been programmed, and that programming needs to be changed. This is no surprise to God, of course. He is fully aware of the pressures and the influences that the world places upon us. But He also states very clearly that it doesn't have to stay that way. Change can take place in our minds and our hearts:

> *And do not be conformed to this world, but be transformed by the renewing of your mind, so that you may prove what the will of God is, that which is good and acceptable and perfect. For through the*

grace given to me I say to everyone among you not to think more highly of himself than he ought to think. . . . so we, who are many, are one body in Christ, and individually members one of another (Romans 12:2–5; NASB).

If you want to solve the issue of racism in your own life, it's simple: you've got to believe the Bible and the true account of the history of the human race. That's the bottom line. All of us need to judge our attitudes and our worldview against the absolute authority of the Word of God.

It's Time to Take Action

James 1:22 commands us to be more than just hearers of the Word. We are to prove ourselves "doers of the Word." We are to be people of action. These actions must come from the heart — from a determined conviction that the issues of racism need to be confronted with truth and integrity. Instead of looking at minor outward differences in our physical features or skin tone, it's time to look past the reflection of the small percentage of our DNA and say, "This is my brother; this is my sister. I am one blood with this person." It's time to fully learn and apply the message that the LORD gave to Samuel. God challenged him to not look at someone's physical features, skin tone, size, etc. *Do not look at his appearance or at the height of his stature . . . for God does not see as man sees, since man looks at the outward appearance, but the LORD looks at the heart* (1 Samuel 16:7; NASB).

The next time you see someone who looks slightly different from you, you should ask, "How can I help them? Do they need my love, my care? Do they need the LORD?" We need to treat people as the LORD did. Jesus continually reached across the invisible barriers of prejudice to love people, to care for people, and to speak truth into people's lives. He reached out to touch those who were unclean, or those who were plagued with leprosy. He reached across ethnic and gender divisions to speak truth into the life of the Samaritan woman at the well (John 4).

If you truly want to see your life reflect the life of Christ, then you must begin to allow Christ to love others through you, particularly those who are different than you, just as He did.

What a difference it will make in the lives around you as you begin to think and act that way! What a difference it will make in the world as more and more of us take up this cause! By choosing to act, we are pulling out the weeds of evolutionary thought and replanting with seeds of truth, love, understanding, and compassion as we are taught to do in God's Word. That's what it's all about.

Now we read more genealogical details in regard to Shem's descendants.

The Generations of Shem

These are the generations of Shem. When Shem was 100 years old, he fathered Arpachshad two years after the flood. And Shem lived after he fathered Arpachshad 500 years and had other sons and daughters.

When Arpachshad had lived 35 years, he fathered Shelah. And Arpachshad lived after he fathered Shelah 403 years and had other sons and daughters.

When Shelah had lived 30 years, he fathered Eber. And Shelah lived after he fathered Eber 403 years and had other sons and daughters.

When Eber had lived 34 years, he fathered Peleg. And Eber lived after he fathered Peleg 430 years and had other sons and daughters.

When Peleg had lived 30 years, he fathered Reu. And Peleg lived after he fathered Reu 209 years and had other sons and daughters.

When Reu had lived 32 years, he fathered Serug. And Reu lived after he fathered Serug 207 years and had other sons and daughters.

When Serug had lived 30 years, he fathered Nahor. And Serug lived after he fathered Nahor 200 years and had other sons and daughters.

When Nahor had lived 29 years, he fathered Terah. And Nahor lived after he fathered Terah 119 years and had other sons and daughters.

When Terah had lived 70 years, he fathered Abram, Nahor, and Haran.

Now these are the generations of Terah. Terah fathered Abram, Nahor, and Haran; and Haran fathered Lot. Haran died in the presence of his father Terah in the land of his kindred, in Ur of the Chaldeans. And Abram and Nahor took wives. The name of Abram's wife was Sarai, and the name of Nahor's wife, Milcah, the daughter of Haran the father of Milcah and Iscah. Now Sarai was barren; she had no child.

Terah took Abram his son and Lot the son of Haran, his grandson, and Sarai his daughter-in-law, his son Abram's wife, and they went forth together from Ur of the Chaldeans to go into the land of Canaan, but when they came to Haran, they settled there. The days of Terah were 205 years, and Terah died in Haran (Genesis 11:10–32).

So we come to the end of Genesis 11. This chapter ends with details concerning Abram who would later on be called Abraham. It's this lineage, from Adam to Shem to Abraham, and eventually to the babe in a manager, through which the Messiah (who came as the babe in a manger), promised in Genesis 3:15, would step into history through Shem's line. The promise of the seed of the woman would be fulfilled.

The following Hebrew Table of Nations developed by Bodie Hodge, the author of *Tower of Babel*, shows the line of Terah to Abraham and then to the 12 tribes of Israel which then as we know goes to Christ. This helps us understand how all these details can be used to trace the lineage of Jesus back to Adam.

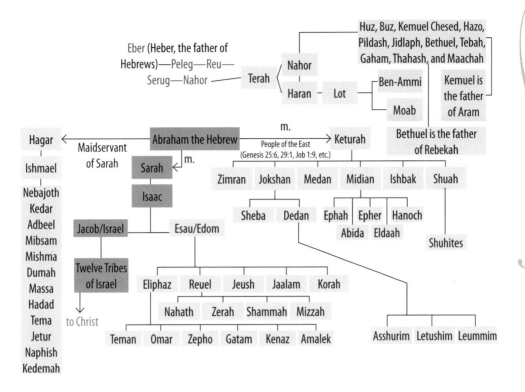

The rest of the Bible details the history of the people of Israel leading up to the birth of Christ as the Godman. But the literal history of these first 11 chapters of Genesis are foundational to the rest of the Bible, foundational to all doctrine, foundational to our Christian worldview, and foundational to all doctrine.

History is not the aimless fumbling of men and nations. Interwoven through all this history, we see the hand of the infinite Creator who directs the affairs of men for His purposes — for man's good and God's glory.

Chapter 18

A Tribute

From a young age, my parents taught me to stand unashamedly and boldly on the Word of God from the very first verse. They never doubted God's Word in Genesis and were dismayed when Christian leaders would try to add man's evolutionary ideas to Genesis. They taught us to defend the Christian faith against the secular and liberal attacks of our day. As my father would tell us, "If you doubt and reinterpret God's Word beginning in Genesis, then that opens a door to do that through the rest of Scripture."

When my father was dying in a hospital in June 1995, my now late brother Robert was sitting with him and asked, "Dad, why do you love God's Word so much?" Robert told me our father replied, "My father died when I was 16 years old, so I no longer had an earthly father and I turned to the Words of my Heavenly Father and read them over and over again."

Dad saturated himself in the Word of God.

For the word of God is living and active, sharper than any two-edged sword, piercing to the division of soul and of spirit, of joints and of marrow, and discerning the thoughts and intentions of the heart (Hebrews 4:12).

. . . so shall my word be that goes out from my mouth; it shall not return to me empty, but it shall accomplish that which I purpose, and shall succeed in the thing for which I sent it (Isaiah 55:11).

I'll never forget what my parents taught me. Here is just some of what they communicated to me that remains indelibly impressed in my mind:

A. When I discussed the gap theory found in the Scofield Bible study notes, my father said, "Always remember, the notes are not inspired like the text, and the text should always be the commentary on the notes — not the other way round."

B. While discussing that many Christians, as well as secularists, believed the universe was supposedly billions of years old, my father said, "I don't have all the answers to how they get the billions of years. But always go to the text of Scripture and ensure you are taking it as written, according to the literature and language. Always take a grammatical historical approach to interpreting Scripture. If you are then sure it doesn't allow for millions of years, then there is something wrong with what others are saying. And just because we don't have answers, doesn't mean there are not answers. It just means we don't know everything, and we can pray and ask God to show us the answer. But we may never get some answers, because only God knows everything, and He expects us to trust His Word. But nothing in God's Word will contradict truth."

C. When discussing Genesis, my father would say, "If you can't trust Genesis, how can you trust the rest of the Bible, because the rest depends on Genesis being true?"

D. I'll never forget my mother kneeling with me at night and teaching me to pray and saying over and over again, "It's only what is done for Jesus that lasts."

When I went to high school, my parents obtained a copy of the new science textbooks the school was going to use. They went through it carefully (what a lesson for all parents!) and then sat down with me to discuss what these books were teaching, particularly the large section teaching evolution as fact and that humans evolved from apes. At that stage they didn't have all the answers (particularly the ones dealing with the scientific aspects) that we have today, which have been published in various Answers in Genesis books, on our websites, in presentations, and through exhibits at the Creation Museum and the Ark Encounter. But they made sure I understood how what was being taught conflicted with God's Word. They didn't want me to be led astray. And over time, through various books, God brought along the answers to some of the questions we didn't know how to answer at the time.

That's why I say that truly, the Answers in Genesis ministry, the Creation Museum, and the Ark are a legacy of parents who faithfully taught their children God's Word. And they lived their faith in ways I could write books about.

This commentary is really a compilation of what I've learned about Genesis 1–11 over the years, because godly parents taught their children to trust God's Word from the very first verse of Genesis.

Thanks, Mum and Dad.

> . . . and how from childhood you have been acquainted with the sacred writings, which are able to make you wise for salvation through faith in Christ Jesus (2 Timothy 3:15).

May this book be used to help raise up generations of godly offspring. Come and visit the Creation Museum and see the Ham Family Legacy exhibit and the spiritual legacy they have left in this world.

Appendix
1

This article is taken from chapter 13 of the book, *Tower of Babel*, by Bodie Hodge entitled, "What about Extra-biblical Tables of Nations and Genealogies That Go Back to Noah?" I would encourage you to read the entire book if you want to know more about the dispersion of people from the Tower of Babel event.

Genesis 10 gives an outline of family groups that left Babel. These people moved throughout the world and populated virtually every continent. (Was Antarctica ever settled in the past? At this point, I am unaware.) On the following page is the Table of Nations from the Bible.

Historians such as Josephus (1st century), Snorri Sturluson (13th century), James Anderson (1732), Nennius (9th century), and many others have commented on various cultures and their genealogical records in the past and the origins of various peoples.[1]

Though there are many to pick from, a few examples of tables of nations should show that historians, especially prior to evolutionary re-writing of history which is common in the past 150 years, even unbeknownst to themselves sometimes, were offering a great confirmation of Genesis.

---

1. Nennius, *Historia Brittonum*, edited in the 10th century by Mark the Hermit, with English version by the Rev. W. Gunn, rector of Irstead, Norfolk, printed in London, 1819; Flavius Josephus, *The Complete Works of Flavius Josephus the Jewish Historian* (~ A.D. 100), trans. William Whiston (~ A.D. 1850) (Green Forest, AR: Master Books, 2008).

Table of Nations (Genesis 10)

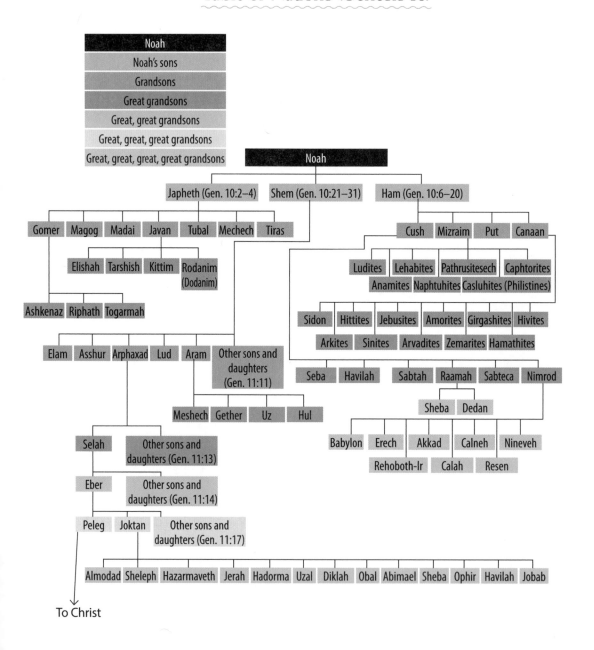

Legend:
- Noah
- Noah's sons
- Grandsons
- Great grandsons
- Great, great grandsons
- Great, great, great grandsons
- Great, great, great, great grandsons

Noah

Japheth (Gen. 10:2–4) — **Shem (Gen. 10:21–31)** — **Ham (Gen. 10:6–20)**

Japheth: Gomer, Magog, Madai, Javan, Tubal, Mechech, Tiras
- Javan: Elishah, Tarshish, Kittim, Rodanim (Dodanim)
- Gomer: Ashkenaz, Riphath, Togarmah

Shem: Elam, Asshur, Arphaxad, Lud, Aram, Other sons and daughters (Gen. 11:11)
- Aram: Meshech, Gether, Uz, Hul
- Arphaxad: Selah, Other sons and daughters (Gen. 11:13)
  - Selah: Eber, Other sons and daughters (Gen. 11:14)
    - Eber: Peleg, Joktan, Other sons and daughters (Gen. 11:17)
      - Joktan: Almodad, Sheleph, Hazarmaveth, Jerah, Hadorma, Uzal, Diklah, Obal, Abimael, Sheba, Ophir, Havilah, Jobab
      - Peleg: To Christ

Ham: Cush, Mizraim, Put, Canaan
- Mizraim: Ludites, Lehabites, Pathrusitesech, Caphtorites, Anamites, Naphtuhites, Casluhites (Philistines)
- Canaan: Sidon, Hittites, Jebusites, Amorites, Girgashites, Hivites, Arkites, Sinites, Arvadites, Zemarites, Hamathites
- Cush: Seba, Havilah, Sabtah, Raamah, Sabteca, Nimrod
  - Raamah: Sheba, Dedan
  - Nimrod: Babylon, Erech, Akkad, Calneh, Nineveh, Rehoboth-Ir, Calah, Resen

Josephus, who was surely drawing from Genesis, completed his table of nations nearly 2,000 years ago. A discussion of this is detailed in Chapter 17, but it is in graphic form on the following pages. So let's start here.

Some genealogies connect prominent modern houses and royal lines with the Table of Nations listed in the Bible.[2] Anglo-Saxon chronologies feature six royal houses that go back to Noah.[3] In these genealogies, Noah is found on the top of the lists in many of these documents, some of which feature variant spellings such as *Noe* or *Noa*.

One historian discovered a relationship between the ancient name of *Sceaf* (*Seskef*, *Scef*) and the biblical *Japheth*.[4] This seems reasonable, as Japheth has traditionally been seen as the ancestor of the European nations. Some of the European genealogies researched have a variant of *Sceaf*, with the exception of Irish genealogies, which still used the name *Japheth*.[5] One table of European nations by historian Nennius is following.

An eighth-century Roman historian, Nennius, developed a table of nations of the lineages of many of the European people groups from Noah's son Japheth: Gauls, Goths, Bavarians, Saxons, and Romans. Nennius's table of nations is reproduced on page 249.[6]

Though it repeats the Goths in two different areas, Nennius's chart bears strong similarities to the history that Josephus recorded, as well as the Bible's Table of Nations. However, there are clearly enough differences to show that it was neither a copy from the biblical text nor from the Jewish historian Josephus.[7]

Chinese records also describe *Nuah* with three sons, *Lo Han, Lo Shen,*

---

2. For a number of these, see Anderson, *Royal Genealogies.* James Anderson, Royal Genealogies (London: James Bettenham Publisher, 1732)
3. Bill Cooper, *After the Flood* (Chichester, England: New Wine Press, 1995), p. 84–86.
4. Ibid., p. 92–96.
5. Ibid., p. 108.
6. Ibid., p. 49.
7. Ibid., chapter 3.

Josephus's Table of Nations

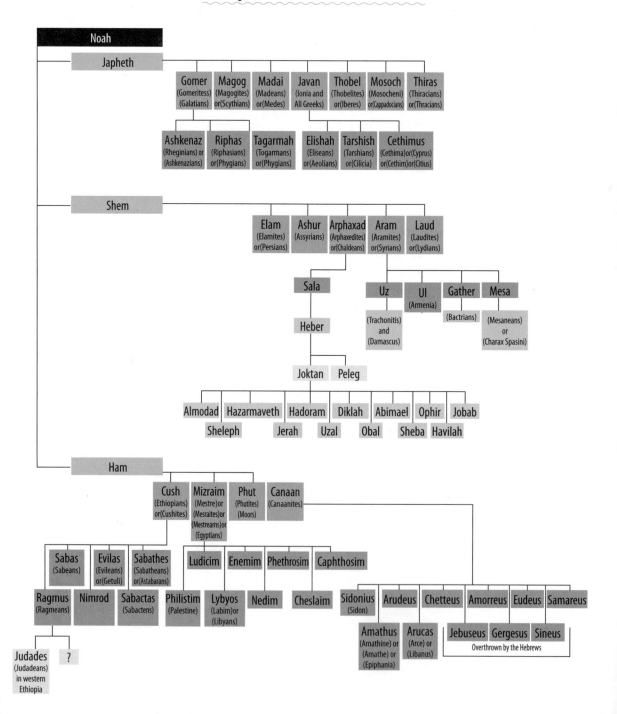

Nennius's Table of Nations

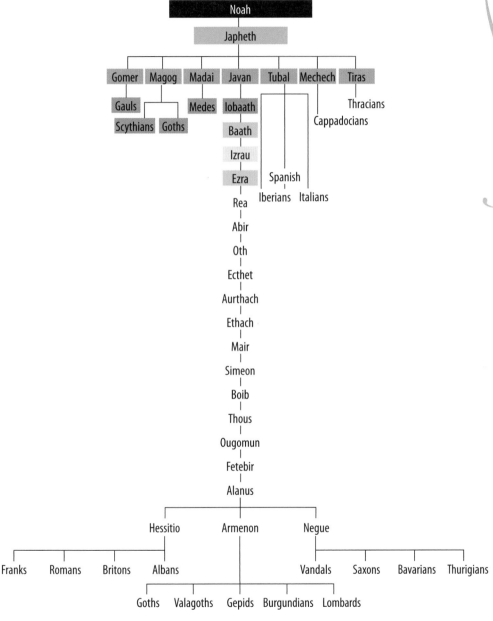

(Chart originally from page 49 of *After the Flood: The Early Post-Flood History of Europe Traced Back to Noah* written by author Bill Cooper and published by New Wine Press; used with permission of the Creation Science Movement in the UK.)

and *Jahphu*, according to the Miautso people of China.[8] Although original documents of ancient sources sometimes no longer exist and one has to rely on quotes from other ancient books, it is interesting how, in many places, we find similarities to the Table of Nations given in the Bible.

Another questionable Table of Nations appears in the book of Jasher (or Jashar). For those familiar with the book of Jasher, it is mentioned twice in the Old Testament.

> *And the sun stood still, and the moon stopped, until the nation took vengeance on their enemies. Is this not written in the Book of Jashar? The sun stopped in the midst of heaven and did not hurry to set for about a whole day* (Joshua 10:13).

> *And he told them to teach the children of Judah the Song of the Bow; indeed it is written in the Book of Jasher* (2 Samuel 1:18; NKJV).

It was assumed that this book had been lost to history. Yet, there are three copies floating around today. So what is the story?

As it turns out, these copies are later books, not the one that is mentioned in Scripture. One book is a collection of legends from creation to the conquest of Joshua (and was written in Hebrew). It is believed by most scholars that this book did not exist until about 1625.

Another book of Jasher is supposed to be an 18th-century translation of a book by Alcuin from the 8th century. Of course, there is a science fiction book by this title as well. So what we can learn from this book of Jasher is not what is reference material to what is stated in Scripture, *but instead* what people believed or researched within the past millennium. Essentially, we can only know what the author believed when this was written.

After researching the book of Jasher from the 17th century, we find a record of genealogies as well. It is not merely a copy of the Bible or of Josephus or of anything else directly referenced in this volume either.

---

8. Edgar Traux, "Genesis According to the Miao People," *Impact*, April 1991; available online at www.icr.org/article/341/.

This is known because there is information here not given in any of the other references and vice versa; the other references give information not mentioned here. On the following pages are charts of what we have.

Some of this makes sense too. I have been able to trace the Turks in Asia Minor (modern-day Turkey) to Noah's great grandson Togarmah's descendants migrating into part of modern-day Turkey. Later, they conquered the whole of Asia Minor and had the Turkish Empire, which was quite powerful. The Bible simply gives his name (Togarmah), but where did the name "Turk" come from? Was it a variation of Togarmah? If the author of Jasher is somewhat correct, then this is now explained by one of the ten sons of Togarmah (Tugarma). One of his sons was Tarki.

In some cases, the name of a descendant became the name of a language or people. For example, in the Bible, the Anakim were people named for descendants of Arba through his son Anak, and the Jews (named for Judah) became a name for the Israelites. So Turk may have that same connotation.

The Uzbek Turks (living in Uzbekistan, Afghanistan, Tajikistan, Kazakhstan, Kyrgyzstan, and Turkmenistan) may well be named for Zebuc, which sounds strikingly similar to Uzbek, as would the Oguzes or Oguz Turks to Ongal. It is this latter ancestral group that gave rise to Osman I, who founded the Ottoman Turk Empire that lasted for about six centuries (late A.D. 1200s to the 1800s).

Another example is the names of the children of Asshur. The Bible simply gives the name Asshur (Assyria). Jasher fills in the names of Asshur's sons. This makes sense since Nimrod conquered and built up four of these places (Genesis 10:11–12) that were in Asshur's lands (Nineveh, Rehoboth Ir, Calah, and Resen). So did these cities take the names of Asshur's sons or Nimrod's sons? In light of the Bible, I would lean in the direction of Nimrod's sons, but simply that they were in the land allotted for Asshur, but the Scripture is not clear. In this book of

Jasher, they attribute them to Asshur.[9] Regardless, there was a mix of these two people groups in these four places.

There is much to learn, and it could be a book in and of itself to find and record various Tables of Nations found throughout the world. In truth, the book *Royal Genealogies* by James Anderson has a number of these tables. The research was done for a prince of Great Britain, Fredrick Lewis, in 1732. This volume, unlike Jasher, is a much more reliable source. The few listed here and many others that can be tracked down are a great confirmation of the truthfulness of the Scriptures.[10]

---

9. Some have thought these names attributed to Nimrod in the Table of Nations were not sons at all, but that Nimrod simply built these cities. But then we are stuck with two predicaments. How can a city, which is made up of people, exist without progeny? And how could they come out with a new language as indicated in Genesis 10? It makes sense that these cities were named for sons, which was the common way of doing it.
10. Bodie Hodge, *Tower of Babel* (Green Forest, AR: Master Books, 2013), pp. 75-84; https://answersingenesis.org/racism/what-about-extra-biblical-tables-nations-genealogies-that-go-back-noah/.

Ham in Jasher

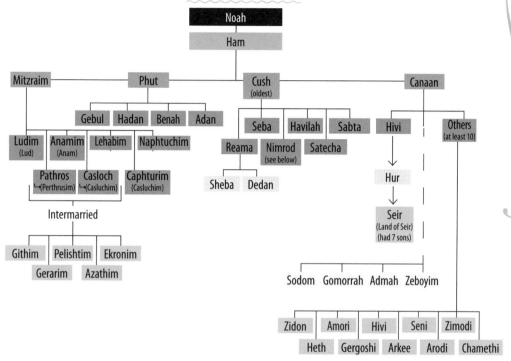

NOTES:

- Nimrod (also called Amraphel) was supposedly born to Cush late in his life and was the youngest.
- Babel, Erech, Eched, and Calnah were not named for sons but the names likely had significance, i.e.:
    1. Babel means: "The Lord confounded their language"
    2. Erech means: "They were displaced from there"
    3. Eched means: "Great battle happened there"
    4. Calnah means: "His Prince's mighty men were consumed there"

- Bible says Abram left Haran at 75 years of age. When did Terah, Abram, et. al. leave Ur?
    * A later queen than Sheba visits Solomon.

Shem in Jasher

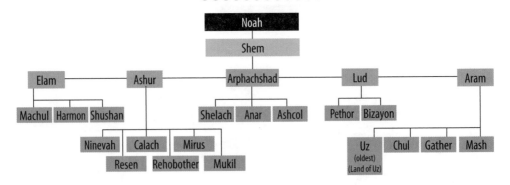

NOTES:
- Chedorlaomer fought and conquered Nimrod's descendants due to their wickedness.
  Abram would have been 49 years of age.
- Bela settled near but away from Sodom and the cities of the plain. New settlement called "Land of Zoar."
- Bible says Abram left Horan at 75 years of age. When did Terah, Abram, et. al. leave Ur?
- About 300 men.

Japheth in Jasher

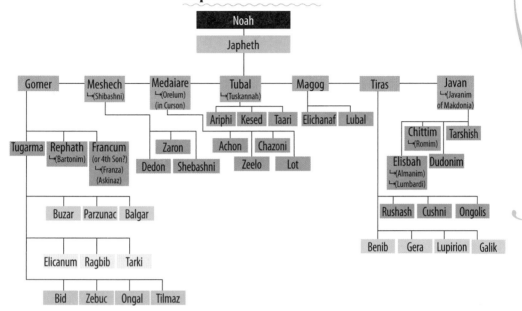

NOTES:

- Genesis 10 and 11 reveal that people like Selah and Eber had other sons. So the listings in Genesis 10 are not necessarily the ONLY sons.
- 460 men at this time.
- Peleg died the 48th year of Abraham's life.

Appendix 2

This article is taken from chapter 17A of the book, *Tower of Babel,* by Bodie Hodge entitled, "Josephus — a Wonderful Stepping-Stone."

Josephus was a first-century Jewish historian with an intriguing history of his own. He served as governor of Galilee, fought against Rome in the first century, and was eventually captured. His surrender ultimately took him to Rome, where his captors became Roman Emperors (Vespasian and his son Titus). He was ordered to write a history of the Jewish nation because of all the strife that had been going on in that area.

But the history to be discussed is not Josephus's life, but something he wrote about. In his book about Jewish history, *The Antiquity of the Jews* (specifically chapter 6), Josephus gave Christians a brilliant "stepping-stone" to the genealogies in Genesis 10.[1]

Table of Nations

Josephus connected many of the nations that formed after the confusion at the Tower of Babel with the nations around him. He often listed the common Greek name for these nations, which provided a solid translation of ancient history into his era. From his work, Christians can connect those nations to the nations we have today. Hence, we have a stepping-stone between nations and people groups soon after the Flood and those today.

---

1. Bodie Hodge, "Josephus and Genesis," Chapter 10, *Answers in Depth*, Volume 4, November 18, 2009, https://answersingenesis.org/genesis/josephus-and-genesis-chapter-ten/.

For example, Josephus mentions that Gomer, one of Noah's grandsons, had descendants that the Greeks called Galatians. Paul wrote an epistle to the Galatians who were living in Asia Minor (modern-day Turkey).

Another intriguing connection is that of Magog — also one of Noah's grandsons. Josephus's research reveals that the Scythians were descendants of Magog. The Scythians are now a variety of people groups living north of the Black Sea.

Another exciting aspect of Josephus is that his Table of Nations gives extra-biblical support to Genesis 10 and the division of the peoples by family group when God confused their languages. Appendix 1 has a chart that shows Josephus's Table of Nations graphically.

Consider how similar this is to the Bible's Table of Nations, which obviously influenced Josephus. And consider how much we can learn from Josephus's comments on the subject.

Conclusions

Although Josephus's work is not infallible, it does confirm biblical accuracy. Take particular notice of some of the names of Canaan's sons. The Bible reveals them as people groups, such as Jebusites, Sinites, Girgashites, and so on. Josephus gives the specific names of Canaan's sons, such as Jebuseus, Gergesus, Sineus, and so on. These are fascinating confirmations of the Bible's teachings.

Excerpts

The following are excerpts from Josephus's *Antiquity of the Jews* as translated by William Whiston and adapted in Online Bible. The names of Noah's grandsons are numbered, and his great-grandsons have a letter associated with their father's number, and so on. Also, if the name is not obvious, the likely connection is linked to the biblical genealogies in brackets.

Japheth

Now they were the grandchildren of Noah, in honour of whom names were imposed on the nations by those who first settled them. Japheth, the son of Noah, had seven sons; they inhabited so that, beginning at the mountains Taurus and Amanus, they proceeded along Asia, as far as the river Tanais, and along Europe to Cadiz; and settling themselves on the lands which they came upon, which none had inhabited before, they called the nations by their own names; for

1. **Gomer** founded those whom the Greeks now call Galatians, [Galls], but were then called Gomerites.
2. **Magog** founded those who from him were named Magogites, but who are by the Greeks called Scythians.
3. Now as to Javan and **Madai**, the sons of Japheth; from Madai came the Madeans, who are called Medes, by the Greeks;
4. but from **Javan**, Ionia, and all the Greeks, are derived.
5. **Thobel** [Tubal] founded the Thobelites, who are now called Iberes;
6. and the Mosocheni were founded by **Mosoch** [Mechech]; now they are Cappadocians. There is also a mark of their ancient name still to be shown; for there is even now among them a city called Mazaca, which may inform those who are able to understand, that so was the entire nation once called.
7. **Thiras** [Tiras, Tyras] also called those whom he ruled over, Thirasians; but the Greeks changed the name into Thracians. And so many were the countries that had the children of Japheth for their inhabitants.
1A. Of the three sons of Gomer, **Ashkenaz** founded the Ashkenazians [Germany], who are now called by the Greeks Rheginians.
1B. So did **Riphas** found the Riphasians, now called Paphlagonians; and
1C. **Togarmah** the Togarmans, who, as the Greeks resolved, were named Phrygians.
4A. Of the three sons of Javan also, the son of Japheth, **Elishah**

gave name to the Eliseans, who were his subjects; they are now the Aeolians.

4B. **Tarshish** to the Tarshians; for so was Cilicia of old called; the sign of which is this, that the noblest city they have, and a metropolis also, is Tarsus, the *tau* being by change put for the *theta*.

4C. **Cethimus** [Kittim] possessed the island Cethima; it is now called Cyprus; and from that it is that all islands, and the greatest part of the sea coasts, are named Cethim by the Hebrews; and one city there is in Cyprus that has been able to preserve its name; it has been called Citius by those who use the language of the Greeks, and has not, by the use of that dialect, escaped the name of Cethim. And so many nations have the children and grandchildren of Japheth possessed. Now when I have premised somewhat, which perhaps the Greeks do not know, I will return and explain what I have omitted; for such names are pronounced here after the manner of the Greeks, to please my readers; for our own country language does not so pronounce them; but the names in all cases are of one and the same ending; for the name we here pronounce Noeas, is their Noah, and in every case retains the same termination.

Ham

The children of Ham possessed the land from Syria and Amanus, and the mountains of Libanus; settling all that was on its sea coasts, and as far as the ocean, and keeping it as their own. Some indeed of its names are utterly vanished away; others of them, being changed, and another sound given them, are hardly to be discovered; yet a few there are which have kept their names entire.

1. For of the four sons of Ham, time has not at all hurt the name of **Cush**; for the Ethiopians, over whom he reigned, are even at this day, both by themselves and by all men in Asia, called Cushites.

2. The memory also of the Mesraites is preserved in their name, for all we who inhabit this country [of Judea] called Egypt

Mestre [**Mizraim**], and the Egyptians Mestreans.

3. **Phut** also was the founder of Libya, and called the inhabitants Phutites, from himself; there is also a river in the country of Moors which bears that name; where it is that we may see the greatest part of the Greek historiographers mention that river and the adjoining country by the appellation of Phut;

2A. but the name it has now, has been by change given it from one of the sons of Mizraim, who was called **Lybyos** [Ludites]. We will inform you presently what has been the occasion why it has been called Africa also.

4. **Canaan**, the fourth son of Ham, inhabited the country now called Judea, and called it from his own name Canaan.

The children of these [four] were these:

1A. **Sabas** [Seba], who founded the Sabeans;

1B. **Evilas** [Havilah], who founded the Evileans, who are called Getuli;

1C. **Sabathes** [Sabtah], founded the Sabathens — they are now called by the Greeks, Astaborans; (135)

1D. **Sabactas** settled the Sabactens; and

1E. Ragmus [Raamah] the Ragmeans; and he had two sons, the one of whom, Judadas, settled the Judadeans [Dedan], a nation of the Western Ethiopians, and left them his name; as did Sabas [Sheba] to the Sabeans.

1F. But **Nimrod**, the son of Cush, stayed and tyrannized at Babylon, as we have already informed you.

Now all the children of Mizraim, being eight in number, possessed the country from Gaza to Egypt, though it retained the name of one only,

2A. the **Philistim** [Casluhites; for the Greeks call part of that country Palestine.

2B. As for the rest, **Ludicim** [Ludites], and

2C. **Enemim** [Anamites], and

2D. **Labim** [Lehabites/Lybybos], who alone inhabited in Libya, and called the country from himself,

2E. **Nedim** [Naphtuhites] and

2F. **Phethrosim**, and

2G. **Chesloim** [8th son that that came after the biblical table of nations?], and

2H. **Caphthorim**; we know nothing of them besides their names; for the Ethiopic war, which we shall describe hereafter, was the cause that those cities were overthrown.

4A. The sons of Canaan were these: **Sidonius**, who also built a city of the same name — it is called by the Greeks, Sidon;

4B. **Amathus** [Hamathites] inhabited in Amathine, which is even now called Amathe by the inhabitants, although the Macedonians named it Epiphania, from one of his posterity;

4C. **Arudeus** [Arvadites] possessed the island Aradus;

4D. **Arucas** [Arkites] possessed Arce, which is in Libanus; but for the seven others [Eueus],

4E. **Chetteus** [Hittites?],

4F. **Jebuseus** [Jebusites founded Jerusalem],

4G. **Amorreus** [Amorites],

4H. **Gergesus** [Girgashites],

4I. **Eudeus** [Hivites?],

4J. **Sineus** [Sinites, Sinai is named for this tribe, and perhaps those that left and settled in the Orient],

4K. **Samareus** [Zemarites] we have nothing in the sacred books but their names, for the Hebrews overthrew their cities; and their calamities came upon them on the occasion following.

Shem

Shem, the third son of Noah, had five sons, who inhabited the land that began at Euphrates, and reached to the Indian Ocean.

1. For **Elam** left behind him the Elamites, the ancestors of the Persians.

2. Ashur lived at the city of Nineveh; and named his subjects Assyrians, who became the most fortunate nation beyond others.

3. Arphaxad named the Arphaxadites, who are now called Chaldeans. Aram had the Aramites, which the Greeks called Syrians;

4. as **Laud** founded the Laudites, which are now called Lydians.

5. Of the four sons of **Aram**,

5A. **Uz** founded Trachonitis and Damascus; this country lies between Palestine and Coelosyria.

5B. **Ul** [Hul] founded Armenia; and

5C. **Gather** the Bactrians; and

5D. **Mesa** [Mechech] the Mesaneans; it is now called Charax Spasini.

3A. **Sala** was the son of Arphaxad;

3A1. and his son was Heber [Eber], from whom they originally called the Jews Hebrews.

3A1A. Heber begat **Joktan** and **Peleg**: he was called Peleg, because he was born at the dispersion of the nations to their various countries; for Peleg among the Hebrews signifies Division.

Now Joktan, one of the sons of Heber, had these sons: Almodad, Sheleph, Hazarmaveth, Jerah, Hadoram, Uzal, Diklah, Obal, Abimael, Sheba, Ophir, Havilah, and Jobab. These inhabited from Cophen, an Indian river, and in part of Asia adjoining to it. And this shall suffice concerning the sons of Shem.

Appendix 3

This article is taken from chapter 14 of the book, *Tower of Babel*, by Bodie Hodge entitled, "Was Nimrod in Charge of Forcing a Rebellion Prior to the Events in Genesis 11:1–9?"

Introduction

Since we just mentioned Nimrod, this is a good time to discuss a controversial subject regarding this famous person. In today's church, many people readily repeat the claim that Nimrod was the instigator at Babel. In fact, if one were to research this, it is not a new idea. About 100 years ago, the Reverend Alexander Hislop presented this idea in his book *The Two Babylons*:

> As the Babel builders, when their speech was confounded, were scattered abroad on the face of the earth, and therefore deserted both the city and the tower which they had commenced to build, Babylon as a city, could not properly be said to exist till Nimrod, by establishing his power there, made it the foundation and starting-point of his greatness.[1]

Further back in history, a Jewish military commander and historian named Josephus was writing about the history of the Jews by order of his Roman conquerors:

> (113) Now it was Nimrod who excited them to such an affront

---

1. Alexander Hislop, *The Two Babylons or the Papal Worship Proved to be Worship of Nimrod and His Wife*, 3rd ed. (Neptune, NJ: Loizeaux Brothers, 1916), p. 23.

and contempt of God. He was the grandson of Ham, the son of Noah — a bold man, and of great strength of hand. He persuaded them not to ascribe to God, as if it was through his means they were happy, but to believe that it was their own courage which procured that happiness.

(114) He also gradually changed the government into tyranny, seeing no other way of turning men from the fear of God, but to bring them into a constant dependence on his power. He also said he would be revenged on God, if He should have a mind to drown the world again; for that he would build a tower too high for the waters to be able to reach! and that he would avenge himself on God for killing their forefathers![2]

In fact, other Jews like the Targum of Jonathan also repeat such things as Nimrod being the one to rebel and challenge God. But let's turn to the Word of God to separate out fact from fiction.

What Does God's Word Say?

Genesis 11:1–9

1 Now the **whole earth** had one language and one speech.

2 And it came to pass, as **they** journeyed from the east, that **they** found a plain in the land of Shinar, and **they** dwelt there.

3 Then **they** said to **one another**, "Come, let **us** make bricks and bake them thoroughly." **They** had brick for stone, and **they** had asphalt for mortar.

4 And **they** said, "Come, let **us** build **ourselves** a city, and a tower whose top is in the heavens; let **us** make a name for **ourselves**, lest **we** be scattered abroad over the face of the whole earth."

5 But the LORD came down to see the city and the tower which the **sons of men** had built.

2. *Revised Works of Josephus,* Chapter 4, Tower of Babel — Confusion of Tongues, 2242 B.C., Lines 113–114; *The Works of Josephus Flavius Josephus* (translated by William Whiston), Tyndale House Publishers: Carol Stream, IL, 1987.

6 And the Lord said, "Indeed **the people** are **one** and **they** all have one language, and this is what **they** begin to do; now nothing that **they** propose to do will be withheld from **them**.

7 "Come, let Us go down and there confuse **their** language, that **they** may not understand **one another's** speech."

8 So the Lord scattered **them** abroad from there over the face of all the earth, and **they** ceased building the city.

9 Therefore its name is called Babel, because there the Lord confused the language of **all the earth**; and from there the Lord scattered **them** abroad over the face of all the earth (NKJV, emphasis added).

Take note of the account of the events at Babel in Genesis 11:1–9. Nimrod is not mentioned, and the Bible clearly reveals that the people were rebelling *in unison* (see bold) against God's command to fill the earth as given in Genesis 9:1 and reiterated in Genesis 9:7.

Furthermore, the people knew the command and were intentionally trying to defy it because verse 4 indicates they were resisting the imperative to be scattered abroad.

The point is that the people collectively resisted God, and the people collectively received this mild judgment of confused languages. Nimrod was not forcing the people to do this; but they were acting of one accord (verse 6) to make a name for themselves (verse 4), which is reminiscent of the rebellion prior to the Flood where people had their own interests in mind to be men of renown (Genesis 6:4).

So where did people, such as Josephus, get this idea that Nimrod was in charge of forcing a rebellion? Let's look at Genesis 10:

Genesis 10:8–12

8 Cush begot Nimrod; he began to be a mighty one on the earth.

9 He was a mighty hunter before the Lord; therefore it is said,

"Like Nimrod the mighty hunter before the LORD."

10 And the beginning of his kingdom was Babel, Erech, Accad, and Calneh, in the land of Shinar.

11 From that land he went to Assyria and built Nineveh, Rehoboth Ir, Calah,

12 and Resen between Nineveh and Calah (that is the principal city) (NKJV).

A repetition of this is found in 1 Chronicles 1:10 where it says:

10 Cush begot Nimrod; he began to be a mighty one on the earth (NKJV).

Researchers note the first center, or more properly the "beginning," of Nimrod's kingdom was at Babel (Genesis 10:10). So people logically conclude that Nimrod *founded* Babel and that he was in charge at Babel because this was his *kingdom*. This sounds like a brilliant deduction until one realizes that this now causes some insurmountable theological problems.

Theological Problems

The first problem has already been discussed in the previous section. That is, throughout Genesis 11:1–9, there is no hint of Nimrod's charge, and the Bible repeatedly makes it clear that this rebellion was a collective rebellion against God by all the people involved (descendants of Noah) who were traveling east[3] (obviously of Noah's settlement and vineyard).

How could Nimrod be the one who founded Babel, when Genesis 11:3–4 says the people were building it in unison? This is a problem!

Another theological problem is that Nimrod would have been obedient to God by filling the earth and scattering. Recall Genesis 10:10.

---

3. The Hebrew word translated "east" (*qedem*) in Genesis 11:2 can mean "from the east" or "toward the east." Either was Babel. This first settlement was in an east-west direction from Noah's original settlement.

The first center of Nimrod's kingdom was not Babel, but four places: Babel, Erech, Accad, and Calneh. So there was not one place that everyone was at, but instead four! So this would call into question Genesis 11:4 where it says they built *a* city and *a* tower. If the above is true, Genesis 11:4 should read "four cities." And this brings us to another related problem.

Nimrod then went into someone else's land and made cities there too (Genesis 10:11)! Nimrod went into Asshur (Assyria), one of Shem's son's land and began building and expanding his kingdom there.

But what is the implication of this? Simply that other people such as Asshur must have also been listening to God's command, had been spreading out, and were not at Babel. If such things are accurate, then God would have been in error when He said that all these people were indeed at Babel and made one city, and that they were being disobedient to Him by defying His command to scatter and fill the earth.

But the fact is that God is never wrong, which means Nimrod could not have entered Asshur until after the event of the scattering occurred, where the earth was divided into various languages, and people really did begin to fill the earth.

And this is how these alleged problems are solved. The simplest solutions often make all the facts fall into place.

Solving the Problem

When we look at Genesis 1:1–2:3, we find the chronological account of creation. When we hone in on Genesis 2:4–25, we find that this does not follow chronologically. But instead, the bulk of Genesis 2 is actually a breakdown of what is going on during the sixth day of creation. If one mistakenly reads Genesis 2:4–25 as chronologically following Genesis 1:1–2:3, then all sorts of theological problems arise.

In fact, we find a theological problem in Jewish mythology that is a direct result of misreading Genesis 1–2 as though it were chronological. That is the mythical account of Lilith, the supposed first wife of Adam.

Many Jews in the past read Genesis 1 and saw that when mankind was created they were both male and female (Genesis 1:27). The word for "man" in Genesis 1 is *Adam*, so they understand that he was indeed the first man. Then they read Genesis 2 and find the creation of Eve. So thinking that Genesis 2:4–25 follows Genesis 1 chronologically, they want to know who this first female was (in Hebrew it is *nᵉqe-bah* meaning "female"). And so mythology takes over and they invent Lilith, the supposed first wife of Adam in Jewish mythology.

Such Jewish mythologies are unnecessary when one realizes Genesis 2:4–25 is a breakdown of what is happening on day six of the Creation week and hence, the female created in Genesis 1:26–28 is Eve. Genesis 2 simply gives us more details as to the specifics.

Why is all of this important? I suggest that the same thing has happened with Genesis 10–11. Genesis 11:1–9 is the chronological account of the events, and Genesis 10 is a breakdown of the language divisions and genealogies of those rebellious descendants of Noah at Babel. In other words, what is discussed in Genesis 10 is actually the result of Genesis 11:1–9, and Genesis 11:1–9 does not follow chronologically from Genesis 10.

This should be obvious since about 78 language families (minimum) are coming out of Genesis 10, and yet Genesis 11:1 opens with, "Now the whole earth had one language and one speech." But if people mistakenly think Genesis 10 precedes Genesis 11 chronologically, then they will be left with problems that seem to elevate mythologies to fill in the gaps. And Jewish mythologies began to fill the pages with Nimrod founding Babel, which the Bible does not say. Jesus warned about the tradition of the Jews (e.g., Mark 7:13), so we need to test everything against the Scriptures.

But with an understanding that Genesis 10 follows chronologically, then things fall into place and theological problems subside.

All Is Not Lost

Was Josephus, et, al, completely wrong? Not at all. With a proper understanding of the timing of the events between Genesis 10 and 11, we can deduce that Josephus was essentially accurate, but just had the timing wrong.

Nimrod *did* take over at Babel, it just makes more sense that it had to be after the scattering occurred (Genesis 10:10); pay close attention to Genesis 10:10. The Bible never says that Nimrod founded or began Babel. It says that it was the *first center or the beginning* of his kingdom (with three other places simultaneously).

After the scattering occurred, Nimrod takes over Babel and some other early settlements in that area (Erech, Accad, and Calneh) to be the first center for his kingdom. From there, he entered into the land allotted to Asshur and began building there as well (Genesis 10:10–12).

He *may* well have been angry with God and wanted to rebel as Josephus and others relate (the name *Nimrod* literally means "to rebel"), but not necessarily for what happened prior to the Flood, but more likely for what happened at Babel. It is possible that as a hunter, his status was likely very high and with the scattering and language division, much of this status was now lost. Consider that Esau's status as a hunter was also highly favored by his father; and as many have pointed out, Nimrod's hunting capabilities made him capable of being a "hunter of men" or a military leader as opposed to being a more mild-mannered person like Jacob was (Genesis 25:27); that is, in a comparative between Jacob and Esau.

Many have commented on the meaning of "mighty hunter before the LORD" and pointed out the negative connotations behind it. H.C. Leupold, an Old Testament scholar, says of the meaning:

> The course that our interpretation of these two verses takes will be determined very largely by the meaning of the word "Nimrod." For the meaning of the verb form *nimrodh*, without a doubt, is "let us revolt." Now the other words employed are, if left by themselves, either good or evil in their connotation, depending on the connection in which they appear. Gibbor may mean "hero" or "tyrant." "Hunter" (*gibbor tsáyidh*) may be

a harmless hunter of the fields, or he may be one who hunts men to enslave them. The phrase, "in the sight of Yahweh," in itself expresses neither approval nor disapproval. But each of these terms acquires a bad sense in the light of the name "Nimrod." The tendency of this Cushite must have been to rise up against, and to attempt to overthrow, all existing order. In fact, he must have used this motto so frequently in exhorting others to rebellion, that finally it was applied to him as a name descriptive of the basic trait of his character. If this be so, then *gibbor* must be rendered "tyrant," or "despot" — a use of the word found also #Ps 52:1, 3; and #Ps 120:4, for which passages K.W. justly claims the meaning *Gewaltmensch*. So this inciter to revolt (Nimrod) came to be the first tyrant upon the earth, oppressing others and using them for the furtherance of his own interests.[4]

If one is familiar with Leupold's positions from other comments, he holds to Nimrod leading a revolt and making the events at Babel occur. Though Leupold is right about Nimrod's name and the meaning of the following phrase (mighty hunter before the LORD), why assume this is *prior* to the events at Babel and not post-Babel?

---

4. H.C. Leupold, *Exposition of Genesis*, commentary notes on Genesis 10:8 (Columbus, OH: The Wartburg Press, 1942), p. 366.

Conclusion

To conclude, Josephus, and many others since who have repeated the view that Nimrod was forcing a rebellion prior to the language division, may not be the best interpretation, and we should always compare such things to Scripture (Titus 1:14). However, I suggest we not "throw the baby out with the bath water" as some of their conjectures may be valid.

Though much of what Josephus and others have taught is excellent, we need to compare all things to the Word of God with humbleness as we too fall short — for even I have taught that Nimrod founded Babel and was the one forcing the rebellion at Babel in the past. When we recognize that Nimrod took over Babel *after* the events of Genesis 11:1–9, things make more sense and theological problems are averted.

Appendix 4

What Is the State of the Canopy Model?

Bodie Hodge

If there is one thing you need to know about biblical creationists . . . they can be divided on a subject. This isn't necessarily a bad thing. Though we all have the same heart to follow Christ and do the best we can for the sake of biblical authority and the cause of Christ, we can have differences when it comes to details of models used to explain various aspects of God's creation.

When divisions occur over scientific models, this helps us dive into an issue in more detail and discover if that model is good, bad, needs revision, and so on. But note over *what* we are divided; it is not the Word of God nor is it even theology — it is a division over a *scientific model*.

This is where Christians can rightly be divided on a subject and still do so with Christian love, which I hope is how each Christian would conduct themselves — in "iron-sharpening-iron" dealings on a model while still promoting a heart for the gospel (Proverbs 27:17).

The debate over a canopy model is no different — we are all brothers and sisters in Christ trying to understand *what the Bible says and what it doesn't say* on this subject (2 Timothy 2:15). It is the Bible that reigns supreme on the issue, and our scientific analysis on the subject will always be subservient to the Bible's text.

What Is the Canopy Model(s)?

There are several canopy models, but they all have one thing in common.[1] They all interpret the "waters above" the expanse (firmament) in Genesis 1:7 as some form of water-based canopy surrounding the earth that endured from creation until the Flood.

> Then God said, "Let there be a firmament [expanse] in the midst of the waters, and let it divide the waters from the waters." Thus God made the firmament [expanse], and divided the waters which were under the firmament [expanse] from the waters which were above the firmament [expanse]; and it was so (Genesis 1:6–7).

Essentially, the waters above are believed to have formed either a vapor, water (liquid), or ice canopy around the earth. It is the vapor canopy that seemed to dominate all of the proposed models.[2] It is suggested that this canopy was responsible for several things such as keeping harmful radiation from penetrating the earth, increasing the surface atmospheric pressure of oxygen, keeping the globe at a consistent temperature for a more uniform climate around the globe, and providing one of the sources of water for the Flood.

Some of these factors, like keeping radiation out and increasing the surface atmospheric pressures of oxygen, were thought to allow for human longevity to be increased from its present state (upwards of 900 years or so as described in Genesis 5). So this scientific model was an effort to explain several things, including the long human life span prior to the Flood. Other potential issues solved by the models were to destroy the possibility of large-scale storms with reduced airflow patterns for

---

1. This is not to be confused with canopy ideas that have the edge of water at or near the end of the universe (e.g., white hole cosmology), but instead the models that have a water canopy in the atmosphere (e.g., like those mentioned in J.C. Whitcomb and H.M. Morris, *The Genesis Flood*) (Phillipsburg, NJ: Presbyterian and Reformed Publishing, 1961); J.C. Dillow, *The Waters Above: Earth's Pre-Flood Vapor Canopy*, Revised Edition (Chicago, IL: Moody Press, 1981); or John C. Whitcomb, *The World that Perished* (Winona Lake, IN: BMH Books, 2009).
2. This is in large part due to the influence of Joseph Dillow, whose scientific treatise left only the vapor models with any potential. He writes on page 422 of his treatise: "We showed that only a vapor canopy model can satisfactorily meet the requirements of the necessary support mechanism." Dillow, *The Waters Above: Earth's Pre-Flood Vapor Canopy*.

less extreme weather possibilities, have a climate without rain (such as Dillow's model, see below) but instead merely dew every night, and reduce any forms of barrenness like deserts and ice caps. It would have higher atmospheric pressure to possibly help certain creatures fly that may not otherwise.

A Brief History of Canopy Models

Modern canopy models can be traced back to Dr. Henry Morris and Dr. John Whitcomb in their groundbreaking book *The Genesis Flood* in 1961.[3] This book triggered a return to biblical authority in our age, which is highly commendable and much is owed to their efforts. In this volume, Whitcomb and Morris introduced the possibility of a vapor canopy as the waters above.

The canopy models gained popularity thanks to the work of Dr. Joseph Dillow,[4] and many creationists have since researched various aspects of these scientific models, such as Dr. Larry Vardiman with the Institute for Creation Research.

Researchers have studied the possibility of solid canopies, water canopies, vapor canopies, thick canopies, thin canopies, and so on. Each model has the canopy collapsing into history at the time of the Flood. Researchers thought it could have provided at least some of the water for the Flood and was associated with the 40 days of rain coming from the "windows of heaven" mentioned along with the fountains of the great deep at the onset of the Flood (Genesis 7:11).

However, the current state of the canopy models have faded to such an extent that most researchers and apologists have abandoned the various models. Let's take a look at the biblical and scientific reasons behind the abandonment.

---

3. Whitcomb and Morris, *The Genesis Flood*.
4. Dillow, *The Waters Above: Earth's Pre-Flood Vapor Canopy*.

Biblical Issues

Though both will be discussed, any biblical difficulties that bear on the discussion of the canopy must *trump* scientific considerations, as it is the authority of the Bible that is supreme in all that it teaches.

Interpretations of Scripture Are Not Scripture

The necessity for a water-based canopy about the earth is not directly stated in the text. It is an *interpretation* of the text. Keep in mind that it is the *text* that is inspired, not our interpretations of it.

Others have interpreted the waters above as something entirely different from a water-based canopy about the earth. Most commentators appeal to the waters above as simply being the clouds, which are water droplets (not vapor) in the atmosphere. For they are simply "waters" that are above.

But most do not limit this interpretation as simply being the clouds, but perhaps something that reaches deep into space and extends as far as the *Third Heaven* or *Heaven of Heavens*. For example, expositor Dr. John Gill in the 1700s said:

> The lower part of it, the atmosphere above, which are the clouds full of water, from whence rain descends upon the earth; and which divided between them and those that were left on the earth, and so under it, not yet gathered into one place; as it now does between the clouds of heaven and the waters of the sea. Though Mr. Gregory is of the opinion, that an abyss of waters above the most supreme orb is here meant; or a great deep between the heavens and the heaven of heavens. . . .[5]

Gill agrees that clouds were inclusive of these waters above but that the waters also extend to the heaven of heavens, at the outer edge of the universe. Matthew Poole denotes this possibility as well in his commentary in the 1600s:

---

5. John Gill, *Exposition of the Bible*, Genesis 1:7.

. . . the expansion, or extension, because it is extended far and wide, even from the earth to the third heaven; called also the firmament, because it is fixed in its proper place, from whence it cannot be moved, unless by force.[6]

Matthew Henry also concurs that this expanse extends to the heaven of heavens (third heaven):

The command of God concerning it: Let there be a firmament, an expansion, so the Hebrew word signifies, like a sheet spread, or a curtain drawn out. This includes all that is visible above the earth, between it and the third heavens: the air, its higher, middle, and lower, regions — the celestial globe, and all the spheres and orbs of light above: it reaches as high as the place where the stars are fixed, for that is called here the firmament of heaven Ge 1:14,15, and as low as the place where the birds fly, for that also is called the firmament of heaven, Ge 1:20.[7]

The point is that a canopy model about the earth is simply that . . . an interpretation. It should be evaluated as such, not taken as Scripture itself. Many respected Bible interpreters do not share in the interpretation of the "waters above" being a water canopy in the upper atmosphere of earth.

Stars for Seasons and Light and other Implications

Another biblical issue crops up when we read in Genesis 1:14–15:

Then God said, "Let there be lights in the firmament [expanse] of the heavens to divide the day from the night; and let them be for signs and seasons, and for days and years; and let them be for lights in the firmament [expanse] of the heavens to give light on the earth"; and it was so.[8]

The stars are intended by God to be used to map seasons. And they

---

6. Matthew Poole, *A Commentary on the Holy Bible*, Genesis 1:7.

7. Matthew Henry, *A Commentary on the Whole Bible*, Genesis 1:7.

8. See also Genesis 1:17.

were also to "give light on the earth." Though this is not much light, it does help significantly during new moon conditions — that is, if you live in an area not affected by light pollution.

Water

If the canopy were liquid water, then in its various forms like mist or haze, it would inhibit seeing these stars. How could one see the stars to map the seasons? It would be like a perpetually cloudy day. The light would be absorbed or reflected back to space much the way fog does the headlights of a car. What little light is transmitted through would not be sufficiently discernable to make out stars and star patterns to map seasons. Unlike a vapor canopy, clouds are moving and in motion, one can still see the stars to map seasons when they moved through. Furthermore, if it was water, why didn't it fall?[9]

Ice

If it were ice, then it *is* possible to see the stars but they would not appear in the positions one normally sees them, but still they would be sufficient to map seasons. But ice, when kept cool (to remain ice), tends to coat at the surface where other water molecules freeze to it (think of the coating you see on an ice cube left in the freezer). This could inhibit visibility, as evaporated water from the ocean surface would surely make contact — especially in a sin-cursed and broken world.

Vapor

But if an invisible vapor canopy existed in our upper atmosphere, then it makes the most sense. But there could still turn out to be a problem. As cooler vapor nears space, water condenses and begins to haze, though as long as the vapor in the upper atmosphere is kept warm and above the dew point, it could remain invisible. But there are a lot of

---

9. Would one appeal to the supernatural? If so, it defeats the purpose of this scientific model that seeks to explain things in a naturalistic fashion.

"ifs." In short, the stars may not serve their purpose to give light on the earth with some possibilities within these models.

But consider, if there were a water *vapor* canopy, what would stop it from interacting with the rest of the atmosphere *that is vapor*? Gases mix to equilibrium, and that is the way God upholds the universe.[10] If it was a vapor, then why is it distinguished from the atmosphere, which is vapor?

The Bible uses the terms *waters* above, which implies that the temperature is between 32°F and 212°F (0°C and 100°C). If it was meant to be vapor, then why say "waters" above? Why not say vapor (*hebel*), which was used in the Old Testament?

Where Were the Stars Made?

If the canopy really was part of earth's atmosphere, then all the stars, sun, and moon would have been created within the earth's atmosphere. Why is this? A closer look at Genesis 1:14 reveals that the "waters above" may very well be much farther out — if they still exist today.

The entirety of the stars, including our own sun (the greater light) and moon (lesser light) were made "*in the expanse.*" Further, they are obviously not in our atmosphere. Recall that the waters of verse 7 are above the expanse. If the canopy were just outside the atmosphere of the young earth, then the sun, moon, and stars would have to be in the atmosphere according to verse 14.

Further, the winged creatures were flying *in the face of* the expanse (Genesis 1:20; the NKJV accurately translates the Hebrew), and this helps reveal the extent of the expanse. It would likely include aspects of the atmosphere as well as space. The Bible calls the firmament "heaven" in Genesis 1:8, which would include both. Perhaps our understanding of "sky" is similar or perhaps the best translation of this as well.

---

10. Again, would one appeal to the supernatural? If so, it defeats the purpose of this scientific model that seeks to explain things in a naturalistic fashion.

Regardless, this understanding of the text allows for the stars to be in the expanse, and this means that any waters above, which is beyond the stars, is not limited to being in the atmosphere. Also, 2 Corinthians 12:2 discusses three heavens, which are likely the atmosphere (airy heavens), space (starry heavens), and the heaven of heavens (Nehemiah 9:6).

Some have argued that the prepositions in, under, above, etc., are not in the Hebrew text but are determined from the context, so the meaning in verses 14 and 17 is vague. It is true that the prepositions are determined by the context, so we must rely on a proper translation of Genesis 1:14. Virtually all translations have the sun, moon, and stars being created *in* the expanse, not *above* as any canopy model would require.

In Genesis 1, some have attempted to make a distinction between the expanse in which the birds fly (Genesis 1:20) and the expanse in which the sun, moon, and stars were placed (Genesis 1:7); this was in an effort to have the sun, moon, and stars made in the second expanse. This is not a distinction that is necessary from the text and is only necessary if a canopy is assumed.

From the Hebrew, the birds are said to fly "across the face of the firmament of the heavens." Looking up at a bird flying across the sky, it would be seen against the face of both the atmosphere and the space beyond the atmosphere — the "heavens." The proponents of the canopy model must make a distinction between these two expanses to support the position, but this is an arbitrary assertion that is only necessary to support the view and is not described elsewhere in Scripture.

Expanse (Firmament) Still Existed Post-Flood

Another issue that is raised from the Bible is that the waters above the heavens were mentioned *after* the Flood, when it was supposedly gone.

Praise Him, you heavens of heavens, and you waters above the heavens! (Psalm 148:4).

> *So an officer on whose hand the king leaned answered the man of God and said, "Look, if the LORD would make windows in heaven, could this thing be?" And he said, "In fact, you shall see it with your eyes, but you shall not eat of it"* (2 Kings 7:2; see also 2 Kings 7:19).

> *"Bring all the tithes into the storehouse, that there may be food in My house, and try Me now in this," says the LORD of hosts, "If I will not open for you the windows of heaven and pour out for you such blessing that there will not be room enough to receive it"* (Malachi 3:10).

The biblical authors wrote these in a post-Flood world in the context of other post-Flood aspects. So, it appears that the "waters above" and "windows of heaven" are in reference to something that still existed after the Flood. So "the waters above" can't be referring to a long-gone canopy that dissipated at the Flood and still be present after the Flood. This is complemented by:

> The fountains of the deep and the windows of heaven were also stopped, and the rain from heaven was restrained (Genesis 8:2).

Genesis 8:2 merely points out that the two sources were stopped and restrained, not necessarily *done away* with. The verses above suggest that the windows of heaven remained after the Flood. Even the "springs of the great deep" were stopped but did not entirely disappear, but there may have been residual waters trapped that have slowly oozed out since that time; clearly not in any gushing, spring-like fashion.[11]

Is a Canopy Necessary Biblically?

Finally, is a canopy necessary from the text? At this stage, perhaps not. It was promoted as a scientific model based on a possible interpretation of Genesis 1 to deal with several aspects of the overall biblical creation model developed in the mid-1900s. I don't say this lightly for my brothers and sisters in the LORD who may still find it appealing. Last century, I was introduced to the canopy model and found it

---

11. I would leave open the option that this affected the ocean sea level to a small degree but the main reasons for changing sea level was via the Ice Age.

fascinating. For years, I had espoused it, but after further study, I began leaning against it, as did many other creationists.

Old biblical commentators were not distraught at the windows of heaven or the waters not being a canopy encircling the earth. Such an interpretation was not deemed necessary in their sight. In fact, this idea is a recent addition to scriptural interpretation that is less than 100 years old. The canopy model was a scientific interpretation developed in an effort to help explain certain aspects of the text to those who were skeptical of the Bible's accounts of earth history, but when it comes down to it, it is not necessary and even has some serious biblical issues associated with it.

Scientific Issues

Clearly, there are some biblical issues that are difficult to overcome. Researchers have often pointed out the scientific issues of the canopy model, as well. A couple will be denoted below.

This is no discredit to the *researchers* by any means. The research was valuable and necessary to see how the model may or may not work with variations and types. The development and testing of models is an important part of scientific inquiry, and we should continue to do so with many models to help us understand the world God has given us. So I appreciate and applaud all the work that has been done, and I further wish to encourage researchers to study other aspects to see if anything was missed.

Temperatures

To answer the question about how the earth regulates its temperature without a canopy, consider that it may not have been that much different than the way it regulates it today — by the atmosphere and oceans. Although there may have been much water underground prior to the Flood, there was obviously enough at or near the surface to sustain immense amounts of sea life. We know this because of the well-known figure that nearly 95 percent of the fossil record consists of shallow-water marine organisms. Was the earth's surface around 70 percent water before the Flood? That is a question creationist researchers still debate.

An infinitely knowledgeable God would have no problem designing the earth in a perfect world to have an ideal climate (even with variations like the cool of the day as mentioned in Genesis 3:8) where people could have filled the earth without wearing clothes (Genesis 2:25, 1:28). But with a different continental scheme that are remnants of a perfect world (merely cursed, not rearranged by the Flood yet), it would surely have been better equipped to deal with regulated temperatures and climate.

A vapor canopy, on the other hand, would cause major problems for the regulation of earth's temperature. A vapor canopy would absorb both solar and infrared radiation and become hot, which would heat the surface by conduction downward. The various canopy models have therefore been plagued with heat problems from the greenhouse effect. For example, solar radiation would have to decrease by around 25 percent to make the most plausible model work.[12] The heat problem actually makes this model very problematic and adds a problem rather than helping to explain the environment before the Flood.[13]

The Source of Water

The primary source of water for the Flood was the springs of the great deep bursting forth (Genesis 7:11). This water in turn likely provided some of the water in the "windows of heaven" in an indirect fashion. There is no need for an ocean of vapor above the atmosphere to provide for extreme amounts of water for the rain that fell during the Flood.

---

12. For more on this see "Temperature Profiles for an Optimized Water Vapor Canopy" by Dr. Larry Vardiman, a researcher on this subject for over 25 years at the time of writing that paper; http://static.icr.org/i/pdf/technical/Temperature-Profiles-for-an-Optimized-Water-Vapor-Canopy.pdf.
13. Another issue is the amount of water vapor in the canopy. Dillow's 40 feet of precipitable water, the amount collected after all the water condenses, has major heat problems. But Vardiman's view has modeled canopies with 2 to 6 feet of precipitable water with better temperature results and we look forward to seeing future research.

For example, if Dillow's vapor canopy existed (40 feet of precipitable water) and collapsed at the time of the Flood to supply, in large part, the rainfall, the latent heat of condensation would have boiled the atmosphere! And a viable canopy would not have had enough water vapor in it to sustain 40 days and nights of torrential global rain as in Vardiman's model (2–6 feet of precipitable water). Thus, the vapor canopy doesn't adequately explain the rain at the Flood.

Longevity

Some have appealed to a canopy to increase surface atmospheric pressures prior to the Flood. The reasoning is to allow for better healing as well as living longer and bigger as a result. However, increased oxygen (and likewise oxidation that produces dangerous free radicals), though beneficial in a few respects, is mostly a detriment to biological systems. Hence, antioxidants (including things like catalase and vitamins E, A, and C) are very important to reduce these free radicals within organisms.

Longevity (and the large size of many creatures) before and after the Flood is better explained by genetics through the bottlenecks of the Flood and the Tower of Babel as opposed to pre-Flood oxygen levels due to a canopy. Not to belabor these points, this idea has already been discussed elsewhere.[14]

Pre-Flood Climate

Regardless of canopy models, creationists generally agree that climate before the Fall was perfect. This doesn't mean the air was stagnant and 70°F every day, but instead had variations within the days and nights (Genesis 3:8). These variations were not extreme but very reasonable.

Consider that Adam and Eve were told to be fruitful and multiply and fill the earth (Genesis 1:27). In a perfect world where there was no need for clothes to cover sin (this came after the Fall), we can deduce

---

14. Ken Ham, ed., *New Answers Book 2* (Green Forest, AR: Master Books, 2008), p. 159–168; Bodie Hodge, *Tower of Babel* (Green Forest, AR: Master Books, 2013), p. 205–212.

that man should have been able to fill the earth without wearing clothes, hence the extremes were not as they are today or the couple would have been miserable as the temperatures fluctuated.

Even after the Fall, it makes sense that these weather variations were minimally different. But with the global Flood that destroyed the earth and rearranged continents and so on, the extremes become pronounced — we now have ice caps and extremely high mountains that were pushed up from the Flood (Psalm 104:8). We now have deserts that have extreme heat and cold and little water.

Biblical Models and Encouragement

Answers in Genesis continues to encourage research and the development of scientific and theological models. However, a good grasp of all biblical passages that are relevant to the topic must precede the scientific research and models, and the Bible must be the ultimate judge over all of our conclusions.

The canopy model may have a glimmer of hope still remaining, and that will be left to the proponents to more carefully explain, but both the biblical and scientific difficulties need to be addressed thoroughly and convincingly for the model to be embraced. So we do look forward to future research.

In all of this, we must remember that scientific models are not Scripture, and it is the Scripture that we should defend as the authority. While we must surely affirm that the waters above were divided from the waters below, something the Bible clearly states, whether or not there was a canopy must be held loosely lest we do damage to the text of Scripture or the limits of scientific understanding.